POLITICAL TRENDS IN THE ARAB WORLD

Author's Publications in English

Islamic Studies

WAR AND PEACE IN THE LAW OF ISLAM
The Johns Hopkins Press

LAW IN THE MIDDLE EAST
Edited, in collaboration with H. J. Liebesny, for the Middle East Institute

ISLAMIC JURISPRUDENCE: Shafi'i's *Risala*
The Johns Hopkins Press

THE ISLAMIC LAW OF NATIONS: Shaybani's *Siyar*
The Johns Hopkins Press

Studies on the Modern Arab World

INDEPENDENT 'IRAQ: *A Study in 'Iraqi Politics, 1932–58*
Oxford University Press

REPUBLICAN 'IRAQ: *A Study in 'Iraqi Politics Since the Revolution of 1958*
Oxford University Press

MODERN LIBYA: *A Study in Political Development*
The Johns Hopkins Press

POLITICAL TRENDS IN THE ARAB WORLD
The Johns Hopkins Press

POLITICAL TRENDS IN THE ARAB WORLD

The Role of Ideas and Ideals in Politics

Majid Khadduri

THE JOHNS HOPKINS PRESS
BALTIMORE AND LONDON

Manufactured in the United States of America

The Johns Hopkins Press, Baltimore, Maryland 21218
The Johns Hopkins Press Ltd., London

ISBN 0-8018-1122-8 (clothbound edition)
ISBN 0-8018-1440-5 (paperbound edition)

Originally published, 1970
Johns Hopkins Paperbacks edition, 1972

DEDICATED

TO THE MEMORY OF

my Mother

CONTENTS

The Prophet Muhammad, upon his return from one of the campaigns, remarked to his Companions:

"We have just fulfilled the lesser jihad; it is now our duty to embark on the greater jihad."

"What is the greater jihad?" asked one of the Companions.

"It is the struggle to save one's own soul," replied the Prophet.

PREFACE

For centuries, Islam provided a self-sufficient way of life embodying norms and values which Arabs have long honored. Today, under changing conditions, Islamic polity is manifestly in a state of decadence and can no longer adequately meet growing needs and expectations. Should the Islamic way of life change or should it be replaced by another? Although the debate on this issue began soon after Napoleon descended upon Egypt in 1798, Arab reformers, especially in Egypt and the Fertile Crescent, began to urge the adoption of new concepts and institutions shortly before World War I. Nationalism and parliamentary democracy, to which Arab leaders were first attracted, began gradually to supersede traditional loyalties and institutions after World War I, but neither nationalism nor democracy could provide the desired strength for the progress needed in modern conditions of life, and Arab experiences with these institutions during the inter-war years demonstrated their inadequacy (Chapters 2 and 3). As a result, a group of conservative reformers began to call for the revival of Islamic institutions (Chapter 4); others, especially young men, called for the adoption of radical ideas and ideologies (Chapter 5). None of these groups, however, was able to achieve power to carry out its ideas while the cry for social reform and progress continued unabated. This situation gave an opportunity to young Arab officers, who had already fallen under a variety of ideological influences, to intervene in politics and carry out agrarian reforms even before they began to experiment with their own eclectic reform programs (Chapter 6). Meanwhile, the debate on reform among Arab thinkers has continued, but, to the present day, no political system which would command general respect has yet emerged, and every reform-minded thinker or group of thinkers displays a bias in favor of one particular ideology or another (Chapter 7).

But life pays no heed to abstract doctrines: Arab society, under the impact of the West, has been undergoing change, irrespective of the ideas and desires of theorists. In the circumstances, Arab thinkers have tried either to rationalize the change or to modify it by advocating the views of one school of thought or another. Trends in contemporary Arab thought have become essentially the products of competing ideals and ideologies generated by recurring crises under the impact of foreign ideas and pressures (Chapters 8–9).

The purpose of this work is to study the mainstreams of contemporary Arab thought and to assess its elements and character in relation to political movements as well as to express briefly certain personal views on the inherent problems (Chapter 10). In the last chapter of the work, I have tried to explain Arab world views on some major problems in which the Arabs have been, or are still being, involved. Since Arab political ideas have not yet crystalized into concrete systems capable of superseding the traditional Islamic system, I have characterized my work as a study in political trends. I have deliberately avoided a discussion of the role of leadership; a study of this problem will be undertaken in another volume, *Arab Contemporaries: The Role of Personalities in Politics.*

Needless to say, *Political Trends in the Arab World* lays no claim to studying the political ideas of all Arab thinkers; it is devoted only to the mainstreams of political thought in the Eastern Arab world. North Africa is dealt with only indirectly, whenever the main concepts of Arab thought were relevant to its political movements. No attempt is made to study the special trends in North African political thought.

It is a pleasure to acknowledge the kindnesses of all who have readily given me assistance. To cite the names of all former classmates, students, and friends who are now in positions of responsibility in the Arab world—both civil and military—would be impossible. They all contributed directly or indirectly to this work by way of personal contacts or by providing counsel and expressing personal opinions. A number of colleagues and friends in Western institutions have read the manuscript either in whole or in part. In particular, I should like to mention Albert Hourani, who read the whole work, and Emil Lang and William Sands who read some parts of it. Sami al-Khuri, a former member of the Syrian Nationalist Party, read the section devoted to that party. The section on Israel and the Arab World has been read by a number of Jewish and Christian friends—Bernard Lewis, J. C. Hurewitz, Don Peretz, General Sir John B. Glubb, Quincy Wright, Charles B. Marshall, John Anthony, and others. Michael Van Dusen, Robert Mertz, and Miss Eileen Donlin rendered invaluable assistance while the work was in preparation. None of them, however, is responsible for any errors contained in this work.

Finally, I should like to acknowledge the intellectual debt I owe to my mother, who above all taught me at an early age to learn from my social environment.

MAJID KHADDURI

School of Advanced International Studies
The Johns Hopkins University

POLITICAL TRENDS IN THE ARAB WORLD

Chapter 1

INTRODUCTION

When the state becomes senile and weak, it begins to crumble at its extremities. The center remains intact until God permits the destruction of the whole state. Then, the center is destroyed. But when a state is overrun from the center, it is of no avail to it that the outlying areas remain intact. It dissolves all at once. Were the heart to be overrun and captured, all the extremities would be routed.

Ibn Khaldun

Writing on Islamic reform in 1882, Wilfrid Scawen Blunt citing an Arab proverb remarked:

> Fear not. Often pearls are unstrung
> To be put in better order.[1]

The words of the great admirer of Islam sum up the age-old debate of Muslim thinkers: in order to reform Islam, its order needs to be re-formed. Blunt was confident that the new order would be a "better order," but he never outlined the precise form it should take. Proposals for reform have varied from thinker to thinker, but all agreed on the need for it.

Western experts who have taken an interest in Islamic lands have studied its society from many viewpoints and have offered many panaceas for its ills. Long ago, missionaries and orientalists recognized the decadence in Islamic society and the cures they prescribed ranged from conversion of Muslims to Christianity to the acceptance of Christian ethical values. Other experts, historians most notably, viewed Islam's decadence as an inevitable legacy of its confrontation with Western

[1] W. S. Blunt, *The Future of Islam* (London, 1882).

civilization. The Muslim who wishes to enjoy the progress Western man has achieved, those experts argued, must submit to the Westernizing forces which are now engulfing the whole world.[2] More recently specialists in economic and behavioral sciences, avoiding value judgments, have offered the novel criteria of "development" and "modernization" and suggested that nations in search of progress must submit to changes compatible with the laws of economic and political development. Social or material progress can never be achieved, they argued, until the stage of the "developed" nations is reached.[3] These Western analysts, despite their divergent methodological approaches, seem to agree on one basic point—Islam's salvation from decadence lies in acculturation. None maintains that acculturation has failed to produce the desired rehabilitation, although it has been in progress for over a century.

In earlier times, Islam's confrontations with other civilizations—Greek, Persian, and Indian—produced an enhancement of its power and its glory, as it assimilated borrowings from foreign cultures into its body politic. But in modern times, the outcome has been otherwise. The confrontation between Islam and the West has triggered a loss in power and dignity and generated continuous tensions and violent changes. These changes call for an explanation since they differ in nature from those arising in the past.

First, the creative capacity which enabled Muslims to blend foreign cultural elements so as to achieve a high level of civilization has entered into a steady decline following the fall of the Arab caliphate. Foreign ideas and innovations which are not assimilated can exert a devastating impact on a decadent society. To many Arabs this decadence remains a mystery, to be explained only by the traditional viewpoint that something has gone amiss with God's ordering of life. But to

[2] This view attained a high degree of refinement in the writings of A. J. Toynbee. See *A Study of History* (London, 1954), VIII, 216–72; and *Civilization on Trial* (New York, 1948), pp. 184–212.

[3] For formulation into laws of economic development, see W. W. Rostow, *The Stages of Economic Growth* (Cambridge, 1960); and W. W. Rostow (ed.), *The Economics of Take-off in Sustained Growth* (New York, 1963).

thinkers who are more articulate and who understand better what has gone amiss, there is no doubt that Islam's creative capacity has been outdistanced by the dynamic forces of Western society the like of which Islam had never encountered before.

Secondly, Islam's contacts with the West in modern times, in contrast with earlier contacts, produced a threat to its sovereignty and power. The self-assurance with which Muslims met foreigners in earlier days has been shaken by the succession of European victories in the more recent era. Since the days when Napoleon set foot in the Nile Valley, Islamic lands suffered so many defeats and threats that their power and glory have become a memory of a remote past. The threats grew even more alarming when Western pressures continued, in one form or another, long after political domination had begun to recede. These unhappy experiences produced a cumulative effect, an indelible feeling of indignity and injured pride.

The reaction to decadence, intended to rehabilitate Islam, was inspired by internal no less than by external pressures. The response to internal pressures came first and arose in areas nearly isolated from Western influences. It took the form of "revivalist" movements, inspired by "century-reformers" who called for a puritanical regeneration of Islam, the purging of age-old accretions, and the re-establishing of a pristine system based on divine revelation and the Prophet's model conduct.[4] These movements drew their inspiration from the past. They addressed themselves to reform directly without an apologia, since they lacked all feelings of injured dignity characteristic of those movements inspired by foreign pressures. Two of the movements—the Mahdiya and the Sanusiya—were momentarily crushed when exposed to foreign pressures

[4] By Islamic tradition, no prophet could have arisen to reform Islam, but by an utterance attributed to the Prophet Muhammad, a great reformer from his house was destined to appear at the end of every century to serve as an inspired leader and guide men along the true path. In modern times, three "century-reformers" have appeared to lead three revivalist movements—the Wahhabi, the Sanusi, and the Mahdiya movements in Arabia, Cyrenaica, and the Sudan.

because the type of reform they offered failed to generate the material strength Muslims needed to resist European encroachments, although they did provide a sense of unity which remained immanent and paved the way for the eventual emergence of fully sovereign states as in the case of the Wahhabi movement. The positive approach to reform furnished by these three revivalist movements has touched the very foundations of Islam and may well prove more constructive in the long run than other movements, stimulated by external pressures such as the lack of material and technological innovations made available by Western civilization and considered essential for modern conditions of life. Exposed to recent Western influence, some of these movements have tended to assume a defensive attitude and to share the outlook of Islamic movements already affected by Western influence.

External pressures, especially the threat to Islamic sovereignty, have produced repercussions which have not yet reached their fullest development. In the course of their soul-searching, Arab thinkers have been sharply divided in their attitudes toward the West, although they have agreed on the need for reform and on Islam's capacity to achieve progress that had been demonstrated in the past. The reform viewpoints have ranged from the extreme of a complete break with the past and wholesale acceptance of Western ideas and ideals irrespective of their compatibility with existing traditions and practices to the other extreme of re-establishing the classical Islamic system with little or no heed paid to the inescapable impact of foreign influences.

Discussions of these approaches produced sharper conflicts among the various schools of thought than were ever expected, and the ensuing "great debate," pregnant with protests, reprisals, and reappraisals, was instrumental in inciting social upheavals of far-reaching consequences. The stress in the controversy has shifted from period to period, as the relevance of each issue to the needs and aspirations of the people changed while progressing from one stage of development to another. Three successive stages may be noted since the "great debate" began.

In the first stage, which occupied Muslims from the latter part of the eighteenth century to the end of the nineteenth, the issue was whether reform should draw exclusively either on Western or on Islamic sources. The Islamic school insisted on the reinstatement of the ideal Islamic system, while the Westernizing school advocated the importation of Western ideas of modernization irrespective of their relevance to traditional concepts and values. These uncompromising attitudes stemmed essentially from a conflict between two rival vested interests representing the ruling elite and their opposition, and reduced the impact of both, except in the middle of the nineteenth century, when a few enlightened thinkers reconciled the two conflicting views for a brief period. The controversy has virtually run its course by now, since any thinker who proposes a purely traditional or completely foreign set of ideas is not likely to win much of a following.

In the second stage, which began after World War I and reached its peak in the latter years of the inter-war period (although its roots may go back to pre-war times), the debate turned on the particular set of ideas and principles that were to be adopted from foreign societies without regard to the sensitivities of religious and conservative groups. This period was characterized by a growing influx of Western ideas and concepts without a critical examination of their suitability to the new social milieu. At the outset, the Islamic school was silenced by a climate overwhelmingly favorable to Westernization. It drew a clear distinction between Western material and spiritual values although it was ready enough to accept the material benefits of Western civilization. But the Westernizing school made no deliberate effort to assimilate Western ideas and ideals or to merge them with Islamic concepts so as to create a new synthesis. When progress under the imported institutions fell short of expectations, the religious leaders contributed in no small measure to the collapse of those institutions by entering into an unholy alliance with the newly arising ideological groups.

In the third stage, which began after World War II, the debate may prove in time to be the most constructive. Today,

Arab thinkers are deliberately striving to assimilate imported ideas as well as to blend them with Islamic concepts in an effort to create a synthesis of two or more ingredients. The experiment has reached beyond a modest beginning and the outcome remains in doubt, but it could lead to positive results if it were regulated by reason and conducted by dexterous hands. The new civil codes, prepared by a leading Egyptian jurist for several Arab countries, blend Western and Islamic legal elements and suggest possibilities for accomplishments in other fields.[5] New attempts at integrating heterogeneous ideas—e.g., Islamic culture, nationalism, and socialism, to mention but one of the most recent experiments, may well provide foundation stones for a new social order. Thinking on these lines remains, it must be admitted, in its formative stages.

The great debate on reform continues in Arab lands. It has released many dynamic forces and produced social and political upheavals. Violent change, in contrast with peaceful and evolutionary development, is the most striking and persistent phenomenon that has arisen since Islamic society was first exposed to Western influence. Arab thinkers who advocated reform along Western lines may have failed to anticipate the eruption of violent upheavals. Yet in traditional societies upheavals of that character seem inherent in social change and some release of violence is probably unavoidable. Shifts in ways of life and values tend to stir conflicts of loyalty between the old generation insisting on preserving old ways and values and the new generation readily prepared to accept the new scale of values while not being capable of conforming to it. Small wonder that a multiplicity of values and practices can prevail in a society undergoing social change while life can be neither easy nor comfortable for either the old or the new generations. It should indeed weigh heavily on the reformer's conscience to find that social upheavals intended to promote progress often promote destruction instead, at any rate in their earlier stages. Not infrequently the social reformer has found himself driven to repressive measures in

[5] See pp. 239–44 below.

order to maintain public order before another reform measure could be undertaken or even considered.

Social change which began over a century and a half ago has failed to date to penetrate very deeply into Arab lands or to produce a uniform transformation. The shift from a traditional to a modern society is visible most notably on the Levant coast, in the region first exposed to foreign influence, although even there certain aspects of traditionalism may still continue. In Lebanon, where Islam has not been the sole basis of social polity, the transformation is nearly complete, and the confessional division of society can scarcely be regarded as a barrier to progress.

Other portions of the Arab world, even those which have barely been touched by foreign influence and which have preserved their traditional concepts and institutions, are all but intact. The Yaman, Hadramawt, and 'Uman (Oman), varying though they may in their attachment to traditionalism, are perhaps the best examples. Social stability in these countries has not shifted greatly, although social change has begun to threaten some aspects of their traditional way of life.

The vast intermediate area between the Westernized and the traditional regions forms the core of the Arab world. In my opinion, it has the greater claim on our attention. It is in these lands that traditional and new institutions are functioning side by side, with all the inevitable conflicts that arise between them. Here Arab society is experiencing its greatest turbulence and instability while undergoing sweeping changes through an interplay of ideas and forces originating within that society as well as outside it. It is a "society in transition" par excellence, as it is passing through a period of ongoing crisis on the road to complete social transformation.[6]

[6] In terms of progress and development, the division of the Arab world into traditional, transitional, and modernized was suggested by the present writer in his article "Governments of the Arab East," *Journal of International Affairs*, 6 (1952), 37–50; see George Lenczowski, "Political Institutions," *Mid-East: World Center*, ed. N. A. Anshen (New York, 1956), pp. 118–19. For the impact of the West on Islamic society, see C. Ernest Dawn, "Islam in the Modern Age," *Middle East Journal* (1965), pp. 435–46; and Manfred Halpern, *The Politics of Social Change in the Middle East and North Africa* (Princeton, 1963), chaps. 1–2.

Chapter 2

RISE OF NATIONALISM

Mankind was but one nation, then it fell into variance.
Qur'an X, 20

Second only to Islam, the idea of nationalism has dominated the minds of Arabs to a greater extent than any other ideology. It is significant that this new concept, in contrast with other imported ideas, has gained acceptance with but little opposition, and has spread so rapidly, despite Islam's tacit or expressed disapproval, that it represents the greatest challenge to Islam today. Moreover, nationalism has encroached upon certain domains of life which in Islam had gone uncontested for centuries. Perhaps for this very reason the early reformers did not become very enthusiastic advocates of the concept, fearing that it might encroach upon traditional loyalties. Instead, they sought to borrow only those concepts which would not enter into direct conflict with Islam. Very soon, however, these early imports brought nationalism in their train, which proceeded to supersede the Islamic loyalty in varying degrees. With the exception of strictly religious concepts, all other concepts have been subjected to a wholesale re-examination by Arab thinkers, in the hope of transferring them from a religious to a national basis. In their recent speculations on the idea of nationalism, many Arab thinkers have consciously sought to associate religion with nationalism in an effort to reintroduce Islam as an element in this ideology; but religion is bound to take a subordinate position in such a blend, and thus become a component rather than an opponent of nationalism.[1]

Islam and Nationalism

As a type of allegiance, patriotism was known among Muslims before it gained currency in the West, but this patriotism was not necessarily territorial. In the tribal community, it was a narrow mode of loyalty confined to the tribe and was often referred to as the *'asabiya*; [2] in urban communities, however, it manifested itself in an attachment to specific localities. Islam superseded this parochial feeling by shifting the loyalty of believers from a narrow local plane to a broader plane of loyalty stressing religious and moral values, although the former was never completely suppressed. Islam conceded that its followers stemmed from many lands and races, but it stressed the overriding principle of equality and the supremacy of one system of law and religion, thereby creating a sense of unity among these diverse groups so that every believer became more aware of his identification with one Great Society—the Islamic brotherhood (the *umma*). Like the medieval *Respublica Christiana*, the *umma* was the ecumenical community *par excellence*.

Despite Islam's tolerance of diverse ethnic and cultural affinities, a latent resentment to Arab ascendency was felt by non-Arab elements. Arab *'asabiya* was manifested as a distinct mode of loyalty by the Arabicized believers who sought to maintain Arab ascendency. Their opponents, especially the Persians were called *shu'ubiyyin*, or the advocates of the principles of "multiple nationalities." This inner conflict revealed an inherent "national" feeling within the Islamic superstructure. The Persian *shu'ubiya* denounced by Arabs

[1] See Chapter 8.

[2] The 'asabiya is a tribal sense of unity derived from a claim to one fatherhood, or an ancestor, real or fictitious. This tribal feeling, described by Ibn Khaldun as the driving force in inter-Arab warfare, is a form of social solidarity. See Ibn Khaldun, *Muqaddima*, trans. F. Rosenthal (London, 1958), I, 264–65; II, 302–7.

as in opposition to Islam, was a form of latent Persian "national" feeling stemming from a rich culture and a vivid historical memory which did not submit completely to domination.

Nor did Islam impose conformity to one religious belief among adherents of other religious systems who lived in Islamic lands. It is true that the majority of the inhabitants of the Islamic state were converts from other religions, yet religious minorities, despite certain legal disabilities, enjoyed considerable freedom in the exercise of religious and civil rights which were denied to minorities in the contemporary society of Europe. This policy was continued by Ottoman sultans in the newly occupied territories of Eastern Europe where the majority remained Christian, because the Ottoman empire inherited the ecumenical character of Islamic society in which non-Muslims had the right to enjoy considerable religious freedom. The Ottoman empire was essentially a religious state, and Turks and Arabs, the primary ethno-cultural groups of the empire, found spiritual satisfaction under the rule of sultans who proved to be worthy successors to the Arab caliphs.

The Break-up of Islamic Unity

The division of Islam into political units was a significant factor in facilitating the introduction of nationalism. Before its break-up in the sixteenth century, the Islamic world had undergone internal changes which helped to transform the state from a unitary to a decentralized form. Such a transformation is inherent in all ecumenical empires and not confined to Islam. The tendency to promote the growth and spread of Islamic political ideas and institutions has always existed, for the maintenance of the empire required continuous social and material development and a growth in wealth, population, and communication. As civilization was spreading more uniformly throughout the empire, the distribution of power tended towards an equilibrium, and authority came to be necessarily shared by an increasing number of component units of the state. At that stage of growth, the empire would have been likely to change into a federation of sub-entities of some sort or split into independent states. As the experience of Islam demonstrated, a long period of time is frequently required for the devolution of a decentralized regime into several political units.

One of the centrifugal forces which contributed to the decentralization and final break-up of the Islamic empire was the spread of its political authority over a vast geographical area; yet geography alone could not cause these divisions. Territorial segregation must be explained, or rationalized, by a set of ideas and ideals which sum up the internal tensions. Whenever these ideals served to alienate the loyalty of a group or groups within the larger political community, the state was likely to split into independent political units. Doctrinal schisms recurred in Islam and led to the formation of rival religious-political parties (Kharijis, Shi'is, and others), each of which spread over a given geographical area. But such schisms in creed never produced permanent territorial divisions until the distribution of power had attained an equilibrium capable of maintaining separate political entities.

The most lasting division, of course, occurred at the opening of the sixteenth century when Ottoman power was challenged by the newly established Safavid dynasty in Persia. The two rival dynasties, Ottoman and Persian, relegated their doctrinal differences to the domestic level, following a long period of competition and conflict, and recognized the sovereign existence of one another. This situation became possible after the fall of the 'Abbasid dynasty, for its disappearance eliminated balancing forces and created a vacuum in the Islamic world. For over three centuries, especially from the thirteenth to the sixteenth, the Islamic world abounded in political entities, small and great, and their rivalries and struggles for survival resulted in the emergence of three principal Islamic states (Ottoman, Persian, and Mughal), each rationalizing its existence on the strength of one of the two credal divisions of Islam—the Sunni and the Shi'i. This territorial segregation was the first to endure and coincided with the absorption of

Islam's peripheries by neighboring powers. The division of Islam into sovereign territorial units, whether regretted as the dissolution of a great ecumenical society or hailed as the progressive evolution of the state in adapting itself to modern conditions, was a necessary background for the subsequent acceptance of nationalism as the basis of the new state-system.

The break-up of Islam into sovereign political entities was not unprecedented, for Christendom, a prototype of an ecumenical political community and older than Islam by some six centuries, had already undergone a similar transformation. The impact of politically fragmented Christendom on Islam was significant, first because of providing a model for the form a nation-state might assume, and then because of support given to the rise of the territorial state in the Islamic world. Christian support of this process, however, did not necessarily imply that the fragmentation of Islam was created by Christian pressures, since such a process, as noted earlier, had already been in the making for centuries.

Persia was the first political entity to secede from Islamic unity, rationalizing its separate existence on credal differences. Up to the sixteenth century, the advocates of Sunnism and Shi'ism were intermingled throughout the Islamic world. Thereafter, they became segregated geographically. This segregation brought about the rise of Persia as a territorial state with Shi'ism as its "national" religion. Not only did the rivalry between the Sunni and Shi'i states separate Persia from Islam's ecumenical society, but it drove her to seek the support of European powers. This caused the newly rising Islamic state-system to be linked inescapably with the power balance of the already developed European state-system. Persia had yet to be transformed from a dynastic to a modern national state. That development occurred only in the twentieth century and is deemed outside the scope of the present study.[3]

Persia's secession bequeathed the burden of bearing the symbolic mantle of Islamic unity to Ottoman shoulders for the next four centuries. The Arabs, weak and divided, wel-

[3] See R. K. Ramazani, *The Foreign Policy of Iran, 1500–1941* (Charlottesville, 1966).

comed their inclusion in the territory lying west of Persia, under Ottoman control. Ottoman rule over Arabs and other ethnic groups necessarily affected the character of the empire, rationalizing its structure on a religious foundation and invoking Sunni Islam as a valid claim for loyalty. The Ottoman empire, to survive as a political entity, had to remain religious and ecumenical in character. It was all the more essential, because the Ottoman ruling class failed to feel any national identity. Neither the government nor the Turkish people ever labeled their empire as "Turkish"—the name was in use only by European writers. In the true Islamic sense, the creed and the sacred law provided the foundations of authority, and the names of the sultan's subjects were inscribed in the government registers on the basis of their faiths and not of their ethnic identities. Hence, despite attempts to transform it into a national entity, the ecumenical nature of the empire remained essentially unchanged until its final dissolution. More significantly, it was inherently opposed to the idea of nationalism.

Outside the Ottoman empire, the three most important territories to secede from the Islamic unity—Morocco, Persia, and Afghanistan—began to develop as independent dynastic states, yet they never became modern national states. When Persia and Morocco seceded from the Islamic unity in the sixteenth century, Western Christendom itself had not yet developed into truly national entities. It was only in the nineteenth century that modern nationalism spread to other countries under the impact of the French Revolution. That wave of nationalism, on its way to encircle the entire globe, reached the Islamic lands as well, and established in them the foundation of the modern state-system. Muslim countries that had reacted against the existing ecumenical unity were the first to respond to nationalist aspirations with varying degrees of enthusiasm.

The Genesis of Arab Nationalism

Turks and Arabs, the two major ethno-cultural groups which maintained Ottoman power, remained the least affected by the forces disrupting Islamic unity. But the decadence of

Ottoman rule, arising from internal as well as external forces, became visible by the latter part of the eighteenth century. Islamic power, which was always held to be invincible, since it was ultimately derived from a divine source, began to suffer successive defeats and humiliations at infidel hands. These defeats inspired reformers to study the secrets of European superiority. This led initially to the adoption of European military techniques, for Ottoman superiority had rested on military discipline in earlier times. But the continuing decline in Islamic power prompted the adoption of additional, wider measures which eventually brought the idea of nationalism in their wake.

The Christian subjects of the Sultan were the first to catch the echoes of nationalism. By the nineteenth century, the Ottoman grip on the Balkan provinces had already weakened. The Christian princes, supported by the European powers, revolted at Ottoman domination and sought to set up independent states on the principles of nationalism. The triumph of nationalism in the Balkans made itself felt in other provinces of the empire. By the end of the nineteenth century, many Muslim thinkers had taken alarm from the steady decline in Islamic power and lost patience with the sultan's despotism, enforced in the name of Islam. These thinkers, under the influence of European liberalism and nationalism, urged the adoption of these very ideas in the hope that the Ottoman empire might regain its strength. The religion on which Sultan 'Abd al-Hamid had formulated a Pan-Islamic policy, they argued, was inadequate to promote loyalty, and they called for its replacement by nationalism. Thoughts along these lines were confined at first to a small circle of intellectuals, but liberal and national ideas began to spread wider following the overthrow of Sultan 'Abd al-Hamid in 1908. Once nationalism had gained acceptance as the official policy, it stirred fears among 'Abd al-Hamid's successors about its possible adverse effects on the unity of the empire. A unifying force in a society enjoying cohesion and social solidarity, nationalism can prove disruptive in a population as composite as the Ottoman. It was feared that adoption of nationalism might tempt the non-Muslim communities to seek their salvation in the collapse rather than in the perpetuation of the structure under which they lived.

When faced with the problem of what national policy to formulate for the maintenance of unity, the new rulers envisioned three possible courses of action: (1) Pan-Islamism, (2) Ottomanism, and (3) Turkish nationalism. A clear policy was never adopted officially owing to the complexities of the situation and the conflicting views of the leaders.[4] The new generation, in the majority, acting under the influence of nationalist thinkers, seems to have favored Turkish nationalism. Pan-Islamism was discredited because it failed to rehabilitate Islam under Hamidian rule, while Ottomanism was put forward too late to create cohesion among diverse groups who had adopted conflicting national identities. It was Turkish nationalism which gradually came to dominate the new rulers and they sought to impose new loyalties on all the non-Turkish elements of the empire with a policy of Turkification.

The Arabs, long faithful to Islamic unity, gradually began to react against Turkification. Most were willing to cooperate with Turkish leaders to maintain unity as long as certain concessions were offered them, but the Turkish-extremist insistence on assimilation drove the reluctant Arab leaders into the arms of liberals who had long called for an "Arab awakening" based on nationalism.

The Christian Arab thinkers were the first to advocate the idea of Arab nationalism without reference to Islam. Although the status of Christians improved considerably after the reform measures of 1839 and 1856 which placed them legally on an equal footing with the Muslims, they nevertheless questioned the religious basis of Ottoman power which separated them from their compatriots. Recalling Christian contributions to early Arab culture, Christian intellectuals aspired to play an important role in the Arab empire were it reestablished. Arab nationalism, as they advocated it, was implic-

[4] The leaders of the so-called triumvirate were not in agreement on the issue. Enver Pasha was reputed to favor Pan-Islamism, Tal'at Pasha Ottomanism, and Jamal Pasha Turkish nationalism.

itly secular. Only a handful of Muslim Arabs of liberal mind accepted it. The majority of Muslim Arabs hesitated to break Ottoman unity for their attachment to Islam had not yet suffered erosion by nationalism.[5]

Muslim liberal thinkers who advocated the idea of nationalism did neither demand that Arab lands be detached from the Ottoman empire nor indeed that religion be separated from the state. 'Abd al-Rahman al-Kawakibi, the most radical Muslim thinker who attacked Ottoman rule, called for the restoration of the caliphate from Turkish to Arab hands, but not for a break in Ottoman unity.[6] He failed, however, to define his frequent references to the Arab nation in clear nationalist terms, and his idea of nationalism represented but a transition from the ecumenical to the national stage. Even the Christian Najib 'Azuri, who advocated the liberation of the Arabs from Ottoman rule, accepted an attachment to Ottoman unity in some form. He proposed to divide the Arab lands into two parts, the North (the Fertile Crescent) and the South (Arabia), each with a reorganization all its own. Arabia, the seat of the caliphate, would become an Islamic state, and the Fertile Crescent a modern secular state.[7] Al-

[5] For the theme that the forerunners of Arab nationalism were Christian thinkers, see George Antonius, *The Arab Awakening* (London, 1938). See also Sati' al-Husri, *Muhadarat fi Nushu' al-Fikra al-Qawmiya* [Lectures on the Evolution of the Idea of Nationalism] (Cairo, 1951), pp. 165–75; Albert Hourani, *Arabic Thought in the Liberal Age 1798–1939* (London, 1962), pp. 273ff.

[6] al-Kawakibi's argument that the Turks usurped the caliphate from the Arabs was based on the doctrine that one of the qualifications of the caliph must be his descent from the Arab tribe of Quraysh, according to authoritative legal texts. While the content of this argument was outwardly polemical, its spread among Muslim thinkers betrayed lack of loyalty to Turkish leadership (see 'Abd al-Rahman al-Kawakibi's *Umm al-Qura* [Cairo, 1316/1900]. For a discussion of Kawakibi's life and works, see Khaldun S. al-Husri, *Three Reformers* (Bayrut, 1966), pp. 55–112; Hourani, *Arabic Thought in the Liberal Age*, pp. 271–73.

[7] 'Azuri was a former official under the Ottoman administration and served as a deputy governor of Jerusalem before he resigned and settled in Paris. He published his proposals in 1905 (see Negib Azoury, *Le Réveil de la Nation Arabe* [Paris, 1905]; Hourani, *Arabic Thought in the Liberal Age*, pp. 277–79). Before 'Azuri, another Christian leader called for the separation of Arab lands from the Ottoman empire—Yusuf Karam;

Kawakibi and 'Azuri, to mention but two distinguished writers, made it clear that the idea of Arab nationalism remained vague and nebulous before the Turkish Revolution of 1908.

Turkish nationalism was a liberal movement at the outset. It displayed its aggressive and assimilating propensities toward other nationalities only subsequently. After 1908, it exercised an adverse effect on those Arabs who wished to live under a regime of liberty and in harmony with the Turks. Attempts at Arab assimilation by the Turks stirred Arab fears that they might lose their cultural identity. Turkish and Arab leaders who advocated unity made several attempts to repair the situation, but in vain. Arab societies, civil and military, began to work actively for the spread of Arab nationalism, with the principal aim of bringing pressure on Turkish leaders for granting concessions in order to preserve the unity rather than to shatter it. In that period, Muslim and Christian Arab leaders were successful in bridging their differences on the subject of nationalism and in reaching agreement about a national program of action for the Arab lands. Their compromise was embodied in proposals formulated at an Arab conference held in Paris (June 18–23, 1913) and communicated to the Ottoman Government. They may be summed up as follows:

1. Reforms to be carried out in the Ottoman empire were deemed a necessity for all.
2. The Arabs were to participate more actively in the central government of the empire.

---

but his suggestion was inspired by the Russo-Turkish war of 1877 rather than by nationalism. Karam wrote from Paris to Amir 'Abd al-Qadir al-Jaza'iri, the exiled Algerian leader in Damascus, urging him to come to an understanding with the European powers for a separate existence of Arab lands under his rule after that war (see Sam'an Karam, *Yusuf Beg Karam fi al-Manfa* [Tripoli, 1950], pp. 330–36, 346–62). When the war was over and Blunt suggested a separate existence for Syria under Jaza'iri's rule, Britain was no longer interested in such an arrangement (see W. S. Blunt, *Secret History of the English Occupation of Egypt* [London, 1907], pp. 118–19).

3. A decentralized administrative regime was to be established in every Arab province (the wilayat of Bayrut demanded the expansion of the powers of its Provincial Council and the right of employing foreign advisers in accordance with an application submitted on January 31, 1913).
4. The Arabic language was to be regarded as official in Arab provinces, and recognized as a second language in the Ottoman Parliament.
5. Military service was to be confined to the needs of the Arab provinces, except in extraordinary circumstances.
6. Economic conditions in Lebanon were to be improved.
7. The Arabs sympathized with Armenian aspirations for a similar decentralized administrative regime.[8]

Had these demands proven acceptable to the Turks, they could have provided a foundation for a binational state.[9] Several Arab and Turkish leaders proposed to establish a Turko-Arab *Ausgleich* (after the Austro-Hungarian model of 1848) in order to reach a lasting settlement with Arabs. But the idea of nationalism which dominated the younger Turks also began to influence Arab opinion shortly before World War I broke out. Arab secret societies, formed in Istanbul, Bayrut, Damascus, and Baghdad, disseminated revolutionary ideas demanding complete separation from Ottoman unity. Syria and Lebanon were hotbeds of Arab nationalism, and they were placed under a rigid Ottoman control. When Jamal Pasha, an exponent of the policy of Turkification, was appointed Military Governor in those countries during World War I, he embittered Arab nationalists and forever alienated

[8] An appendix was added to these points stipulating that no Arab should accept any government position, nor a seat in Parliament, before these demands were accepted by the Ottoman government. For the text of the resolutions, see Muhib al-Din al-Khatib (ed.), *al-Mu'tamar al-'Arabi al-Awwal* [The First Arab Conference] (Cairo, 1913), pp. 113–31.

[9] The Ottoman government showed initial readiness to accept these proposals and an agreement was reached between Tal'at Pasha, Minister of Interior, and 'Abd al-Karim Khalil, representing Arab leaders, incorporating the major points, but it was never carried out. For an account of the agreement and a summary of the text, see Husri, *Muhadarat fi Nushu' al-Fikra al-Qawmiya*, pp. 202–6.

them by hanging their principal leaders. This act marked the breaking point in Islamic unity, and the war gave a fresh impetus to Arab nationalism and its striving for independence.

The Aims of Nationalism

The aims of Arab nationalism were never formulated in a set of principles at the time Arabs grew aware of themselves as a group separate from others in the Ottoman empire. Their aims began to take shape gradually after the nationalist movement got under way. In many instances, the rationale and the principles of significant political movements developed after rather than before these movements had sprung into existence. The Arab nationalist movement followed in that tradition. Each new circumstance widened the horizon of the movement, and these cumulative conditions and forces affected considerably the changing character of the nationalist movement.

Before World War I, while the Arab idea of nationalism was mingled with the idea of Islamic unity, Arab nationalism scarcely aimed beyond the rehabilitation of the Arab race in a multinational empire. Some thinkers called for a restoration of the Arab empire, presumably implying that Arab political leadership should be separated from that of the Turks, but most Arabs were content to remain within the frame of the Ottoman unity, as long as their proper place was recognized by the Turkish rulers. Arab thinkers justified the claims of their race to such a place by recalling the role the Arabs had in the rise and maintenance of the Islamic empire. The aim of Arab nationalism, they argued, was merely to restore the Arabs to their lost role in Islam to which they felt entitled. Some, who had fallen under the influence of European liberal ideas, stressed the national rather than the ecumenical values, but none advocated separation from the Islamic unity. Even Christian thinkers, who advocated complete separation from the Ottoman union, were ready to compromise their extreme nationalist views so as to maintain solidarity with their Muslim compatriots.

The new circumstances introduced by World War I greatly affected the course of Arab nationalism and called for the reformulation of Arab aims. A few Arabs may have harbored revolutionary notions after the Ottoman failure to carry out the Paris proposals, but almost all continued to hope that their differences might be reconciled. When war broke out, they were ready to wait for a redress until its end. British support for Arab claims against the Turks brought to the fore those revolutionary leaders who made their imprint on Arab nationalism and who transformed it from a slow and peaceful movement into a revolutionary and a separatist one. From that point onward, Arab nationalism demanded complete independence, whether from Turkish or some other foreign rule. The revolutionary method was not completely new to the Arabs, but the British alliance with Arab nationalism speeded up the progress of the movement and all but turned it into a rebellion against the traditional modes of loyalty. Under the impact of European ideas, Arab nationalism necessarily became liberal and almost secular in character, since it was reacting against the Islamic unity.

Detached from Ottoman rule before the era of nationalism, the whole of North Africa, from Egypt to Morocco, was stirred by religious zeal, reminiscent of the *jihad,* to resist European encroachment. It followed naturally that nationalism, when it began to develop, became mixed with religion, since no conflict between religious unity and nationalism in these lands had developed along the lines of the conflict in eastern Arab lands which had led to the revolt against Ottoman unity. Even Egypt, which always fostered closer cultural connections with eastern Arabs, shared with the peoples of North Africa their opposition to European influences while her nationalism was also mixed with religion. Hence, it was not surprising that the Arab alliance with Britain in 1916, which helped to separate Arab lands from the Ottoman empire, was viewed with suspicion and disapproval by Egyptian leaders because Egyptian nationalism favored Ottoman unity against European intervention.[10]

However, under the European impact, Arab nationalism, though broad in scope, changed its character from a positive to a negative movement. World War I made it possible for Arab nationalists to demand independence, and they came close to achieving it. But when Arab lands, especially in the Fertile Crescent, were detached from the Ottoman sovereignty, they were placed under foreign tutelage. Arab nationalism thereupon began to assume a negative character, because foreign influence deprived it of the promised unity and independence by creating small and weak states that would be easy to dominate. Had nationalism been allowed to mature peacefully and slowly without foreign intervention, its trends and character, as well as the political map of the Arab world, would have assumed a different form. If administrative decentralization, the aim of Arab nationalism before World War I, had reached its full development, it might have produced a set of self-governing provinces with full independence for the region, in the event of Ottoman unity having been dissolved. Since Egypt was then under the British control and Arabia was virtually independent, the Fertile Crescent might have found it more advantageous to create separate administrative systems without disrupting its political unity, thus allowing large measures of local autonomy in provinces which claimed religious or ethnic exclusiveness, such as the Kurds in 'Iraq and the Christians in Lebanon. Such a development might have spared Arab nationalism of the conflict between the advocates of local independence and the emerging Pan-Arab movement aiming at reuniting Arab lands. During the interwar years, Arab nationalism necessarily remained confined to negative aims, since independence and national unity were

[10] The case of 'Aziz 'Ali al-Misri, an Egyptian patriot who participated in Arab nationalist activities in Istanbul and the Hijaz, presents an example of the mixture of Arab and Islamic loyalties which came into conflict when his compatriots sought cooperation with a foreign power. Failure to reconcile his attachment to Ottoman unity with Arab independence led to his departure from the center of the Arab Revolt (see Majid Khadduri, " 'Aziz 'Ali al-Misri and the Arab Nationalist Movement," *St. Antony's Papers*, ed. Albert Hourani (London, 1960), *Middle Eastern Affairs*, no. 4, pp. 140–63.

regarded as overriding. Social and economic ideals had not yet captured the imagination of nationalist leaders, although some parties, like the Wafd of Egypt, inserted into their programs planks dealing with social questions. In the eyes of nationalist leaders at that time, questions of security and national freedom deserved priority over social and economic needs. Only after World War II did social and economic ideals attract public attention and become national aims.

Components of Nationalism

Before Islam, Arab loyalty was exclusively tribal.[11] Like other narrow loyalties, ethnic, geographical or related ones, this loyalty was superseded by Islam. The Arabs, in Lawrence's words, had "lost their geographical sense, their racial and political and historical memories; but they clung the more tightly to their language, and erected it almost into a fatherland of its own." [12] It was the Arabic language, rich in literature and legend, which provided the source for historical memories and a sense of pride, invoked to fire the imagination of young men who took the lead in arousing their people to achieve national goals. Since the call came first from the Arab-speaking peoples of Syria, Lebanon, and 'Iraq, themselves Arabicized after the early Islamic conquest, Arab nationalism was necessarily cultural rather than ethnic in character. Such an admixture of races had already occurred in the Arab world that ethnic differences were superseded by religious and cultural elements.[13] Anyone who identified himself with the Arab cultural heritage and claimed Arabic as his native language was and is regarded today as an Arab. After the Arab conquest of the lands bordering Arabia, the Christians who made their homes in them contributed so much to Arabic culture, notably its language and literature, that Christians today have been able to identify themselves fully with the Arab cultural herit-

[11] See p. 9, above.

[12] T. E. Lawrence, *Seven Pillars of Wisdom* (London, 1935), p. 45.

[13] For a discussion of the relation between race and nation in the Arab world, see Albert Hourani, "Race, Religion, and Nation-State in the Near East," *A Vision of History* (Bayrut, 1961), pp. 71–105.

age. The Arabic language, praised in the Qur'an and the Traditions as the richest and the most eloquent of tongues, remains as the very foundation of the Arab national consciousness.

The study of the Arabic language and literature in recent times revived awareness of the "past glories" (*al-amjad*) and the Arabs began to take pride in the role their ancestors had played in the establishment of the Islamic empire. This "historical memory," a blend of fact and vivid imagination, became an important ingredient in Arab nationalism, since it created, in the minds of young men, a sense of compelling duty to restore these glories to their people. In all Arab countries, Arab history was and is taught in primary and high schools as an instrument for national indoctrination, and not as an intellectual exercise. Language, literature, and history have come to form the core of the Arab cultural heritage. These were the elements which largely predetermined the character and inner force of the nationalist movement before World War I as well as after it.

Arab nationalism with its ingredients of cultural heritage might have molded Arab national feeling eventually into a mature and positive social force imbued with a liberal and tolerant spirit, were it not for the forces unleashed after World War I. The imposition of tutelage on the more advanced Arab lands against their wishes, while the relatively more backward ones were left free and independent, aroused suspicions of European motives for the denial of their independence, and gradually introduced a negative and antiliberal element into Arab nationalism. Since independence was not in sight despite continuous opposition (except perhaps for 'Iraq which had obtained a formal independence though not its full substance), Arab nationalism, in time, fell under the influence of still another anti-liberal ideology—"integral nationalism." [14] The rise of Fascism, and its proto-

[14] This term, suggested by Carlton Hayes, is based on the assumptions of the corporate and totalitarian state and characterized by authoritarianism (see Carlton J. H. Hayes, *Historical Evolution of Modern Nationalism* [New York, 1931], pp. 164ff). For a discussion of this form of Arab nationalism, see chap. 8, below.

type Nazism, which both developed in reaction to liberalism, greatly influenced Arab nationalism, which fell prey to national frustrations and was lured by the promises of what integral nationalism might achieve. Some tried to identify Arab nationalism with these new forces as a protest to European domination and to Zionism. To religious groups, the new nationalism appeared as a revival of a prototype religious zeal which was not alien to Islam. Thus, when religious groups began to take an active part in politics, they shared with the young nationalists a certain national urge which they had adopted from European integral nationalism.

National Traits

In comparison with other ethno-cultural groups in Islamic lands, the Arabs are perhaps the most highly individualistic and parochial in character. In ordinary circumstances, they manifest narrow loyalties, tribal or local in nature. Contrary to their submissive appearance and pacifist manners, they are robust, violent, and highly sensitive people whose volatile emotions may rise to a very high pitch in moments of excitement. In the absence of an effective internal or external stimulus, the Arabs tend to relapse into local jealousies or intertribal warfare, but when their imaginations are fired by a moving idea or ideal, their narrow loyalties are at once submerged, even superseded, and they can rise to the task they are called upon to fulfill. Such a call must be made by a prophet, i.e., an inspired reformer, or a fiery charismatic leader trusted for his integrity, straightforwardness, and strength of character. As long as the ideal is preached by lesser men, the effect on the minds of Arabs is scanty and the call remains without response. But when a powerful leader arises, the ideal is likely to be translated into a sudden upsurge, even without passing through transitional stages. The outburst releases a store of energy which could lead to a creation or a destruction. If the outburst fails to achieve the cherished goal, it subsides quickly unless it is revived by fresh stimuli, which will stem but rarely from the same source of inspiration.[15]

A comparison of some Arab national traits with those of the Persians and the Turks, the other two major ethno-cultural groups in the Islamic unity, may not be without interest. The Persians are less violent but more articulate in their individualistic impulses and their imaginative and speculative minds rendered them more passive and perhaps less excitable than the Arabs. These traits are not conducive to violent acts; therefore, if a revolt were ever to arise, it must begin as a clandestine movement before it is translated into an open rebellion. Thus Persian movements of opinion must pass through transitional stages before they appear on the surface as sudden outbursts. If the movement fails, it never really dies for it relapses into some form of expectation to be revived by the return of a *Mahdi*, the Messiah who will reappear to fulfill the unfinished task.

Less violent and more submissive to authority than Arabs and Persians are the Turks, yet they are no less courageous. They are so well disciplined in the art of war that Arab tradition described them as the most difficult to defeat in battle. A saying ascribed to the Prophet Muhammad admonishes the Arabs that the Turks should be the last people to attack, owing to their strength of character and toughness.[16] Keen observers of the Turks from the time of al-Jahiz (d. 869) to von Moltke (d. 1891) paid high tribute to their perseverence and military discipline,[17] but these very traits rendered their

[15] T. E. Lawrence has expressed the effect of ideas on the Arab mind in these words: "Arabs could be swung on an idea as on a cord; for the unpledged allegiance of their minds made them obedient servants. None of them would escape the horde till success had come. . . . Then the idea was gone and the work ended—in ruin. Without a creed they could be taken to the four corners of the world (but not to heaven) by being shown the riches of earth and the pleasure of it; but if on the road, led in this fashion, they met the prophet of an idea . . . they would all leave their wealth for his inspiration" (*Seven Pillars of Wisdom*, p. 42).

[16] See Imam al-Bukhari, *Sahih*, ed. Rudolf Krehl (Leiden, 1864), II, 230.

[17] See Abu 'Uthman al-Jahiz, "Risala Ila al-Fath b. Khaqan fi Manaqib al-Turk," *Thalath Rasa'il*, ed. G. Van Vloten (Leiden, 1902), pp. 1–56; cf. Field-Marshal Count Helmuth von Moltke, *Essays, Speeches, and Memoirs* (New York, 1893), vol. 1, 269.

traditional loyalties the more difficult to supplant in favor of new ones. Once the new loyalty has taken root, however, it tends to persist as a stabilizing force in society.

Retrospect

Three major forms of nationalism had arisen in the Islamic world before World War I. The first, Persian, nationalism may be regarded as a protest against the cumulative domination of Sunni Islam over heterodox creeds. In large measure, it was also the assertion of a Persian ethno-cultural identity, disguised in the Shi'i creed and providing the foundation of modern Persian nationalism. The second and third, Turkish and Arab, nationalisms remained latent owing to their subordination to orthodox Islam; they arose essentially in reaction to a failure to create common loyalty which might have replaced Islam as a point of reference. Thus while religion (Shi'ism) provided the basis for Persian nationalism, Turkish and Arab nationalisms were impeded by religion (Sunnism). The three types of nationalism, however, eventually subordinated religious values to national values before they could develop as separate loyalties. Only one, Turkish, nationalism succeeded in separating religion from nationalism after World War I, mainly because it refused to view Islam as the product of its cultural heritage; the two others could not possibly dissociate religion from nationalism because they considered their creeds as legacies of their own culture.

In a broad sense, the three nationalisms may be regarded as manifestations of failure of the ecumenical Islamic society to hold its own in the face of European ascendency. At the outset, social reformers sought to adopt reform measures without compromising Islam, but the continuous decadence of Islamic power prompted later reformers to turn to nationalism, a movement whose full development has not yet been reached.

In its early stages, nationalism received the support of European powers because it was closely linked with European liberalism; later on, however, it reacted against European ascendency after several Islamic lands had passed under European control.

Like similar movements in the West, nationalism in Islamic lands passed through two major stages of development before it began to mature into a mode of loyalty to a modern nation-state. The first stage produced the territorial state governed by a dynasty whose interests were identified with interests of the nation. Justified as *raison d'état*, the dynasty always sought to defend itself against foreign encroachment. In the second stage, when authority passed from the dynasty to the nation, the will of the people determined the national interest. This stage of development obviously has not yet been attained by the Arabs.

Finally, unlike nationalism in Europe, nationalism in Islamic lands (especially in the Arab world) is based essentially on cultural rather than on ethnic grounds. But, as in Europe, it has been compromised by cross-current nationalities —essentially ethnic in Europe and ethno-cultural in Arab lands. In the latter area, some minorities, especially religious ones, are not opposed in essence to major national unities; but when religion is augmented by cultural variation, militant cross-current nationality tends to arise. So varied and intermingled are these national and religious minorities that the Arab world all but resembles a mosaic of minorities.[18]

During the inter-war years, nationalism and political democracy were accepted by the ruling elites in Egypt and the Fertile Crescent as working concepts and institutions to replace traditional loyalty and institutions. The first ideology succeeded in becoming the basis of polity, but the second one, for complex factors to be explained in the following chapter, failed to provide a working substitute for traditional institutions.

[18] See Albert Hourani, *Minorities in the Arab World* (London, 1947).

Chapter 3

CONSTITUTIONALISM AND DEMOCRACY

Governments cannot be constructed by premeditated design. They are not made, but grow . . . from the nature and life of that people: a product of their habits, instincts, and unconscious wants and desires, scarcely at all of their deliberate purposes.

John Stuart Mill

The movement to provide Islamic countries with constitutional charters embodying the fundamental principles of government and a bill of rights was inspired by Europe. Traditional Islam did formulate general principles governing the incidence and exercise of authority, but it failed to provide checks on the absolute authority of rulers, many of whom violated the very spirit of the Islamic system. Modern constitutionalism, a movement to limit authoritarianism, was initiated by European nations which sought to curb the powers of autocratic rulers. It was emulated by Muslim reformers who strove for a similar objective to limit the traditional powers of their rulers—power originally derived from Islamic sources but no longer regarded as compatible with Muslim interests. In a broader sense, constitutionalism dealt with the political system as a whole and the methods and the instruments by which the people can participate in it, as well as with the ways and means of exercising authority by rulers.

The Rise of Constitutionalism

Reformers were already grappling with the notion of constitutionalism by the beginning of the nineteenth century, but fears arose that a drastic step of this description might arouse the opposition of the forces of conservatism and inertia. However, neither the early reform measures (the decrees of 1839, 1856, and others) nor traditional Islam itself could offer correctives to the existing system of government, although all sides subscribed in principle to the need for reform. The liberal reformers, some of whom had fled to Europe and began to call for constitutionalism and representative government in their own lands, were inspired by the European liberal movements of 1830 and 1848. Their agitation reached its highest pitch in 1866, when they submitted a petition to the sultan in the form of a letter accompanied supposedly by draft constitutional proposals, and urged him to take the lead in the constitutional-representative movement.[1]

But Jamal al-Din al-Afghani, the leading religious reformer, alarmed by the widespread corruption and inefficiency in traditional institutions, stirred the interest of religious groups in the constitutional-representative movement, and encouraged liberals to apply pressure on their rulers to accept the principles of constitutionalism and representative government. Representative institutions, Jamal al-Din maintained, were necessary because they were prescribed by religion under the general principle of "shura," and because they were essential to progress.[2] To support his argument, he called on the Quranic story of Solomon and the Queen of Sheba, which set a precedent for consultation with the people's representatives. The story relates that the Queen, after receiving an important message from Solomon, called upon the notables for advice and said:

> O my nobles, give an opinion in my affair; for I am not in the habit of resolving an affair until you are present with me.[3]

More specifically, the principle of consultation is expressed

[1] Fazil Pasha, grandson of Muhammad 'Ali Pasha of Egypt; his letter is entitled *Lettre Addressé au feu Sultan Aziz feu Prince Mustafa Fazil Pacha, 1866* (Cairo, 1879). For a discussion of his political views, see Şerif Mardin, *The Genesis of Young Ottoman Thought* (Princeton, 1962), chap. 9.

[2] Literally, *Shura* means consultation, but constitutionally it means the ruler's consultation with his people's representatives on public affairs.

[3] *Qur'an* XXVII, 32.

in the Qur'an in the following terms: "... their affairs are subject to consultation among themselves."[4] These texts, cited by Jamal al-Din from the primary source of Islam, can be taken as clear evidence that Muslim rulers should call on the people's representatives for advice before taking decisions on public affairs. But Jamal al-Din was not content to halt there. On the strength of these texts, he went on, authority ultimately belongs to the people and rulers have no right to govern without the consent of their subjects.[5] These ideas, coming from an influential religious leader, had an immense impact on the religious groups who supported the European-inspired constitutional movement. It was on the momentum of Jamal al-Din's efforts that religious groups in Istanbul, Cairo, and Tehran supported the constitutional experiments launched by Turkey in 1876, Egypt in 1881, and Persia in 1905. In similar fashion, the Tunisian statesman-reformer Khayr al-Din Pasha sought religious justification in support of representative institutions and promoted his views by taking an active part in the preparation of a draft constitution for his country in 1860.[6]

When the leaders of the constitutional movement finally succeeded in establishing representative institutions, they paid no heed to those religious doctrines which continued to hold the public in their grip. The constitutions of Tunisia, Egypt, and Turkey took no notice of Islamic principles save for reference to Islam as the official religion of the state.[7] They were framed under the exclusive influence of European

[4] *Qur'an* XLII, 36.

[5] See *Khatirat Jamal al-Din al-Afghani,* ed. Muhammad al-Mukhzumi (Bayrut, 1931), pp. 46–47, 58, 91, 162–63. Jamal al-Din was quite willing at the outset to cooperate with autocratic rulers, but he soon found the difficulties involved in carrying out reform and began to advocate the adoption of representative institutions.

[6] For Khayr al-Din's ideas, see his *Kitab Aqwam al-Masalik fi Ma'rifat al-Mamalik* (Tunis, 1284/1868); translated by L. Carl Brown, *The Surest Path: The Political Treatise of A Nineteenth-Century Muslim Statesman* (Cambridge, Mass., 1967).

[7] The Ottoman Constitution of 1876 added that the Sultan was the Caliph of Muslims, for the obvious reason of asserting allegiance of non-Turkish elements of the empire.

models and thereby lost touch with religious groups whose support was essential for the operation of those novel institutions. Explanation for the failure of the constitutional experiments have sometimes stressed certain legal and technical weaknesses, e.g., cabinets were not responsible to their parliaments, the sovereign's powers were not sufficiently curbed, and elections were not completely free.[8] But the fundamental weakness has not been in these structural defects alone; the constitutions failed because they provided no procedures which could mobilize popular support. A nexus to traditional institutions seems to have been a necessity. As a result, the new institutions began to operate side by side with older ones and an ever-widening rift began to open between them, as the newly created vested interests began to clash with the old ones. Nor did the new institutions prove efficient enough as instruments for progress to overpower the opposition of religious leaders who called for the reassertion of the traditional Islamic system.

As the decades passed, the constitutional movement suffered a setback from which it recovered only by an ultimate resort to violence—an abnegation of the very spirit implied in that liberal movement. The religious groups, fearing that the liberal constitutional movement might lead to the ultimate destruction of Islam, came to the inescapable conclusion that the support of authoritarianism rather than its destruction would best serve their interests. Towards the end of the nineteenth century the realization began to grow among liberals that to achieve reforms by peaceful means was no longer possible.

Both in Persia (1905) and in Turkey (1908), the liberals resorted to violence in an effort to overthrow the opposition and to establish representative institutions. In Turkey, the army first brought the liberals to power, for popular agitation was impossible under the previously strict police surveillance. Until the end of World War I, representative institutions in

[8] Only the Constitution of Egypt (1881) stated that the Cabinet was responsible to parliament.

Turkey and Persia operated under the strains and stresses produced by foreign wars and internal conflicts, yet they seemed to provide a working substitute for traditional institutions, despite the novelty and the complexity of their procedures. Leaders of the constitutional movement found it essential to come to a *modus vivendi* with religious groups and to enlist the cooperation of their leaders in parliamentary representation. When the war ended, the advantages of representative institutions in either the mother country or in the successor states were not questioned.

The Twilight of Democracy in Arab Lands

Outside Egypt, no significant Arab writings on constitutionalism and representative government reached publication before World War I, largely because the Arab thinkers were so preoccupied with the major question of Arab-Turkish relationships that they gave little attention to the form of government their countries should adopt following independence. Even al-Kawakibi, who emptied the vials of his wrath on Hamidian despotism and Ottoman administration, mentioned but casually the form of government he advocated when he called for the restoration of the caliphate to Arab hands and the establishment of consultative councils.[9] However, the participation of Arab leaders in Turkish constitutional and parliamentary activities in 1908 proved invaluable when the task of erecting constitutional structures in the newly created Arab states fell upon them, although the new political systems followed closer the Western democratic models than the models of traditional Ottoman institutions.[10] Nonetheless, most Arab leaders were mentally unprepared for these innovations.

[9] See 'Abd al-Rahman al-Kawakibi, *Taba'i' al-Istibdad* (Cairo, n.d.); and *Umm al-Qura* (Cairo, 1931). For discussion of his political views, see Khaldun S. al-Husri, *Three Reformers* (Bayrut, 1966), pp. 63ff.

[10] Egypt, which passed under British control since 1882, had undergone constitutional experience apart from the eastern Arab lands, although it remained formally part of the Ottoman empire until World War I.

Unlike the Turks and the Persians who were at liberty to make free choices in political systems, the Arabs were not fully at liberty to do so; their decisions were dependent on guidance and advice of the European powers which had extended their control to Arab lands after World War I. Political institutions erected at that time did not spring from the social forces existing in those societies nor did they express the true desires of its peoples. Nevertheless, many Arab leaders, the young nationalists above all, were not discouraged at the outset from experimenting with these institutions despite the limitations that foreign control imposed on the independence of their countries. They seemed ready to accept the notion that democratic institutions were not inherently incompatible with national dependence and they hoped that British and French influence would recede once the new institutions functioned to the satisfaction of foreign as well as national interests.

That hope was not immediately realized. No sooner did the European powers establish themselves in the newly occupied Arab lands than they began to exploit those internal conditions that were unfavorable to democratic institutions in order to strengthen their own positions. The public did not gain the impression that these institutions were erected for their own national benefit, while political subjugation to foreign control caused indignity and injured pride, as has been pointed out before. Even if these institutions had as their purpose the instruction in the art of self-government of the "peoples not yet able to stand by themselves," as the Western powers claimed,[11] their sincerity was questioned: Why were countries which had gained some experience in self-government, Egypt, Syria and 'Iraq, placed under British and French control, while the hinterlands of Arabia which were more backward by far in the art of self-government, allowed to remain immune to foreign influence?

The European powers and their allies who sought to make the world safe for democracy by spreading liberal institutions

[11] See Article 22 of the Covenant of the League of Nations.

never grasped the problems inherent in the transplanting of democratic institutions into the new Arab countries. Apparently, they encouraged native leaders to adopt political institutions modeled after their own systems—the French pattern in the countries under French control and the British pattern in countries under British control—but they paid little heed to whether these institutions were compatible with local conditions. Moreover, the newly created systems were not permitted to function freely in order to adapt themselves to existing conditions; too often limitations were imposed wherever conflicts with foreign interests loomed up.

British and French policies in issuing constitutional and political guidance were frequently inconsistent. Britain appeared to champion the Egyptian constitutionalists who favored parliamentary control of government against the King's desire to exercise authoritarian powers, but her proconsuls in 'Iraq and Transjordan were known to favor powerful heads of state. The conflicts between authoritarian tendencies and democratic aspirations created compromise systems which vested the heads of state with veto powers, including the right to dismiss the heads of government, and which recognized the theoretical right of parliaments to control cabinets, although during parliamentary recesses the governments retained the right to legislate by decree. The granting of dual responsibility for government to heads of state and to parliaments proved an inherent weakness in the political system. Parliamentary democracy came to appear as a travesty to those who aspired to a true democracy. As to France, she proved so eager to strip away the advantages of democratic institutions by continuous resort to the suspension of parliamentary life, that those institutions could never hope to take root.

In Western countries, the existence of a multiple party system which permits the participation of the people in democratic processes is a necessary requisite for the proper functioning of democratic institutions. But in Arab lands, the political parties organized to consolidate parliamentary democracy were more absorbed, from the very outset, in the struggle to bring foreign domination to an end at the earliest moment possible, than in preparing an enlightened population to participate in parliamentary elections. Small wonder that the people were encouraged to support only the party, or parties, that raised the cry of nationalists, and a multiple party system in the Western sense proved too weak to take root. A one-party system could scarcely provide a secure foundation for democratic institutions. Britain and France were often obliged to focus their energies on reducing the influence of the nationalist party, or parties, rather than on guiding them toward the role of a responsible opposition, particularly because of the uncompromising attitude of the opposition leaders.[12]

Britain and France also failed to agree on the policies they would follow in the countries under their control. Essentially, their disagreement may have stemmed from two opposing viewpoints relating to the reconciliation between foreign interests and the natural growth of indigenous free institutions. Should the foreign power exercise direct control over the country under its guidance, or should it guide with a minimum degree of control? And how long should foreign guidance continue in order to help operation of free institutions with relative stability and positive effects (i.e., progress, native satisfaction, etc.)? Keenly aware of her formal responsibilities as a mandatory power, France insisted on the need for inserting in the constitutions of Syria and Lebanon stipulations designed to ensure that prior every official action French approval was granted. Britain, willing to subordinate form to substance, demanded no such formal powers, and preferred to rely on indirect rather than on direct influence.[13] Provisions for foreign tutelage were deemed unnecessary in the 'Iraqi constitution, but the Syrian and Lebanese constitutions defined in detail the powers of France's official represen-

[12] For the failure of party systems to consolidate parliamentary democracy, see pp. 44–46, below.

[13] "The most successful Anglo-Egyptian officials," says one experienced British official in colonial administration, "have been those who have relied most on their own powers of persuasion, and have rarely applied for diplomatic support" (Lord Cromer, *Modern Egypt* [London, 1908], II, 283).

tatives *vis-à-vis* the heads of state. This direct control of government by foreign advisers was unacceptable to Arab leaders, in whose eyes it inflicted indignities on the heads of state and of government and hampered any Arab assumption of responsibility. Conflicts between Arab leaders and French advisers over constitutional issues became continuous.

How long could a control, direct or indirect, last? Ideally, the French practice, though limiting native ability to learn by experience, might have been more effective in achieving swift progress and development, while the British method, though encouraging initiative, was likely to make progress slow and tedious. But foreign control, no matter how beneficial in material progress it might be, was bound to be resented as an affront to Arab pride. True, the British resorted to persuasion, which tended to satisfy the *amour propre* of native officials, but it called for a long period of tutelage, which could result in weakening the ability to accept true responsibility.[14]

Arab leaders were not entirely ungrateful for the benefits of democratic institutions and the freedom provided by them. The criticisms voiced by them were aimed essentially at the foreign restraints imposed on the operation of free institutions rather than at those institutions in principle. Indeed, parliamentary democracy provided opposition leaders with a forum for attacking foreign control with impunity. Short of rebellion, they could scarcely gain such impunity anywhere outside of the walls of parliament. It was that very reason which prompted Syrian nationalists to demand the resumption of parliamentary life whenever the French authorities suspended

[14] "The steady progress which 'Iraq has made since the termination of the mandate in 1932," said Captain V. Holt, a former Oriental Secretary, in a letter to the present writer, "has strengthened me in my belief that the ability of any people to govern themselves does not, as many may seem to think, develop in ratio to the length of the period during which they are under tutelage. On the contrary, prolonged tutelage weakens and ultimately destroys the qualities on which the capacity for self-government depends. The one way for any people to learn how to govern themselves is by assumption of real responsibility for the management of their own affairs" (cited in my *Independent 'Iraq*, 2d ed. [London, 1960], p. 321).

their Parliament following a stormy session. These advantages prompted an ardent Syrian nationalist who was expelled from his country after raising a rebellion to suggest that he favored parliamentary democracy as long as his country remained under foreign control, although a benevolent dictatorship was personally more congenial to him.[15]

When foreign control began to weaken and the task of operating the democratic institutions fell to nationalist leaders, virtual oligarchies arose as vested interests came to dominate these institutions more and more. Nationalist leaders who inherited authority from foreign powers showed little respect for free institutions and began to display traditional authoritarian inclinations. Political parties atrophied and their leaders, relieved of popular pressure, continued in their old ways instead of meeting the demands of new independence by making significant change. The people who expected development and progress under national rule began to discover how scandalously unscrupulous politicians could misuse democratic processes. The new generation that grew to manhood in the period following independence lost confidence in their rulers, although they earnestly desired to participate in truly democratic institutions. Democracy lost its meaning to the majority of the people, while the rulers—the oligarchs—were too preoccupied by a struggle for personal power to plan for reform and development.

In 1936, four years after it gained independence, 'Iraq, the first Arab country to be relieved of tutelage (though not completely free of foreign influence), passed under military control. In 1949, Syria, where foreign tutelage came to an end after World War II, passed under military domination only four years after she had gained independence. Egypt, relieved by partial British evacuation in 1936, escaped domestic military rule until 1952, although some Egyptian army officers seem to have considered the seizure of power as early as

[15] See 'Abd al-Rahman al-Shahbandar, *al-Qadaya al-Ijtima'iya al-Kubra fi al-'Alam al-'Arabi* (Cairo, 1936), pp. 93–94. Shahbandar's views were then shared by several other nationalist leaders.

1940.[16] It remained under British military occupation for over a decade following independence and was kept under British military control throughout World War II. Evacuation began in 1946, but reached completion (the Canal base excepted) only in 1949. Lebanon proved the only Arab country to maintain its institutions relatively free owing to the operation of a checks-and-balances system based on the confessional structure of society, but the social and economic progress achieved must also have resulted in some satisfaction with those institutions. The prolonged British presence in Jordan may account for the survival of the parliamentary regime in that country, but the regime itself fell into a precarious state following departure of the British. In the countries of North Africa west of Egypt—the region which had long remained under a rigid foreign control—democratic institutions could scarcely be expected to develop. When these countries passed from foreign to native hands, they all fell under a varying degree of authoritarian rule because significant popular checks were never permitted to develop. Algeria, governed directly by the French, began to establish free institutions after independence in 1962, but the country passed under a military rule three years later. Libya followed the same pattern of political change. Military rule in this country had been expected to follow the death of an old monarch who achieved independence after long and bitter struggle with foreign rule. The young officers would not even wait for the death of a charismatic ruler and the country, with virtually no resistance, passed under a military dictatorship.

The failure of the democratic experiment in Arab lands calls for an examination of the conditions in which free institutions functioned, and the forces which acted upon them. Meanwhile, rival ideas and ideals of government began to attract attention and contributed to the collapse of free institutions. The failure of the democratic experiment will be discussed presently, while the rival ideas of government will become the subject of discussion in the chapters which follow.

[16] See Anwar al-Sadat, *Revolt on the Nile* (London, 1957), chaps. 3–4.

Failure of Democracy

During the years between the wars, Arab thinkers observed that those Islamic lands which remained free of foreign control had either chosen political systems modeled on contemporary European dictatorships (i.e., Turkey and Persia) or continued to be governed in accordance with traditional authoritarianism (Saudi Arabia, the Yaman, Masqat, etc.). The Arab countries that had fallen under foreign control chose parliamentary democracy on encouragement of European powers, but this encouragement was taken by some to mean foreign intervention in domestic affairs and by others (especially religious groups) as Christian encroachment on Islamic loyalty.

Superficial as this observation may seem, it distorted the image of democracy from the start and added to the difficulties of operation by liberal leaders. The European powers which had participated in the shaping of the new democratic systems, had they but known Arab society better and cherished a greater awareness of the political processes then in progress, might have given the Arab lands under their tutelage an opportunity to adopt Western political concepts and institutions more slowly. Under Western guidance, these countries might have developed their own forms of political democracy to fit their own needs and aspirations. The Arab leaders who cooperated with the European Powers never tried to reconcile Western concepts with traditional concepts and vested interests. As a result, democracy failed to command respect from its very inception; progress and development were expected but not achieved, and democracy had to shoulder the blame.

The argument that European powers and Arab leaders were solely responsible for the failure of democracy might imply that the role played in the operation of political systems by the forces inherent in society has been overlooked. The Arab leaders who participated actively in the shaping of the newly established political systems borrowed concepts in then current fashion. As to the European powers, with the approval of Arab leaders, they sought to introduce into Arab lands political ideas and concepts familiar to them from their own countries that were viewed at the time as elements of strength in Western society. These Western innovations provided only the outward structure of the political system, not the substance, while the forces and conditions which had a bearing upon the substance of the system were found in traditional Arab society. In a word, the form alone was borrowed from the West, while the operating forces were necessarily derived from existing socio-economic conditions and past traditions. An interplay between the form and the operating forces necessarily led to the adaptation of the form to the forces. To achieve progress and development, such an adaptation should not have entirely subordinated the form, expressing needs and aspirations, to the existing conditions which represented traditional patterns. Internal conditions might have undergone gradual modification as new traditions favorable to democratic systems developed, but adjustments of this description needed strong governments that could restrain or change traditional political patterns, as Kamalist Turkey had done, or else external pressures that could maintain the stability of the form as it had been established under European tutelage. There existed no well-informed and responsible public opinion upon which enlightened leaders could rely for the adaptation and consolidation of free institutions. As noted before, democratic institutions were transformed into virtual oligarchies as soon as foreign control came to an end. Turkey's experiments with European political concepts, viewed in retrospect, may well prove to have been more thoroughgoing than those in Arab lands. Before they could develop new political systems, the Arabs had yet to modify the traditional patterns of society.

Islam and Democracy

Constitutionalism and representative government, as we have already had occasion to notice, received the approval of religious groups on the assumption that they were compatible with Islamic principles of government. This Islamic validation for the adoption of Western concepts enabled early reformers to establish parliamentary regimes in several Islamic countries. But at the moment when these institutions began to function, the conflict between the new and the old broke into the open, and the gulf between them grew almost too wide to bridge. It is true that, once the liberals succeeded in establishing modern institutions, they ignored the role of religious groups and in consequence gained the opposition of vested-interest groups. To close the rift became more and more difficult, as each fresh attempt revealed deeper causes of conflict. At bottom, an inherent incompatibility between two political philosophies was at fault.

For centuries, Islam provided a political system which commanded the allegiance and respect of its believers. It prescribed that authority belonged to God. The caliph, though enthroned by the people to enforce God's law, was not constitutionally responsible to the people, but the caliph and his subjects were equally bound by the sacred law, and the violation of it would make them equally subject to punishment. Obviously, the people represented a passive element in principle, for their basic duties were to obey God's law and his mortal representatives on earth. A theory of the state, placing ultimate responsibility in God or his representatives or in both, is certainly not inherently democratic in principle. The believers were satisfied that their political system was an ideal that could not possibly be superseded or matched by any other system, since authority was derived from God, the embodiment of good and justice.[17]

The religious and conservative groups reacted slowly but firmly to the attempts to change Islamic institutions under the impact of Western ideas and concepts. Aghast that traditional codes of law should be superseded by secular legislation without reference to the shari'a (Islamic law), they were also jolted that the very essence of the Islamic system had suffered

[17] For a more detailed statement on the theory of the Islamic state, see my *War and Peace in the Law of Islam* (Baltimore, 1955), chap. 1; Louis Gardet, *La Cité Musulmane* (Paris, 1954).

encroachment, since the liberals called for a complete breach with the past and the adoption of Western secular institutions. Following World War I, the caliphate was formally dissolved in Turkey and subsequently relapsed in Arab lands. The new rulers accepted democratic institutions without attempting to adapt them to existing conditions. The people were neither able nor seriously permitted to participate in the political processes, while intense rivalries divided leaders who were vying for power. Democracy failed to command either the respect or the allegiance of the common people in the way that God's law and the Islamic system had done in the past. Above all, democracy failed to rehabilitate Islam and to repair injured Arab pride. But apart from the slogan "back to Islam," the religious groups offered little in constructive reform programs which might have combined the best of Islamic and Western concepts. The conflict between religious and liberal groups remained unresolved: the liberals denounced the Islamic system as incompatible with modern conditions of life, and the religious leaders, witnessing an impending breach with Islam—such a breach had actually taken place in Turkey—vented their wrath upon those in authority for permitting this change. In practice, Islam proved an impediment in the development of democratic institutions, although religious apologists continued to maintain that Islam was inherently democratic.[18]

Democracy in the Shadow of Nationalism

Democracy, based on the doctrine of popular consent, is closely linked with the idea of nationalism. No nation is expected to respond to nationalist calls unless it is participating in major national decisions, directly or indirectly. The liberals who advocated the adoption of democratic institutions in Arab lands were nationalist leaders who sought to erect new political systems on nationalistic foundations.

[18] Cf. Humayun Kabir, *Science, Democracy and Islam* (London, 1955), chaps. 1–2.

Before World War I, nationalism was restricted to a small circle of young men imbued with liberal ideas, but after the war it began to spread among the masses who developed an anti-Western bias in reaction to the domination of their lands by Western influence. Nationalism became a lay ideology, mixed with traditional Islamic zeal, and swept the entire Islamic world from the Atlantic to the Indian Ocean. An uprising in one country often served as a signal to revolutionaries in other lands. No one expressed that emotional feeling better than Marshal Lyautey, who styled the Islamic world as a "sounding box."

The upsurge of nationalism, intensified by a feeling of indignation against foreign domination, brought to the forefront political leaders who identified themselves more outspokenly with nationalist objectives. The advocates of democracy subscribed to nationalist objectives in principle but suffered losses largely because democracy and foreign influence were identified as one in the public eye. Their insistence on democratic freedoms was often interpreted as harmful to the national interest, because energies might be diverted from the struggle against foreign domination to an absorption with internal issues. It was therefore the slogan of "national unity," demanding the subordination of divergent views on national affairs to a single national objective—independence—to be achieved by concerted action, which exercised a popular appeal greater than any conceivable call to public debate on national issues. As a result, the advocates of democracy received little or no credit for public debates in parliament and their supporters were often denounced as deficient in patriotism. Small wonder that the loudest applause went only to leaders who clamored for national unity and demanded sacrifices in the struggle against foreign domination at the expense of leaders who called for democratic freedoms.

The very notion of freedom, as expounded by democratic leaders, was never fully fathomed by the nationalists. Freedom to nationalist leaders meant freedom from foreign domination and not freedom from authoritarian rule. Hence nationalist leaders were never prepared to permit criticism of their policies in parliament, because they viewed the national objective as sacrosanct and beyond criticism. Zaghlul's retort to his political opponents that those who would challenge him would challenge the Egyptian national interest expressed the true feelings of nationalist leaders in other Arab lands, although Zaghlul struggled as devotedly against Britain in the effort to achieve national freedom as he did against the King's authoritarianism in the effort to assert parliamentary control of government.

In stressing freedom from foreign control, the nationalist may not have strayed too far from political realities, for the individual can achieve no true freedom before the country is freed from foreign servitude. Yet, paradoxically, nationalist leaders displayed a traditional authoritarianism which was incompatible with individual liberty once national independence has been gained. Authoritarianism is nothing new in Islamic polity, but the urgent need to achieve nationalist objectives hampered liberal efforts to denounce it as inconsistent with the effective functioning of democratic institutions.[19]

The Role of Political Parties

In the West, the multiple-party system has been viewed as an essential setting for the workings of parliamentary democracy, even though written constitutions failed to make special provision for political parties. Such parties, operating within the framework of the political system, are not expected to undermine or to negate the principles enshrined in constitutions or their very spirit, but to achieve their goals through parliamentary means. But a party which is opposed to the very

[19] An interesting example of the conflict between national and traditional patterns of authority is revealed in the debate between Faysal, King of Syria in 1920, and Rashid Rida, President of the Syrian (National) Congress. During the debate when the Congress was drawing up a constitution for Syria, there was a suggestion from the floor to put the Syrian Cabinet to a vote of confidence to which King Faysal denied such a right to Congress and said: "I have created the Congress and will not concede to it a right which might impede the action of the Government." To this Rashid Rida replied: "It was the Congress which created you [as King of

basis of the political system under which it functions is transformed thereby into a revolutionary party and no longer remains a mere "loyal opposition." In several democratic systems in the West, such parties have been charged with disloyalty to the democratic system and denounced as unlawful.

Under the Islamic system, political parties were never recognized, and those that existed were never viewed as a loyal opposition. On the contrary, political parties invariably represented heterodox sects, and their doctrines were denounced as irreconcilable with the official orthodox creed. The doctrinal differences sharpened political conflicts, although in origin they may have stemmed from differences in social and economic backgrounds. Following a revolutionary course of action, heterodox religious-political groups were denounced as unbelievers by religious authorities and suppressed by the armed forces of the state. This pattern of political opposition, so characteristic of political activities throughout the course of Islamic history, survives as a legacy in Islamic society today.[20]

From the outset of the new political systems established in Arab lands, interest was keen in organizing political parties on a Western pattern because they were considered essential to the effective functioning of democratic government. But the political parties organized under these circumstances betrayed traditional patterns and some, in the guise of opposing foreign control, refused to act as a "loyal opposition." From their beginnings, political parties were therefore divided into

---

Syria], for you were one general among Allied generals, under General Allenby's command, and [the Congress] proclaimed you King of Syria. It is true that you had called Congress to session . . . but once it convened in the name of the nation, in which authority ultimately resides in accordance with Islamic law as well as the modern principles of law, you and the Government became responsible to it in all matters relating to the independence of the country and the Government's program" (see "The General Syrian Congress," *al-Manar,* 23 [1920], 392–93). Even after he became King of 'Iraq (1921–33), Faysal continued to control the Government, notwithstanding that he learned to pay greater respect to constitutional processes in 'Iraq than he did in Syria.

[20] For the activities of a modern Islamic prototype, see discussion of the Muslim Brotherhood in Chap. 4.

pro-government and anti-government parties. The basic difference which divided them, and often became the subject of parliamentary debate, pertained to the most suitable means of ending foreign control as swiftly as possible. The opposition parties, obeying traditional patterns of political activity, often engaged in anti-government activity, because they could count on the support of those people for whom the pro-government parties (including the one in power) and foreign influence were identical. Democratic procedures became subordinated to nationalist considerations, and every leader who accepted a high government post or was prepared to play the loyal opposition in parliament was viewed with suspicion and disfavor. Only those who proved to be anti-government and identified their goals with "national interests," were accepted as *bona fide* "opposition parties," because they violently attacked foreign influence. Nationalism became the yardstick to distinguish one set of parties from the other, rather than their platforms and parliamentary activities. When foreign control came to an end, these nationalist parties died natural deaths for the most part, because the *raison d'être* for their existence had vanished.

The political parties that survived independence failed to reorganize on democratic lines, since leadership and party loyalty hinged on personal and family affiliation more than on public support. Parties came to represent a mere handful of personalities, gravitating about a leading political figure, who exerted no efforts whatsoever to reach the masses. The Egyptian Wafd party, although it could claim a mass support greater than that of any other in Arab lands, failed to support the parliamentary system by educating the people in democratic methods.

Lack of an Enlightened Public Opinion

In Western countries, public opinion plays an indispensable role in the functioning of democratic institutions, because the theory of democracy rests on the assumption that government is an instrument in the service of the people and must be controlled by them. Public opinion may be vague and wavering in many instances, yet it may become so firm on certain issues of national policy that no democratic government could long survive in power if its policies ran counter to dominant opinion. But public opinion cannot play any significant role if a high percentage of literacy is not attained or if the people are not kept constantly enlightened on public affairs.

In the traditional Islamic society, no deliberate effort was ever made to win the active participation of the public in government processes, owing to the negative attitude towards authority taken by that public and the wide gulf separating the governing and the governed. In tribal society, the tribesmen obeyed their chiefs (the shaykhs), but the tribe as a whole almost invariably viewed central authority as an alien force and looked upon urban society with contempt and suspicion. For centuries, Islamic authority was mainly preoccupied with raising taxes and maintaining mercenary armies in an effort to protect town dwellers from tribal raids. The urban subjects of caliphs and sultans submitted to authoritarianism as a safeguard against raids and plunder.

The Islamic state did not rest on any assumption that the public should act as a check restraining the ruler, even if he transgressed the sacred law. It is true that the caliph, the head of the state and government, was enthroned by the consent of the people, but owed them no responsibility, in practice or in theory. In matters such as the interpretation of law and religion, the caliph was expected to consult the 'ulama. But if the caliph ignored the 'ulama's advice or chose to act without it, they might warn him of evil consequences or pray that God might change his heart. Rarely did the 'ulama ever seek to influence the caliph via public opinion. Witnessing the shifting fortunes of the caliph's authority and the instability of Islamic polity, the 'ulama preached quietness and submission to authority rather than incitement of the public, arguing that tyranny was preferable to disorder and anarchy. In the circumstances, the 'ulama all but supported authoritarianism, because the maintenance of public order concerned them more than the opposition to oppressive rule. As a result, the gulf between the governing and the governed grew ever wider and public opinion could never develop to bridge the gap.

During the years between the wars, after democratic institutions in Arab lands had been established, Arab leaders began to cultivate public opinion in the hope of reaching power with its support or of carrying out declared policies after they gained power. Through the press and radio broadcasting, Arab leaders often succeeded in exciting the public to a pitch so high that violence in times of crisis became almost a daily affair. The government was denounced by opposition leaders as subservient to foreign pressures, and often proved incapable of controlling violence and street demonstrations. To set on fire a public already prepared to rise against authority was far easier than any counter attempts at lowering the temperature. But this upsurge in public emotionalism could not be regarded as an expression of an enlightened public opinion nor as being helpful to public authorities seeking to trim their policies to public demand. Rival leaders sought to use public opinion as a pawn in vying for power rather than as an arbiter of power. Political leaders, whether in opposition or in power, never took pains to inform the public and to prepare it for its proper role in democratic processes. The public was often kept in ignorance on public issues and political leaders refrained from speaking frankly after making extreme promises which could never be met. The public remained ill-informed, frequently hearing only the accusations and counteraccusations among leaders, and often lacking the very faintest notion of what differences of opinion divided them.

Public opinion could never become enlightened in a society stricken with poverty and illiteracy. For centuries, the percentage of literacy was insignificant and the masses remained in ignorance and subservient to superstitions and fetish beliefs. After the national regimes were established, interest was keen in introducing elementary education, and in some countries elementary education became compulsory. Sudden rises in the percentage of literacy were not expected, although it grew more rapidly in Lebanon and Syria than elsewhere. Appeals to emotionalism by Arab leaders could help but little in creating an enlightened public opinion, for beyond the struggle to eliminate foreign influence and to achieve independence (and, more recently, to oppose Israeli claims), the public understood but vaguely the sophisticated slogans of young reformers or the intrigues and manoeuvers of older politicians. Such a public was obviously unready to participate actively in democratic politics or to grasp the value of its complicated processes.

Democracy in a Society Unprepared for It

Democracy, as noted before, met the opposition of religious and conservative elements who viewed it as incompatible with traditional patterns of authority. It failed to win the support of the lay public which forms the backbone of any democratic society, since the very class that identifies its interests with those of democracy was lacking. In Western Europe, democracy was championed by a strong middle class which stood up to the autocracy of the privileged and feudal classes. No comparable middle class has arisen anywhere in Arab lands so far—a middle class which would champion democracy in opposition to authoritarianism. In countries like Lebanon, where a small middle class began to assert itself, democracy is beginning to make headway.[21] But in other countries, which are made up essentially of a two-class society, the democratic system succumbed to authoritarian forces shortly after its establishment or never entered into existence at all.

From medieval times, Islamic society has been divided into the nomadic tribes and the town-dwellers on the one hand and into the relatively wealthy ruling few and the exploited masses on the other. No important middle class, with interests

[21] There was a relatively large middle class before the Egyptian Revolution composed of a high percentage of Copts and foreign colonies, but their influence in politics was mainly exercised through individuals in high government positions rather than by the direct support of the democratic system (see M. Berger, *The Arab World* [New York, 1963], pp. 270–84).

ranging between those of the few rich or of the many poor, ever sprang into existence to bridge the gap between the two. This division of the population naturally gave rise to the dual rivalry between the nomads and the central authority, and between the ruling oligarchy and the masses. The desert areas in the Arab world were inhabited by tribesmen whose habitual occupation was fighting. When the caliphs were strong enough to wage the jihad (popularly called holy war) against unbelievers in neighboring countries, the tribesmen were loyal to the central authority, since their superfluous energy was directed against the external enemy and they found ample compensation in the spoils of war. But when these conquests came to a standstill, idleness did not agree with the restless tribesmen. Often they became a serious threat to the central authority and they turned their energies against the cities. In time, the problem of how to protect the cities from periodic tribal raids became one of the great concerns of the caliphs and of their governors. For centuries, the function of the state was reduced to the collection of taxes from the urban population and the maintenance of mercenary armies against tribal raids. After the decline of the 'Abbasid caliphs, the feudal lords of the various provincial administrators inherited those functions. The Ottoman sultans, who assumed control of Arab lands in the sixteenth century, adopted a policy essentially of tribe-smashing, aggravating thereby the tensions between urban and tribal populations on the one hand, and between tribesmen and the central authorities on the other. Only in the latter part of the nineteenth century did the Ottoman Porte embark on a policy of settlement by offering lands for cultivation to the tribal shaykhs of Syria and 'Iraq. This new policy, which aided in reconciling the shaykhs to authority and in "detribalizing" their followers, also strengthened the power of the landlords. The newly established governments of Syria, 'Iraq, and Transjordan (later Jordan), while helping to settle the tribes and to encourage them to engage in agriculture, proved unable either to control them completely or to gain their full cooperation. The tribal shaykhs, in 'Iraq in particular, often revolted against the government in defense of their feudal rights.[22]

The town-dwellers were divided into a small but relatively wealthy class and the wretched and exploited masses. Many of the latter were, and still are, without homes, without land, without schools, and even without personal property; many were frequently threatened by starvation and disease. The gap between them and the relatively rich was, and still remains, so wide that those on the lowest rung can scarcely ever hope to reach even the one above. These conditions developed because of the striking absence of an important middle class and because of the exploitation by the landlords, especially before the revolution in Egypt and 'Iraq. The vested interest, whether in past or present, supported whatever authority there was in power as long as it protected their positions. The rank and file were utterly neglected. Despairing of any hope for improvement, these masses became a great source of unrest. In the past, they revolted on a variety of pretexts, such as religious and sectarian differences. Today, ideological slogans attract them, but the true cause of their unrest lies in the deplorable social and economic conditions they live in.

In a complex social structure, torn between vertical (tribal *v.* town-dweller) and horizontal (rich *v.* poor) rivalries and without any middle class of consequence, democracy could scarcely be expected to flourish. It was an artificial creation by liberal groups, which hoped that its beneficiaries might eventually muster sufficient strength to support it. It is true that in predominantly agricultural countries, where feudalism (representing the dual influence of land-owners and tribal shaykhs) had survived for so long, the rapid rise of a middle class could not be expected.[23] After World War II, when a small middle class began to develop in Syria and 'Iraq, the new generation was unable to participate in the political processes dominated by older politicians, and began to view their futures in terms of gaining the support of workers and peas-

[22] See my *Independent 'Iraq*, pp. 49–51, 55–58, 113–16.

[23] Lebanon is perhaps the exception where a relatively important middle class began to develop after World War I.

ants. The appeal of these young men to the masses rather than to the emerging middle class was another blow to democracy.[24]

Individual Liberty and Democracy

Democracy as practiced in the West seeks to emphasize the liberty of the individual, sometimes at the expense of his equality with others in the social order. Political democracy that stresses individual initiative and free enterprise may lead to greater rather than smaller differences in wealth and social status. To a people accustomed to authoritarian rule for centuries, an ideology that promises equal rights and opportunities to the poor and the rich, even at the cost of submission to authoritarian rule, appeals far more than individual liberty which permits the enrichment of the few at the expense of the many.

Democracy was further discredited among the Arabs when liberty and license in political criticism became identical, and the press often indulged in wild and profane attacks on political opponents. The lack of restraint among rival leaders and professional politicians, which was revealed in general elections and in a relatively free press, reflected a number of political activities that were unprincipled, fanatical, and dissolute. Prior to democracy, the prohibition of freedom produced disguised intrigues and underground political machinations which came to the notice of the public only if they resulted in the arrest of the conspirators or in a change of rulers. The freedom provided under democracy disclosed traditional political abuses, but failed to put a stop to them; again, democracy had to shoulder the blame. Moreover, the administrative system which had been designed to provide justice and to conduct the government with efficiency, fell victim to similar traditional practices, such as favoritism,

[24] The rise of military rule and the heavy dependence on governments to modernize and industrialize militated against the growing influence of a middle class (see chaps. 6–7).

nepotism, and corruption, although the externalities of Western bureaucratic procedures were often rigidly observed.

The tribesmen and their chiefs were also unfamiliar with the working of democracy and failed to grasp its relatively complicated processes. Tribal society, it is true, enjoyed a social democracy of sorts, but political democracy ran contrary to traditional patterns of government in which the shaykh, after listening to opposing opinions, made his final decision irrespective of the advice of counsellors. The tribal shaykh, though *primus inter pares,* conducts the business of government as a supreme ruler, in harmony with traditional patterns of authority and without restrictions by his tribal council. The counsellors offer advice, but share no authority. No better example exists to illustrate the views on the point held by a tribal shaykh, than his discourse on the meaning of democracy when he was told that it would lead his tribe to share authority with him:

> The other day a Shamar Sheikh up from Hail drops in to call [on the Naqib of Baghdad, Sayyid 'Abd al-Rahman al-Gaylani, the Prime Minister of Iraq in 1921]. "Are you a Damakrati [Democrat]?" says the Naqib. "Wallahi [by God], no!" says the Shammari [shaykh], slightly offended. "I'm not a Magrati. What is it?" "Well," says the Naqib, enjoying himself thoroughly, "I'm Sheikh of the Damakratiyah [the democrats]." "I take refuge in God!" replied the Sheikh, feeling he had gone wrong somewhere. "If you are the sheikh of the Magratiyah, then I must be one of them, for I'm altogether in your service. But what is it?" "Damakratiyah," says the Naqib, "is equality [i.e., sharing authority equally by all]. There's no big man and no little, all are alike and equal [in power]." With which the bewildered Shammari plumped on to solid ground. "God is my witness," said he, seeing his tribal authority slipping from him, "if that's it I'm not a Magrati!" [25]

The cause of democracy in Arab lands is rendered even more hopeless by the rise of competing ideologies propagated

[25] Lady Florence Bell (ed.), *The Letters of Gertrude Bell* (London, 1927), II, 618.

by religious groups which had opposed it to begin with, or by young men disillusioned with the results of its operations. The Arabs, unaware of the capabilities of democracy, have judged it by the results visible to date in their lands. At this point, they have reached the judgment that their leaders have deceived them and that democracy has failed to measure up to expectations.[26]

[26] For a discussion on the new notions of democracy and emerging trends, see chaps. 7 and 10.

Chapter 4

REVIVAL OF ISLAM

At the turn of each century there will arise in my nation a man who will call for religious revival.

The Prophet Muhammad

For centuries, Islam provided for the believers a way of life the validity and perfection of which no believer ever questioned. When the decadence in Islamic society became apparent and the reform measures that had been adopted from the West failed to rehabilitate Islam, the pious Muslim underwent a moral crisis. Not only was he shocked that Islamic institutions were replaced by Western institutions and the sacred law (*shari'a*) superseded by secular legislation, but also that Western Powers should be encroaching upon Islamic lands with impunity. The leaders who had debated conflicting approaches to reform failed to agree on a constructive program acceptable to all because no common ground for reconciling their conflicting views had been found except perhaps during a short-lived period when Jamal al-Din al-Afghani encouraged religious leaders to support the constitutional movement. Even then, the process of reconciling Islam with Western thought was not given full expression, and the movement suffered a setback resulting in a radical change in the character of Islamic thought.

When the caliphate was abolished and secular institutions were set up under the impact of Western ideas following

World War I, the religious groups in Arab lands reacted unfavorably and began to revive interest in Islamic reform along traditional lines. Lay religious leaders, combining religious zeal with nationalism, expressed their ideas about reform in terms completely different from earlier liberal reformers. But these preachers had little to offer in the way of a constructive program which might combine the best of Islam with newly adopted concepts from the West. An appraisal of these trends calls for a brief discussion of the inception of the modernization movement.

The Modernization of Islam

Like liberal reformers, the advocates of the re-establishment of the Islamic system, though imbued with regard for a vanished past, had to meet the same immediate external threat. As a result of foreign pressures, the Islamic reaction, like the Westernizing movement, suffered from an identical inherent weakness—the need for self-defense against European ascendancy which prompted some leaders to assume an apologetic attitude in contrast with others who were concerned directly with reforms. This defensive movement, often referred to as Pan-Islamism, appeared to be more preoccupied by issuing elaborate apologiae addressed to European critics of Islam on the one hand and by leveling sharp criticism against all thinkers who called for the adoption of European ideas on the other hand, than in positive reforms. The European-oriented reformers were denounced as traitors of Islamic culture and were charged with the deliberate intention of destroying Islam itself. This negative attitude often inspired lay religious leaders to stir popular emotionalism and religious fanaticism which prompted Western writers to characterize Pan-Islamism as a reactionary movement. The advocates of Pan-Islamism, however, failed to offer any constructive ideas of reform beyond the vague concept of Islamic unity and the reinstatement of the Islamic system.

The Pan-Islamic movement probably would have remained negative and reactionary had it not received a positive impetus from Jamal al-Din al-Afghani (1839–97). Like earlier revivalist leaders, Afghani represented the spirit of the traditional reform movement, and he carried it forward without the need to declare himself a *Mahdi* or the century-reformer. After short periods of service in high government positions in Afghanistan and Persia, he visited many Muslim countries and the principal European capitals. In his endeavors to emancipate Muslims from internal lethargy and foreign rule, he often appeared as the agitator who sought to manipulate the masses against oppressive rulers. His energy, courage, and eloquence enabled him to arouse a spirit of discontent wherever he went. Dissatisfied with the slow progress achieved under Muslim rulers, he did not shrink from resorting to violent methods for the achievement of his objectives.

Afghani's immediate goal was to liberate Muslims from oppression internally and from foreign encroachments externally; but his aim was neither to unite all Muslim lands under one ruler (as some of his biographers seem to imply), nor to restore glory and power to Islam by arousing religious zeal only.[1] The significance of his approach to reform lies partly in his attempt to support religious leaders who sought to revive Islam and partly in his tolerant attitude toward those who advocated the adoption of European civilization, although he saw certain weaknesses in each of these two approaches. His observation of European society, which he had seen at first hand, led him to the conclusion that Europe's strength lay in modern science and technology. Islam, as he told his contemporaries, was never against science; for, as history demonstrates, men of science received great encouragement at the time of Islam's ascendancy. Afghani went on to say that Christendom, under the influence of Islamic scientific progress, achieved power and ascendancy, while Islam slipped

[1] Afghani's name has often been associated with the ideal of Muslim unity, but his writings seem to stress reform rather than unity. Even his often quoted article on unity stresses liberation from foreign control and only vaguely the integration of one Muslim country with others. See Jamal al-Din al-Afghani, *al-Wahda al-Islamiya wa al-Wahda wa al-Siyada*, ed. 'Izzat al-'Attar (Cairo, 1938).

into decadence when it turned its back on scientific development. So Afghani urged Muslims to acquire European scientific and technological skills, the adoption of which, he argued, had never been opposed by Islam; but, in the meantime, he advocated the preservation of Islamic religious and moral values.[2] His combination of European materialism with Islamic spiritualism was, perhaps, his most important contribution to Islamic thought, because it laid the foundation for other thinkers trying to bridge the gulf between the advocates of Western and Islamic thought. Afghani, though a brilliant thinker, never cared to reformulate his ideas into a coherent system, and he often expressed his views in abstract and terse sentences, not making any attempt to indicate their relevance to every day problems. He was too impatient to put his words in writing, preferring to communicate them in speeches before private and public audiences, and he seems to have been satisfied that his spoken words, eloquently expressed, might produce the desired effect. His objectives devolved, therefore, upon his disciples who sought to work out a more consistent and practical program of reform in circumstances permitting freer expression of opinion than under Ottoman rule.[3]

[2] Afghani, it is true, denounced European "naturalism" but his criticism was directed mainly against agnosticism rather than against the scientific attitude. See Jamal al-Din al-Afghani, *Risalat al-Radd 'Ala al-Dahriyyin*, trans. Muhammad 'Abduh (Cairo, 1925).

[3] In the last five years of his life, Afghani, after settling in Istanbul in 1892, became closely linked with Sultan 'Abd al Hamid II. The Sultan, who tried to justify his supreme spiritual authority over Muslims by proclaiming himself caliph, sought the indirect support of Afghani by inviting him to the Ottoman capital. Afghani's association with Sultan 'Abd al-Hamid gave the impression that he had tacitly approved of the Sultan's authoritarian rule, although he often spoke violently against it. His continued residence in Istanbul as the guest of the Sultan compromised his mission for liberal reform and led to conflicts with some of his disciples, especially Muhammad 'Abduh. For Afghani's inconsistencies, see Elie Kedourie, *Afghani and Abduh* (London, 1966). However, these inconsistencies in matter of details, contrary to the conclusions drawn by the author of this book, do not necessarily detract from the moral and intellectual honesty of the man, since Afghani, as we pointed out before, never took pains to write down his spoken words or to work out a coherent system of his own.

Afghani, impatient to prepare a new generation that might achieve his goal, tried by a short cut to achieve reform by starting at the top of the social pyramid. But the failure of his direct appeal to heads of state and government for introducing reforms demonstrated the futility of his approach, since it led to a violent clash with vested interests. His disciples, avoiding direct conflicts with the ruling hierarchy, tried to preach reform to the common man as well as to give fuller meaning to the concept of reform.

It was in Egypt shortly after the British occupation, in an atmosphere of relative freedom, that liberal ideas of reform were expounded by Afghani's disciples. Spared the need for political agitation against autocratic rulers, these disciples concentrated on social and religious reform. Their exposition of Islam set the example of what liberal reforms in one Islamic country could achieve, although their influence was by no means confined to Egypt. It was indeed Muhammad 'Abduh, Afghani's principal disciple, who forcefully and courageously espoused liberal ideas, although others, like Sa'd Zaghlul (founder of the Wafd Party)—to mention but one outstanding example—concentrated on reform in other directions. It is not our purpose to give a full exposition of 'Abduh's ideas and proposals for reform save as far as they relate to the general problem of modernization. His life and works, especially those expounded by Muhammad Rashid Rida, are worthy of a more extended study, and the reader may be advised to scrutinize them in the original.[4] Some

[4] Muhammad 'Abduh's leading theological study is the *Risalat al-Tawhid* (Cairo, 1315/1897; second edition, with notes by Rashid Rida, 1326/1908); French translation by B. Michel and Cheikh Moustapha Abdel Razik, *Cheikh Mohammed Abdou: Rissalat al-Tawhid* (Paris, 1925); English translations by Ishaq Musa'ad and Kenneth Cragg, *The Theology of Unity* (London, 1966). 'Abduh's fundamental ideals of reform may be found in *al-Islam wa al-Radd 'Ala Muntaqidih* (Cairo, 1327/1909), reprinted from *al-Mu'ayyad* newspaper, and translated into French by M. Tal'at Harb under the title *L'Europe et l'Islam* (Cairo, 1950). For 'Abduh's life, see M. Rashid Rida, *Ta'rikh al-Ustadh al-Imam al-Saykh Muhammad 'Abduh* (Cairo, 3 vols., 2nd ed., 1344/1925–1367/1947); Mustafa 'Abd al-Raziq, *Muhammad 'Abduh* (Cairo, 1946); and Osman Amin, *Muhammad 'Abduh* (Washington, 1953).

aspects of them have been adequately studied by several writers.[5]

Educated at the Azhar University of Cairo,[6] 'Abduh received a thorough training in Islam, although he saw while still young the futility of old-fashioned learning which stressed memory rather than reflective thinking. He was at first attracted to mysticism, which encouraged him to withdraw from society, but under the influence of Afghani who came to Egypt in 1869 (and again in 1871–79), he turned from mysticism to active public life. 'Abduh took an active part in the nationalist movement led by 'Urabi and advocated the establishment of representative government. But the failure of the 'Urabi movement, resulting in 'Abduh's exile for almost six years, led to a complete reversal of his approach to reform. While in exile, 'Abduh joined Afghani in Paris and participated with him in political agitation. After his return to Bayrut in 1885, where he resided for the next three years, he devoted his time to lecturing and writing, and his ideas on reform began to take shape independently of his master's influence. Returning to Cairo in 1888 'Abduh devoted the rest of his life (d. 1905), whether in the positions of *Qadi* (judge) and *Mufti* (jurisconsult) or member of the Legislative Council, to social and religious reform. It was in religious reform that his impress remained permanent.

'Abduh's ideas of Islamic reform were based on two fundamental assumptions: first, the inescapable role of religion in the life of nations, especially in nations whose social polity is based on religion; and second, the need for new institutions and technical skills, in the efficiency of which the West has excelled, to meet the demands of modern life. Since it has become fashionable, almost irresistible, throughout the world

[5] See Charles C. Adams, *Islam and Modernism in Egypt* (Oxford, 1933), chaps. 2–8; Osman Amin, *Muhammad Abduh: Essai sur ses idées philosophiques et religieuses* (Cairo, 1945); Albert Hourani, *Arabic Thought in the Liberal Age,* 1798–1939 (London, 1962), chap. 6; Jamal M. Ahmed, *The Intellectual Origins of Egyptian Nationalism* (London, 1960), chaps. 1–2; N. Safran, *Egypt in Search of Political Community* (Cambridge, Mass., 1961), pp. 62–75.

[6] 'Abduh was born in a village northwest of Cairo in 1849.

to adopt these Western novelties, Muslims could no longer afford to ignore them. Some of 'Abduh's contemporaries still held that Western ideas were incompatible with Islam, but 'Abduh argued that Western scientific and technical skills were not inherently incompatible with Islamic religious and moral values. History bears evidence that Islam was never opposed to scientific investigation and that leading Muslim scientists were encouraged by Muslim rulers. 'Abduh maintained that the scientific achievements of the West, to which Islamic science had contributed, could be safely adopted without violating the spirit of Islam. Failure to adopt the achievements of modern science might lead to the indiscriminate importation of Western civilization with the consequent submergence of Islamic values in Western materialism.

Having established a common ground between Islamic and Western thought, 'Abduh turned to examine the problem of modernizing Islam from another angle. He had found, as Afghani did before him, that Islam was in a state of decadence, but both were convinced of Islam's capacity for progress. The concept of "decadence" in the Afghani-'Abduh scheme of thought implied the pressing need for "progress" and "development," if Islam were to catch up with the West.[7] This was a novel concept of reform in Islamic thought, for earlier reformers, as noted before, called for the re-establishment of the ideal Islamic standard as the safest measure of reform. However, neither 'Abduh nor his master ever made the claim that they were *Mahdis* or century-reformers, because their ideas of reform stemmed from their belief in Islam's capacity for progress under the changing conditions of life.[8] Some have attributed 'Abduh's concept of reform to Western sources, in particular his familiarity of Guizot's *History of Civilization*;[9] but it must also be traced to his study of Ibn

[7] See "Inhitat al-Muslimin," *al-'Urwa al-Wuthqa* (April 10, 1884); and "Sunnat Allah fi al-Umam," *al-'Urwa al-Wuthqa* (September 25, 1884); both reprinted in Rida, *Ta'rikh*, II, 244–49, 325–31.

[8] See the opening article of *al-'Urwa al-Wuthqa* (March 13, 1884), reprinted in Rida, *Ta'rikh*, II, 215–23. The tone of almost all other writings of 'Abduh were to this effect.

[9] Adams, *Islam and Modernism in Egypt*, pp. 39 and 44.

Khaldun's philosophy of history which analyzes changes in society in terms of social forces rather than in transcendental values.[10]

In 'Abduh's scheme of thought, Islam could not overcome decadence without abandoning *taqlid*, the time-honored doctrine of conformity, and without resorting to reason. His writings abound in admonitions against *taqlid* and in repeated calls for the exercise of reason, without which, he pointed out, Islam could not achieve progress and development. In his treatise on theology, 'Abduh explained the role of reason in life generally and asserted that Islam was pre-eminently a religion of reason, since the Qur'an gave it a place of first importance by stating that reason is the power which enables men to distinguish truth from falsehood and the harmful from the beneficial.[11] From this basic assumption, 'Abduh suggested that Islamic law must be interpreted by reason, and in the case of conflict between the literal meaning of law and reason, reason must be given priority. He himself demonstrated the significance of reason in the application of law in his capacity as both Qadi and Mufti, by giving legal opinions like the Transvaal *fatwa* (legal opinion), declaring it lawful for Muslims to eat the flesh of animals slaughtered by Christians and Jews, the fatwa permitting Muslims to wear European forms of dress, and the fatwa permitting Muslims to deposit money in Postal Savings Banks which yield interest. These legal opinions were made possible in the absence of any authoritative texts prohibiting such actions.[12]

The key to progress in 'Abduh's eyes was the adoption of Western science and education. In one of his early articles he pointed out that the ascendancy of Europe lay in the superior-

[10] 'Abduh used Ibn-Khaldun's *Prolegomena* as a basis for some of his lectures in Bayrut and he always recommended it for his students. For other influences on 'Abduh's thought, see Hourani, *Arabic Thought*, pp. 132, 135, 138, 139, and 143.

[11] *Risalat al-Tawhid*, see note 4, above; and 'Abduh, *al-Islam wa al-Nasraniya*, pp. 51–53.

[12] For 'Abduh's fatwas, see Rashid Rida, *Ta'rikh*, I, 646–716. For the Transvaal Fatwa, see Charles C. Adams, "Muhammad 'Abduh and the Transvaal Fatwa," in *The Macdonald Presentation Volume* (Princeton, 1933), pp. 11–29.

ity of its educational system and in the advancement of scientific investigation. He said:

> We see no reason for their [European] progress to wealth and power except the advancement of education and science. Our first duty, then, is to endeavour with all our might and main to spread these sciences in our country.[13]

He insisted that Islam was never in conflict with science and that Muslim rulers were patrons of men of science and literature. He believed that, if reason were the basis for the belief in One God who, as stated in the Qur'an, "created for you all that is on Earth," Islam must necessarily be in conformity with science. Science, like religion, reveals to men the secrets of nature. 'Abduh has reconciled this view with prophecy and contended that the Prophet's function was to teach men how to understand nature and profit by it within the limits set forth in the sacred law. Thus he concluded that both religion and science addressed themselves to the study of the same phenomena, each with its own object in view. Frequent references in the Qur'an to natural phenomena gave 'Abduh the justification to equate the study of religion with the study of nature.[14] 'Abduh may have not fully grasped the scientific theory with which he had become acquainted through second hand sources, but he fully understood the significance of supporting the findings of science. He had gone as far as to validate by religion, contrary to his master's views on the subject, the Darwinian theory of the evolution of the human species by interpreting a Quranic citation to the effect that the origin of the human race was not Adam, but a *nafs* (soul) from which all men descended. He also found in the Qur'an references to "the struggle for existence" and "the survival of

[13] Rida, *Ta'rikh,* ii, 43; and Adams, *Islam and Modernism in Egypt,* pp. 39 and 135.

[14] In one of his commentaries on the Qur'an he stated: "God has sent two books [to men], one created, which is nature, and one revealed, which is the Qur'an. The latter leads us to investigate the former by means of the intelligence which was given to us" (*al-Manar,* VIII, 292; and Adams, *Islam and Modernism in Egypt,* p. 136).

the fittest" as the laws of nature.[15] Muhammad 'Abduh laid no less emphasis on education. He had observed European institutions of learning during his visits to Europe and read Spencer's work on education (which he translated into Arabic), believing that the contribution of the West to education would be of great importance to an Islamic revival. In some of his reports, he urged his countrymen to reform the educational system in order to catch up with the West, arguing that the ascendancy of the West lay in the superiority of its educational system and in its scientific investigation. He maintained that if Muslims armed with Islamic religious and moral values were to acquire modern disciplines they would be able to compete with Westerners.

The significance of 'Abduh's approach to reform lies chiefly in the clarity and freshness of his ideas. He made it clear that Islam's decadence was due to a long-standing rigidity in Islamic thought coinciding with the progress and the ascendancy of Europe, especially in fields which Muslims had long neglected. Islam could catch up with European progress if Islamic thought were revived by the exercise of reason and the adoption of European disciplines—disciplines to which Muslims themselves had contributed in the past. He therefore saw no harm, as some contemporary reformers contended, in adopting elements of Western civilization which would enable Islam to be rehabilitated.

By virtue of this approach, 'Abduh provided a common ground for the opposing viewpoints of reform and saw no inherent incompatibility between those who advocated the adoption of Western ideas and institutions without regard for Islamic values and those who insisted on the re-establishment of the Islamic system. He had succeeded in his eloquent defense of Islamic religious and social morality, which gave moral support to religious leaders although some opposed his unorthodox interpretation of Islamic doctrines. His argument in favor of Western disciplines was taken up by modernists who advocated the wholesale adoption of Western civilization,

[15] Cf. Jamal al-Din al-Afghani, *al-Radd 'Ala al-Dahriyyin*, tr. M. 'Abduh (Cairo, 1925), pp. 28–30. See *Qur'an* IV, 1.

to give religious validity for their approach to reform concerning which some may have had certain mental reservations.

It is true that 'Abduh was supported during his lifetime by many who shared his ideas, but only a few were imbued with the same spirit of tolerance and showed sufficient interest in expounding Islam beyond the framework of reform set by him. This was due partly to 'Abduh's failure to carry his argument to its logical conclusion and to reconstruct out of conflicting viewpoints of reform a synthesis acceptable to Islamic and modernist groups and partly to the increasing influx of Western thought which rendered the task of harmonizing conflicting views very difficult after his death. No coherent system of thought emerged out of his school of reform and the basic problem concerning the precise role of Islam as the basis of modern life still remained unresolved.[16] After 'Abduh's death his disciples, though most of them continued to derive inspiration from his teachings, were necessarily divided into two groups, each representing one stream of 'Abduh's thought, but no serious attempt was made to blend the one with the other. The first group, while remaining loyal to 'Abduh's moral values, began to expound the principles of a secular society in which Islam was honored but no longer the basis of social polity. The other groups, claiming to conform more closely to 'Abduh's thought, took an apologetic attitude in order to defend Islamic values in the face of an influx of secular ideas that had already begun to dominate the modernists and cited copious traditions in order to give validity to many vague statements about reform. This conservative attitude, especially as espoused by 'Abduh's principal disciple Muhammad Rashid Rida, stamped the movement with traditionalism, and the movement lost direct touch with the new generation.

Islamic Revival as the Return to the "Elders of Islam": The Salafiya

'Abduh's thought was accepted in principle by all his followers, but only the modernists tried to carry it to its logical

[16] Cf. Hourani, *Arabic Thought*, p. 230.

conclusion and to relegate Islam's role in society to the level of the individual conscience. They regarded Islam as a living doctrine that must continue to develop; the ultimate outcome of this development would be the secularization of Islamic society.[17] But this interpretation was unacceptable to many of 'Abduh's conservative disciples, especially to those who held that 'Abduh himself had made some unnecessary concessions to modernism. Muhammad Rashid Rida, claiming to have comprehended 'Abduh's thought more accurately than others, led this conservative reaction and interpreted 'Abduh's liberal thought more narrowly. Thoroughly learned in the doctrine and traditions of Islam, he was admirably fitted to play that role both temperamentally and intellectually.[18]

Before he joined 'Abduh's circle, Rashid Rida had received an old-fashioned education in Tripoli, mixed with some Western ideas made available to him through second-hand sources. He had studied the writings of al-Ghazzali (d. 1111) and Ibn Taymiya (d. 1328) and for a short while he fell under mystic influences. His interest in reform, stimulated by the writings of Afghani and 'Abduh, made him determined to join the reform circle. Afghani had just died when Rida left Syria for Egypt in 1897, and from that time on Rida remained associated with 'Abduh. He started a periodical, *al-Manar*, which became the organ of Islamic reform according to the Afghani-'Abduh school. Except for a few excursions into politics,[19]

[17] See chap. 9.

[18] Rida was born in a village near Tripoli (then Syria), in 1865, and received his education under the influence of Husayn al-Jisr, a learned scholar who was not completely out of touch with Western thought. For Rida's life and thought, see Rida's autobiography of his early years in *al-Manar wa al-Azhar* (Cairo, 1353/1934), pp. 129ff; Adams, *Islam and Modernism in Egypt*, pp. 177–204; Hourani *Arabic Thought*, pp. 222–44; Malcolm Kerr, *Islamic Reform* (Berkeley, 1966); Sami al-Dahhan, *Qudama' wa Mu'asirun* (Cairo, 1961), pp. 173–79; Ibrahim Ahmad al-'Adawi, *Rashid Rida* (Cairo, n.d.).

[19] He participated in the political activities of Arab nationalist societies in Egypt before and after World War I, became President of the Syrian Congress under Faysal in Damascus in 1920, and supported the Syrian revolt in 1925–26.

Rida remained the editor of *al-Manar* to the end of his life in 1935, the chief interpreter of 'Abduh's ideas as he understood them, and his official biographer.[20]

Following the footsteps of Afghani and 'Abduh, Rida addressed himself to the basic question of Islamic reform. His approach, though outwardly modernist, reflected an inner attachment to traditionalism. He derived his inspiration from the elders of Islam (*salaf*) who, according to him, understood the true meaning of Islamic principles as provided in the Qur'an and Traditions. The underlying cause of Islamic decadence, according to him, was the Muslims' ignorance concerning the true meaning of Islam. He also blamed decadence on bad rulers, who, in an effort to secure their subjects' submission to despotic rule, encouraged their ignorance of the true meaning of Islam.

Western civilization, Rida maintained, is the product of certain intellectual attitudes and social habits which Muslims had lost and in which Westerners came to excel. Yet, he insisted, these traits are the very essence of Islam. But how could Muslims revive these qualities? They can revive them, he said, by an understanding of the true meaning of Islam, the Islam as taught by the Prophet Muhammad. Knowledge of true Islam may be found in the Qur'an and the Prophet's Traditions, as related and understood by the Companions of the Prophet and the elders (*salaf*) of the first generation of Islam. Their opinions constituted the consensus (*ijma'*) which gave a full expression to the principles laid down in the Qur'an and Traditions. That consensus was the only valid and binding one upon Muslims in succeeding generations. Thoroughly learned in the science of Traditions and in the opinions of elders, Rida set for himself the task of interpreting Islam in a manner that would fit modern conditions of life,

[20] Rida was a prolific writer. Some of his works were first published in *al-Manar,* later re-issued in separate volumes, and he edited and wrote 'Abduh's autobiographical fragment and life in a three-volume work, entitled *Ta'rikh al-Ustadh al-Imam*; volume 1 embodies 'Abduh's autobiography (Cairo, 1344/1925–1350/1931).

as indicated by his copious commentaries on the Qur'an and the juristic and theological studies. But it was precisely in this method that Rida departed from 'Abduh's broader outlook since Rida's great attachment to Traditions prompted him to formulate even more precisely the very same principles that rendered these Traditions no longer adequate for the ever growing demands of succeeding generations. Moreover, his stress on orthodox doctrines aroused Shi'i suspicion, which Afghani and 'Abduh avoided, primarily because solidarity among believers was regarded as necessary in the face of Christian encroachment upon Islam. As the gulf between the modernists and the salafi teachings widened, Rida found greater spiritual affinity in puritanical Wahhabism, an attraction which was not altogether devoid of political motives. Reacting against secular trends in northern Arab lands, he hoped that the Saudi dynasty might eventually re-establish Islamic rule in the cradle of Islam.

Rashid Rida, however, did not insist on orthodoxy in all its facets, for he allowed certain measures of flexibility in his system of ideas, especially in the realms of law and political theory. He made a distinction between the sacred law, regulating man's personal behavior, and the law regulating man's actions towards others. The former, he maintained, are prescribed for all time and cannot be changed; the latter is necessarily subjected to revision in accordance with changing circumstances. The criteria of revision, he held, must be the common good (*maslaha*) of the community. These criteria are provided by the law, for Islam forbids injury (*la darar wa la dirar*) and permits relaxation of prescribed rules if there is pressing necessity (*al-darurat tubih al-mahdurat*). These guiding principles, he maintained, were constantly followed by the elders; but they had been applied by other methods of legal reasoning such as analogy (*qiyas*) and consensus (*ijma'*). He stressed, in particular, consensus as a legal procedure, which he reserved to the 'ulama (scholars) who act on behalf of the public. The 'ulama, meeting in an assembly (parliament) as representatives of the people, make decisions and laws on the basis of the general interest and welfare of the people. Thus Rida combined the concepts of consultation (*al-shura*) with consensus in order to demonstrate that representative government is feasible under the Islamic system.

What rendered this system of thought more complicated and out of keeping with the trend of modernism was the role Rida reserved for the caliphate and his insistence that Islam, as a religious and legal system, must remain the basis of polity. He maintained that the caliphate was necessary, for no real Islamic society can exist without it; but he was not clear on the precise relationship between the caliph and the heads of government. The caliph's functions were presumably to preside over the body that makes laws and legal decisions, as well as to supervise their applications, to exercise *ijtihad* (acting upon the advice of the 'ulama), and to communicate his opinion on public matters to Islamic authorities while leaving matters of private affairs to the individual conscience. Rida was not clear, however, on how those functions were to be fulfilled if the trend toward territorial sovereignty was to reach its full development, nor did he touch upon possible conflicts between caliphial and national jurisdictions.[21]

So artificial and outdated to the young men who grew up following 'Abduh's death did Rida's thought seem that it failed to meet the new demands of life exposed to the increasing impact of Western civilization. The modernists had no use for ideas that seemed to reassert traditionalism rather than to stress the progressive evolution of modernism. As a result, during the inter-war years, Rida found himself attacking not the 'ulama who had been criticizing 'Abduh's modernism but 'Abduh's liberal disciples who carried out 'Abduh's reform ideas to their logical conclusions. The new generation, accordingly, began to vacillate vetween two extreme tendencies—secularism and agnosticism on the one hand, and reactionary and lay religious propaganda on the other.[22]

[21] Rashid Rida, *al-Khilafa wa al-Imama al-'Uzma* (Cairo, 1341/1923); French translation by H. Laust, *Le Califat* (Bayrut, 1938).

[22] See chap. 9.

Lay Religious Revival

In the early inter-war years a new generation was swept up by nationalism. There was a tendency to place loyalty to Islam aside in favor of secular thought. Some were impressed by the Kamalist experiment of parting with Islamic institutions, but the majority were influenced by Western secular ideas. Secular manifestations, however, proved to be short-lived, mainly because nationalist leaders failed to achieve nationalist objectives while the influx of Western thought brought in its train the political domination by European powers. This domination, though resented by nationalist and Islamic groups alike, weakened the position of nationalists who were denounced by religious and conservative groups as having prepared the way for European influence by their acceptance of Western secular thought.

This religious reaction, in contrast with earlier movements, took at first the form of organizing social and religious associations which inspired the new generation with religious and social morality rather than abstract doctrines. Since government schools have been looked upon as fulfilling mainly vocational purposes and failing to provide religious and moral instruction, the initial reaction to these religious associations was prompt and favorable. Most important of all was the Association of the Muslim Young Men (Jam'iyat al-Shubban al-Muslimin). The name, which indicates the impact of a Western prototype, may be slightly modified as Young Men's Muslim Association or YMMA, after the initials of the YMCA.

This association, founded in Cairo by a group of religious-minded men in 1927, provided a model for others which took more active part in public life. Because it concentrated on religious and social matters, trying to keep away from political activities, the association survived other religious associations, and its impact upon lay society may well be regarded as more far-reaching. The original founders of the association represented various shades of opinion and included men like 'Abd al-Hamid Sa'id, a member of Parliament and an active member of the Nationalist Party (who served as first President of the association); 'Abd al-'Aziz Shawish, formerly a lecturer in Arabic at Oxford University and a high-ranking official in the Ministry of Education;[23] Ahmad Taymur Pasha, a well-known scientist; Muhib al-Din al-Khatib, editor of several religious reviews; Muhamad al-Khidr Husayn, professor at the Azhar University; and several others well-known in public life.[24] The aims of the association as set forth in its regulations were: (1) to spread Islamic religious and moral values; (2) to endeavor enlightening young men by knowledge in a way that is adapted to modern times; (3) to work against dissension and corrupt practices which may be found in parties and groups; and (4) to take from the cultures of the East and the West all that is considered good and to reject all that is considered bad in them. The association made it plain that it did not intend to interfere in politics.

The objectives of the association were carried out by founding a club, frequented by members as well as sympathizers, where lectures on cultural and social subjects were delivered. Other activities of the club included various sports, games, and musical entertainments, but liquor was not allowed in accordance with Islamic teachings. A magazine,[25] carrying the message of the association beyond its walls, was issued in 1929. Outside Egypt, a number of branches were opened in Palestine, Syria, and 'Iraq. But it was the Egyptian central association, with its journal which had a wide circulation throughout Muslim lands, that laid down fundamental teachings of the association. These teachings, which were never formulated in one particular study but which were discussed in several published lectures and articles in the association's journal, emphasized the revival of the Islamic spirit

[23] Shawish was also known for his Islamic interest as well as for his activities in the Nationalist Party (see Anwar al-Jundi, *'Abd al-'Aziz Shawish* [Cairo, 1965]).

[24] For a brief account of these thinkers, see Adams, *Islam and Modernism in Egypt*: passim.

[25] *Majallat al-Shubban al-Muslimin* [Journal of the Young Men's Muslim Association].

derived directly from the Qur'an, the basic source of the Islamic way of life. "A return to the Qur'an," a phrase from now on often repeated, became a fashionable slogan of this as well as other societies that addressed themselves to Islamic reform. In the first issue (October 1929) of the journal, Yahya al-Dardiri, one of the contributors, expounded the social morality stressed by the association. This morality included: (1) a call to reform and to do good to everybody; (2) freedom of science and thought; and (3) the co-operation and solidarity of mankind. Further articles by various contributors dealt with such problems as the need for religious revival, religious doubts of young men concerning the conflict between science and religion, and many other subjects intended to inspire religious morality.[26]

In 1930, a conference was held in Cairo in which the work of the association was reviewed and plans for the future were laid down. The discussion revealed the aspirations and prevailing idea of stressing religious values through practical steps to be undertaken by the association. Further meetings held in subsequent years were to stress similar tendencies. The principal objective of the association was to stress practical measures, such as religious training for children, spreading information about Islam in various lands, founding co-operative societies, educating women, opposing missionary activities, and persuading Islamic governments to include Islamic law in their legislation and to fulfill its functions in accordance with Islamic principles. Political questions, especially those relating to Islamic affairs, were occasionally touched upon, such as the questions of the caliphate, Zionist infiltration into Palestine, and Western influence, but the association was on the whole able to keep out of politics.

The emphasis on religious morality and avoidance of polemical discussion of doctrines insured the association a continuing appeal to young men who would otherwise have fallen under agnostic and secular influences. The religious

[26] For the early activities of the YMMA, see G. Kampffmeyer, "Egypt and Western Asia," *Wither Islam*, ed. H. A. R. Gibb (London, 1932), pp. 99ff.

groups, however, though pleased with the association's success among the young, were far from satisfied with such a modest achievement. They desired no less an Islamic resurrection than the permeation of religion into all walks of life and the ultimate replacement of secular by religious institutions. The YMMA, continuing its activities inspiring social and religious values, was able to survive the strains and stresses of political upheavals. The revolutionary leaders of Egypt, though opposed to religious organization likely to take part in politics, have allowed this association to continue its activities under the benign leadership of Salih Harb, a retired army officer who had taken part in politics under the monarchy.[27]

The Muslim Brotherhood

The YMMA, though stressing religious ethics in its activities, paid little or no attention to religious instruction and its appeal was essentially confined to young and intellectual circles; it made no effort to appeal directly to the masses. The religious groups, aspiring to a greater manifestation of religious revival, called for an emphasis of religious instruction in their activities. Several societies, devoted to religious and mystical performances, were founded to combat the spread of lax social habits and secular ideas; but none had greater appeal and more profound emotional influence than the Muslim Brotherhood (al-Ikhwan al-Muslimun), founded by Hasan al-Banna in 1928.

The Brotherhood's success, though basically due to moral dissatisfaction with existing conditions, was to a large extent dependent on its leader's strength of character. A little historical background about the life and character of the leader is perhaps necessary.

Born six years after the turn of the century, Hasan al-Banna was the son of a man dedicated to religious activities. Short

[27] For a summary of the activities of the YMMA, see J. Heyworth-Dunne, *Religious and Political Trends in Egypt* (Washington, 1950), pp. 11–14; *Majallat al-Shubban al-Muslimin*; and my interviews with Salih Harb.

and well built, he led a very active life, fully absorbed in Islamic activities. He inherited his father's keen interest in religion and dedication to preaching and religious instruction. From youth, he set out to organize preaching societies, and this avocation became his chief preoccupation after he had graduated from school. He had a charming personality and ability to persuade which attracted the literate no less than the illiterate: he proved to be an effective speaker who had an emotional appeal to the masses. He was not an original thinker, but his organizing ability, which he probably inherited from his father, a watch-maker, made him the real motivating spirit behind the highly organized Brotherhood hierarchy.

The Brotherhood began in Isma'iliya early in 1928, where Banna was appointed as a government-school teacher in the fall of 1927. Isma'iliya, then inhabited mostly by Europeans who were officials of the Suez Canal Company, seemed scarcely the place to start an Islamic movement. Banna's preaching, however, was conducted not among high-ranking officials of the Canal Company, but among the poor and depressed workers. His followers, deprived of the privileges and luxury of the European community, were ready to listen to a preacher stressing non-material values and to receive encouragement and moral uplift. The atmosphere was therefore congenial for the vigilant crusader; for, had he started in the capital where his activities would have invited police supervision or the rivalry of other Islamic societies, he probably could have achieved only limited initial success.

From Isma'iliya, before the Brotherhood's headquarters were moved to Cairo in 1933, the new Islamic spirit radiated far and wide into the lower strata of society almost unnoticed by rulers and privileged classes. Banna visited every important town and locality and preached among workers and peasants. During the five years when the headquarters were in Isma'iliya, it is said that almost fifty chapters had been established throughout the country. Associated with the Brotherhood's building in each chapter, a charitable foundation, a textile or rug factory, a mosque, a dispensary, or an educational institution was established. After the headquarters were moved to Cairo, the number of centers, perhaps not without exaggeration, reached the high figure of 1500–2000, and the followers between 300–600 thousand. Hasan al-Banna once said, shortly before his assassination, that he was speaking on behalf of 500 thousand followers and expressing the aspirations of 70 million Arabs and 300 million Muslims. His followers were no longer confined to the masses, since young men in big towns and cities, including university students and graduates, found in the Brotherhood a revivalist movement the like of which Egypt never had within memory. Branches in the Sudan, Syria and 'Iraq, and perhaps elsewhere, were opened, and the Brotherhood's official organ, books and pamphlets, published in ever increasing numbers, were distributed throughout the Islamic world.

When World War II broke out, Hasan al-Banna had become an acknowledged leader not only to men interested in social and religious reform but also to politicians at all levels, since he had either contacted them personally or issued to them letters, warning against moral decadence and calling attention to the need for religious and moral standards. Following the war, during which Banna's movement reached the height of its influence, the Brotherhood's activities were never rivalled by any other religious organization. The Brotherhood's participation in the Palestine war, which brought the organization into the forefront of Egyptian politics, demonstrated its self-discipline and potential abilities in handling public matters. Hasan al-Banna, hailed by the Brothers as their Guide—as he was officially known to them—came very near to achieving power after the Palestine war; but he came out into the open too soon and clashed with Egypt's ruling oligarchy. Had he proceeded slowly into the political field as he did in the social and religious, Egypt's rulers might have found it difficult to get rid of him; but the Brotherhood's resort to violence and terrorism gave the Government ample excuse to close the headquarters of the organization after Banna was assassinated. Even following Banna's death, the Brotherhood took an active part in the events leading up to the army's intervention in politics, but this aspect of the Brotherhood's activities will be examined later.

The Brotherhood's critics have remarked that Banna's speeches and public statements were devoid of any new approach to reform capable of meeting the new demands of a modern society. Following World War II, when the Brotherhood took an active part in politics, the critics denounced its political activities as inconsistent with its declared religious objectives and saw behind Banna's agitation a bid for power. These critics, however, have overlooked the fact that the Brotherhood's activities were but a manifestation of the previously discussed larger movement of reaction against decadence of Islam and cultural and political ascendancy of the West in the Arab world. There was a short-lived secular movement in the early inter-war years which was superseded by a religious reaction; now the Brotherhood has risen up, led by a Mahdi in the guise of a Guide, in response to a challenge that had been long overdue.

Hasan al-Banna, it is true, offered at first no elaborate program beyond stressing the creed of Islam; he merely tried to sum up the objective of an Islamic revival in such synoptic captions as "the return to Islam," "the Qur'an is our constitution" and the like. In his early preaching, he even went so far as to stress only the essentials of religion, avoiding controversial questions which might affect solidarity among his followers.[28] But Banna, revealing gradually the broad objectives of the movement, declared on more than one occasion that Islam had a very wide meaning, that it regulated all human affairs including modern problems, and that it was not restricted to purely religious and spiritual matters. Islam, he often said, regulates the affairs of this life and the hereafter. It is an all-embracing religion, a religion of peace and brotherhood and of sincere collaboration, but one that cannot approve of party politics.

Questions were put to Banna concerning the compatibility of democracy, nationalism, socialism, secularism, and com-

[28] Hasan al-Banna, *Mudhakkirat* (Cairo, n.d.), p. 69.

munism with Islam. Apart from secularism and communism to which the Brotherhood strongly objected, Banna took pains to explain that anything that was good in the other systems may be found in Islam. Islam, he said, is essentially a system that guarantees freedom and equality, insures welfare and justice for all, and inspires the spirit of brotherhood and social morality.[29] He maintained that it was unnecessary for Muslims to borrow ideas and institutions from other societies, for Islam embraces all conceivable values and systems of ideas needed by its followers. Thus the Brotherhood's aim was not to provide a new set of ideas, but to create a new generation, capable of understanding the true meaning of Islam, as interpreted by the Brotherhood's leaders, and of acting according to Islam, in order to achieve progress and restore to Islam its prestige and power. The Brothers seem to have aimed at becoming the elite of a new nation to be born.

The question was often asked as to whether the Brotherhood sought ultimately to abolish the existing political system and re-establish an Islamic polity presided over by a caliph. From the time when the Brotherhood was founded to World War II, Banna categorically denied that the Brotherhood had anything to do with politics. Indeed, he admonished his followers to keep out of party politics and advised concentration on constructive religious and social work. But this attitude did not mean that the Brotherhood was satisfied with existing political systems or with the course of political development in the Islamic world. Both in written and spoken words, Banna had shown the Brotherhood's dissatisfaction with the intense rivalry among the corrupt and unscrupulous politicians vying for power and called on heads of state and government to follow the precepts of Islam and put an end to this situation. Shortly before the war, the Brotherhood

[29] Banna, *Da'watuna* and *Da'watunna fi Tawr Jadid* (Cairo, n.d.). See also Muhammad 'Abd-Allah al-Samman, *Usus al-Hukm fi al-Islam* (Cairo, 1953); Sayyid Qutb, *al-'Adala al-Ijtima'iya fi al-Islam* (Cairo, n.d.), English translation entitled *Social Justice in Islam* (Washington, 1953), by J. B. Hardie. Sayyid Qutb, one of the editors of the Brotherhood's journal, was one of the intellectual leaders of the society.

showed interest in political activities, and some of its leaders declared that the Brotherhood was not only a social and religious society but also a political organization. In 1941, Banna sought to enter Parliament, but he was dissuaded from taking part in politics since Egypt was under threat of foreign attack. During the Palestine war (1948–49), the Brotherhood's paramilitary leaders, while fighting with an army ill-prepared for war, openly spoke about an eventual control of political authority, if the Brotherhood's objectives were ever to be realized. It was talk of an impending *coup d'état* that prompted the rulers of Egypt to take action against the Brotherhood.

Following World War II, when Islamic lands from Morocco to Indonesia rose against Western domination and when Egypt in particular was in a state of intense agitation, the Brotherhood thought that the time had come to tackle political problems. The Guide's incursions into politics had been at first confined to criticism of the social behavior of men in authority and their neglect of the precepts of Islam; but later he began openly to accuse them of not being active believers and demanded the replacement of secular by Islamic institutions. Egypt's defeat in the Palestine war and failure to force Britain to evacuate the Canal Zone gave ample ground for the opposition to criticize the political regime and demand thorough reforms. Of all the opposition groups, however, the Brotherhood was the only one—except perhaps the communists—that had a program (though often vague on many questions) touching on almost all aspects of public life.[30]

The Brotherhood repeatedly warned that internal conditions in Egypt were progressively deteriorating. The democratic regime, which allowed Western domination to continue, had failed to achieve progress. Short of a communist seizure of power, the nation was moving quickly to the brink

[30] For an account of the history and activities of the Brotherhood, see J. Heyworth-Dunne, *Religious and Political Trends in Egypt* (Washington, 1950); Ishaq Musa al-Husayni, *al-Ikhwan al-Muslimum* (Bayrut, 2nd ed., 1955); C. P. Harris, *Nationalism and Revolution in Egypt* (The Hague, 1964).

of a destructive revolution. The leaders of the Brotherhood made it clear that they felt it was obligatory for them to warn the nation, just as it was obligatory for the Prophet Muhammad to warn his people, and that they had in their possession the answers to all the nation's political ills. The existing political system was incapable of improvement because it was secular in character and paid little or no attention to religion. According to the Brotherhood, men are not free to choose their political system; they would fall into error if their government were not established on a religious basis.

The Brotherhood's teachings, however, were not inflexible. It was again and again stated that Islamic rules were liable to change in accordance with changing circumstances but that basic principles should be maintained. It is not correct to hold that the Brotherhood sought to re-establish the Islamic system without change. It insisted that religion must be the basis of social polity, the details of which would be worked out in accordance with social conditions. According to Islamic political theory, authority is derived from a divine source and its holders must be guided by an ultimate religious objective. Thus religion is necessarily inseparable from politics, and the Brotherhood made it clear that those who held Islam had nothing to do with politics did not understand the true meaning of Islam. It is true that the constitution of Egypt stated that Islam was the religion of the state, but this lip service to Islam was unsatisfactory to the Brotherhood which regarded the democratic regime as essentially secular in character.

What were the basic principles of an Islamic government according to the Brotherhood? Three principles seemed to be particularly stressed; these were the principles of representation, unity of the nation, and the national will. Any government that seeks to be legitimate must satisfy these basic requirements. Sovereignty ultimately belongs to God, but its exercise is entrusted to the nation. An Islamic government must therefore be a representative government and responsible to the will of the nation. Such responsibility implies that the holders of authority are not masters of the people but their servants, in order to insure that God's order and the sacred law (supplemented by human legislation) are carried out.

All believers are brothers and must enjoy equal rights. The citizens of the state are inherently equal and entitled to respect according to the principle of Islamic brotherhood. There should be no discrimination nor should the believer be denied the right to share authority with rulers. Muslims are responsible for their public affairs no less than for their private ones.

Second, all believers must constitute one nation. If divided into various countries, they nevertheless remain united as one *umma* (community) because of their spiritual bond of brotherhood. However, the Brotherhood was vague about the need of a caliph who would assume ultimate authority, although they admitted the necessity of the caliphate in theory. If the Brotherhood were ever to achieve power, the question of the caliphate might be opened and the Guide called upon to speak on behalf of the caliph.

It is important to realize that this system was different from the system of government that existed in Egypt before the revolution. Not only was the Egyptian political system modeled after a non-Islamic pattern, to which the Brotherhood objected, but it also fell short of certain other requisites. It was not clear to whom ultimate responsibility belonged, whether to the head of the state or to the nation, since the constitution of Egypt provided that the government was responsible in certain matters to the head of state and in others to parliament. The constitution failed to state clearly that ultimate responsibility rested with the nation as the Brotherhood desired. The Egyptian government also failed to respect the principle of the unity of the nation, since the party system divided the believers into competing factions contrary to Islamic principles. Muslims must always be united on matters concerning public affairs, for disunity weakens them, especially in their struggle against foreign influence, and diverts their efforts from public to personal affairs. For this reason the Brotherhood demanded the dissolution of the party system as it saw grave dangers in competition and rivalry among politicians who sought to serve their personal interests at the expense of the public. Party politics seemed irrelevant to the community of believing Brothers.[31]

The will of the nation must be exercised by a representative government. However, the Brotherhood did not intend to consult the nation on every matter or detail. The government, in accordance with the principle of consultation (*al-shura*), should be guided by the 'ulama, who represent the people on all matters of religion and law. Parliament, which fulfills one of the functions of the 'ulama, must be truly representative and enacts the laws on the basis of the sacred law. However, the Egyptian parliament was neither truly representative of the people nor adequately attentive to religion, since many of its secular laws were inconsistent with Islamic law. Thus the Egyptian political system failed to measure up to the Brotherhood's standards, and its replacement by one based on Islamic principles was among the Brotherhood's fundamental demands.

Egypt's economic system also appeared unsatisfactory to the Brotherhood. The disparity between rich and poor and the widespread poverty and disease were regarded as the principal barriers to the progress of the country. This situation, said Banna, prompted the Brotherhood to pay proper attention to economic questions.

Egypt, well-known for its prosperity in antiquity, is not a poor country: it possesses great potentialities and rich resources. But Egypt's resources, the Brotherhood held, have long been exploited by foreigners, many of whom had acquired Egyptian nationality, at the expense of native Egyptians. Native Egyptians did not enjoy equitably whatever was left of Egypt's riches. The great disparity between rich and poor, with no important intermediate class between them (most of the Egyptian middle class was made up either of Copts or foreign elements), rendered the economic position of the majority of the population desperate. Some thinkers sought a solution to Egypt's economic problems by an appeal

[31] See Hasan al-Banna, *Risalat al-Mu'tamar al-Khamis* (Cairo, n.d.), pp. 50–51.

to foreign economic doctrines, especially to socialism and communism, but none of these was satisfactory in the Brotherhood's eyes. For each one of these doctrines had arisen in response to particular needs in foreign settings and therefore was not suitable for transplantation to Egyptian soil, although each may have had certain advantages in European countries.

To the Brotherhood, however, it seemed surprising that Muslim thinkers should turn their eyes to foreign economic systems when Islam possesses one of the most ideal and perfect economic systems ever provided for mankind. The combined merits of all foreign economic doctrines may, according to the Brotherhood, be found in the Islamic system. This kind of reasoning is, of course, based on the assumption that Islam is an all-embracing system in which the economic and the political sides of life no less than the religious and ethical are regulated by divine and ideal rules. The true meaning of Islam, the Brotherhood complained, has not been fully understood by Muslims today, especially by Muslim thinkers who received secular education in government schools or abroad. Thus Banna laid down certain broad principles derived from Islam and based on the pressing needs of modern society.

To begin with, Islam recognizes the principle of private property and the individual's right to enjoy, transfer, and dispose of his property, provided it is not contrary to public interest. Nor is the individual's right to accumulate wealth in a lawful manner to be restricted. It is true, said Banna, that Islam condemns the accumulation of wealth for extravagant and licentious living, but it approves of wealth for the promotion of the community's welfare and the increase of production and the national income. Banna's viewpoint was based on a Quranic text which states: "But do not give the fools property that God has assigned to you," [32] and on a Tradition in which the Prophet Muhammad said: "Lawful wealth belongs to him who is good." Islam also urges believers to exploit natural resources for the increase of wealth of

[32] *Qur'an* IV, 4.

their society, since God, in more than one Quranic injunction, ordered men to explore and use the hidden resources of the earth. The Prophet said: "Have you not seen how God has subjected to you whatever is in the heaven and earth," and "He has subjected to you what is in the heavens and what is in the earth." [33] However, Islam prohibits the acquisition of wealth by illegal means, such as usury and gambling, because these practices are included in the broader prohibition of wealth acquired by theft and robbery. Islam also prohibits trade in unlawful property, such as harmful drugs, intoxicating liquids, and others. It discourages practices harmful to the economy of society, such as hoarding and speculation, but it encourages generosity and the circulation of property in order to maintain a healthy social and economic order.

Islam provides ample rules for the regulation of the economic life of believers, including the fiscal and taxation system, which are applicable to modern society. It also provides rules for the way notes and currency should be issued, but it prohibits certain practices as harmful to a healthy economic life, such as the use of gold and silver for licentious purposes. Gold and silver, the Brotherhood advised, should be used for the general welfare of society, such as currency and bank reserves, but not for luxurious and decorative purposes.

Islam does not neglect the relationship of the individual to work; it discourages withdrawal from life and abstention from work and encourages the individual to earn his livelihood by taking an active part in life. He who is able but refuses to work should not receive any compensation. The right to work, said Banna, is inherent in the Islamic system and it should be regulated by legislation. Islam also recognizes the principle of social security by providing rules for those incapable to work—whether on account of age or sickness—to receive compensation. The early Islamic practice was embodied in the levying of legal alms (*al-zakat*) and distribu-

[33] *Qur'an* XXXI, 19; XLV, 12.

tion of charities, but these old methods might be adapted to meet the new demands of life.

Finally, Islam prescribes that the state should be ultimately responsible for the protection and the maintenance of a healthy social and economic system. It should supervise the economic life of the community and enforce rules and regulations in such a way as to promote the welfare of society and protect the interests of the individual on an equitable basis. The state should prohibit men in authority from using their influence at the expense of others, because corruption, bribery, and even the acceptance of gifts by men who enforce the law, are inconsistent with Islam. Men in authority should be regarded as servants, not as masters and exploiters of other men; only God is the ultimate ruler while those entrusted with authority should rule in accordance with His orders.[34]

In order to achieve its goal, the Brotherhood recommended industrialization, Egyptianization of foreign firms and capital, and nationalization of public utilities, on the ground that public welfare necessitates the intervention of the state to put an end to exploitation. It also called for the undertaking of large projects, such as the Aswan Dam and other irrigation projects, as well as for bringing further land under cultivation in order to improve agricultural production. The Brotherhood, though stressing individual enterprise, wanted the state to play a greater role in the organization of the economic life of the community than traditional Islam may imply. There seems to be a contradiction in Banna's economic thought when he permits the individual to own and employ wealth (capital) for production and in the meantime prohibits him to derive profit. Profit, said Banna, is usury, and usury is prohibited in Islam just as it is prohibited in Russia. He went on to explain that economists have argued that profit (usury) is necessary for the promotion of production, but their argument has been refuted by the communist experiment which proved that profit is not necessary under its social order. "It is unfortunate," added Banna, "that communist Russia should

[34] See Banna, *Mushkilatuna*, pp. 70–82.

precede us in abolishing a practice which in Islam had already been declared prohibited."[35] One is tempted to draw the conclusion that Banna's economic system, though declared to be opposed to communism, is essentially based on collectivist ideas for which Islam is invoked to provide religious and ethical rationalization.

The clash between the Brotherhood and authority, though it led to a temporary eclipse in the Brotherhood's position, by no means affected the appeal of its ideas among the people. The new Guide, Hasan Isma'il al-Hudaybi, who assumed his position in 1951, quickly restored the Brotherhood to the position it had lost two years before. But he so radically departed from the course of the first Guide that his leadership of the Brotherhood became the subject of controversy both within the Brotherhood and outside it. Some, in defense of Hudaybi's policy, held that his conciliatory policy with the Government led to the re-opening of the Brotherhood's headquarters without which the Brotherhood would never have been able to resume its activities under the monarchy. Others, criticizing Hudaybi's conduct, were concerned about the impact of his compromise on the country. It soon became apparent that dissension had already crept into the Brotherhood's ranks, and this may well be regarded as the second major blunder in the Brotherhood's life ever since the first Guide plunged his organization prematurely into politics.

Hudaybi, it is true, inherited the legacy of his predecessor's error, despite his declaration that the Brotherhood would no longer interfere in politics, but after the revolution of 1952, he seemed to have changed his mind and openly declared that the Brotherhood would ultimately seek to govern Egypt on the basis of the Islamic system. Until then, no one had ever doubted that the Brotherhood was struggling for power, and this open declaration ultimately brought the Brotherhood into a clash with the military leaders who governed Egypt after 1952.

Hudaybi's fatal blunder, which contributed to the further

[35] *Ibid.*, p. 91.

weakening of the Brotherhood, was his departure from the first Guide's established procedure for avoiding internal dissension. The agreement he concluded with King Faruq created Hudaybi's many opponents who saw in the new Guide's leadership a departure from the Brotherhood's principle that Egypt's rulers should follow the precepts of Islam. Since Faruq was regarded as a secular ruler who had no regard for Islam, Hudaybi's conduct was denounced as contrary to Islam's principles of government.

Following Faruq's fall, Hudaybi, who had followed a moderate policy, took a surprisingly firm stand against the army officers who came to power after the revolution. He insisted that short of actual participation in Government the Brotherhood should be consulted on all public matters. This attitude was unacceptable to the army officers and led Baquri, one of the leading members of the Brotherhood, to resign and accept a cabinet position in the Government in defiance of Hudaybi's policy. Meeting with a growing opposition within the organization, Hudaybi sought to consolidate his precarious position by dismissing a number of leading members. This resulted in further splits within the Brotherhood. Finally, Hudaybi tried to assume control of the secret paramilitary organization which had been set up after the Palestine war and the leadership of which had passed to other hands after Banna's assassination, but he was unable to do so owing to internal opposition. Internal dissension proved to be the Brotherhood's greatest weakness, and the dissenters often rationalized their disagreement on doctrinal grounds, which damaged the influence and prestige of the Brotherhood in the country.

Matters came to a head on the question of the Anglo-Egyptian agreement of 1954 to which the Brotherhood objected on the ground that it gave Britain a pretext to return to Egypt in time of war or threatening war. Perhaps without Hudaybi's knowledge, some of the Brotherhood's leaders resorted to violence and one of them made an attempt on President Nasir's life on October 26, 1954. This move, giving the Government ample reason to liquidate its opponents, sealed the fate of the Brotherhood. The principal leaders, except Hudaybi (who was thrown into prison) were executed, and the Brotherhood was declared illegal. A few members fled the country and became active abroad, but in reality the movement suffered a setback from which it could never recover, although several other attempts were made to overthrow the regime.[36] In 1966, the principal leaders were arrested after an alleged plot to assassinate Nasir, and four of them, including Sayyid Qutb, who played the role of the Guide, were executed.[37] The task of interpreting Islam in a manner compatible with modern conditions of life has passed to other hands.

The Brotherhood's collapse may seem to have been mainly due to its premature intervention in politics and to internal dissension, but in reality fundamental weakness of the movement lay deeper than that. Contemporary critics may differ on the significance of its contribution to the modernization of Islam. True, it showed flexibility in accepting foreign ideas under the guise of their Islamic origin, including almost every Western technological invention, but it could hardly be credited with having improved on 'Abduh's contribution in the realm of non-material values. One could even discern a falling away from 'Abduh's religious toleration by arousing religious fanaticism mixed with nationalism. 'Abduh's appeal to reason which prompted him to advocate a liberal interpretation of Islam was matched by the Brotherhood's insistence on the re-establishment of principles and practices no longer compatible with modern conditions of life. Thus, some of the Brotherhood's proposals seem impractical, since its insistence on the religious basis of authority and the restoration of the caliphate was incompatible with the progressive dissolution of Islam into separate territorial units, each stressing its sovereign attributes.

[36] Sa'id Ramadan, one of the active members of the Brotherhood, led the movement outside Egypt and continued its opposition against the regime.

[37] Sayyid Qutb, one of the Brotherhood's intellectual leaders, edited a review and published several works expounding Islamic doctrines (see note 29, above).

The Brotherhood derived popular support from its opposition to the much criticized democratic system which failed to achieve progress and development. Since democracy failed to inspire confidence and was regarded by religious and reactionary elements as a secular form of government, the Brotherhood was unwilling to reconcile it with Islam, and advocated the re-establishment of the Islamic system. As a result, the Brotherhood failed to provide a corrective to the existing political system and advocated the return to a system of government which earlier Muslim reformers had declared to be incompatible with the new demands of life. Rival groups and ideologies were bound therefore to compete with the Brotherhood even at the time when the Brotherhood was at the crest of favorable circumstances. These groups were the so-called "left-wing" groups, and their ideologies were collectivist in nature.

Chapter 5

THE COLLECTIVIST ALTERNATIVE

Though not in substance, yet in form, the struggle of the proletariat with the bourgeoisie is at first a national struggle. The proletariat of each country must, of course, first of all settle matters with its own bourgeosie.

The Communist Manifesto

Like nationalism and democracy, collectivist ideas were imported from the West and began to compete with other Western concepts in an effort to substitute traditional ideas of society. Beginning as a utopian socialist doctrine before World War I, it was transformed into a communist ideology after that war and contributed in no small measure to the collapse of liberal institutions. Following World War II, this new ideology penetrated almost all Arab lands. Its advocates, in a short-lived marriage with young nationalists, came close to seizing power, but its leaders prematurely precipitated their ideological clashes with other groups and aroused either violent protests from their opponents or dissension in their own ranks. Whether socialist or communist, the impact of collectivist thought has not yet reached its full development and may well be regarded as the greatest challenge to both old and new concepts of government.

Utopian Socialism

Liberal groups displaying sympathy for the ideology reigning in the Soviet world, often give the impression that their ideas were originally derived from Soviet thinkers. Truc, communist leaders opposed to Western thought derived their inspiration and guidance from Soviet prophets, but their forerunners, especially those who appeared before World War I, obtained their ideas from European thinkers.

The fathers of this new ideology were a few intellectuals who had been attracted to European socialist thought and believed that society would be more equitable and prosperous if it were reorganized on a socialist basis. They belonged to the set of Westernized reformers who saw no hope in modernizing Islamic society by drawing on its Islamic past, nor were they satisfied with a European way of life that failed in their view to measure up to ideal socialist standards. They dreamed, like their contemporary European socialists, that mankind would live in peace and harmony if the conflicting interests of social classes were reconciled under some sort of social democracy. According to socialist thought, life would be more abundant and prosperous if co-operative group enterprise were substituted for individual competition. Utopian socialists dreamed that liberty and equality could be shared by all and that the individual thereby would be liberated from the vagaries of social and religious tyranny.

It was perhaps the idealist thinkers who first caught the echo of socialist thought, especially those who had come into direct contact with European socialists. However, most of the educated individuals who had gone to Europe for study were from a relatively well-to-do class and only a few from poorer families. These latter were naturally more receptive to socialist ideas, but after their return home, they had little or no influence on the course of political development. After the adoption of democratic institutions, authority passed into the hands of young men of the upper classes who sought to fashion their political system closer to the then operating European models than the models advocated by radicals. Nationalism and democracy had dominated the minds of Westernized groups whose principal task was to assert the free expression of political opinions rather than to echo the grievances of oppressed classes. Rarely was there a man of an upper class who advocated socialism; it devolved upon

Christian intellectuals, though not necessarily of poorer classes, to advocate socialist ideas and to rid society of traditional shackles. The intellectuals sought to establish the egalitarian social order that was denied them by traditional Islam, in which no social differentials would be acknowledged and in which religious values would be substituted by more rational criteria.

Shibli Shumayyil (1860–1917), a Lebanese Christian domiciled in Egypt, was the first one to expound the doctrine of socialism (*ishtirakiya*), although the idea of socialism was not unknown to Arab thinkers. Shumayyil was better known to his contemporaries for his writings on the theory of evolution and on secularism. As a Christian who sought to rid his community of religious intolerance and who had read Büchner and Spencer, he dreamed of a society in which the individual would be liberated from all kinds of exclusiveness. His socialism was based on the doctrine that only labor should be the source of individual income and it should be regulated by the state in order to insure justice: he called neither for the state ownership of production nor for the abolition of private property. True, he talked about an eventual world socialist revolution, but he stressed peaceful change and called for cooperation among nations.[1]

Shumayyil's writings aroused the criticism of Muslim thinkers, and the debate that ensued centered around the relations between religion and science. Among those drawn to this debate was Farah Antun (1874–1922), another Christian thinker, who, in his debate with 'Abduh on the conflict between religion and science, advocated a vague brand of socialism. He called it "the religion of humanity," which was to replace traditional religion, but he failed to develop these socialist views because he was fundamentally interested in

[1] Shumayyil's writings, originally published in newspapers and periodicals, were reprinted in his *Majmu'a* (Cairo, 1908), II, 152–57, 179–82, 183–86, 187–98. For a summary of his ideas, see 'Ali al-Din Hilal, "Shibli Shumayyil and Salama Musa," *al-Musawwar* (December 19, 1965), pp. 32–33; Albert Hourani, *Arabic Thought in the Liberal Age* (London, 1962), pp. 252–53.

literary and philosophical rather than in socialist thought; he defined "socialism" as synonymous with secularism and opposed to religious intolerance.[2]

Under the influence of Shumayyil and Antun, still another Christian thinker, Salama Musa, who resented religious intolerance and intellectual stagnation, found in socialism and the theory of evolution an "outlet and a revenge" for existing social conditions.[3] His attraction to socialism was further confirmed after an extended visit to Europe between 1908 and 1911. "I was quite in love with *l'Humanité*," he recalled when he was in Paris. "Socialism," he remarked, "was a new way of seeing things, which made me vividly remember the poor classes of Egypt, and thus the spread of socialism in our country became the object of my concern." In England, he found himself with a congenial group when he joined the Fabian Society, and fell under the influence of the writings of G. B. Shaw and H. G. Wells. "Within the first year of my stay in London," he went on to explain, "I felt myself moving towards the left, that is, towards socialism . . . . I became more or less a socialist before I read Marx . . . ." In 1909 he visited Keir Hardie, leader of the Independent Labour Party and a member of Parliament who impressed him greatly. "When I met him," says Musa, "he told me that he was a socialist, and that socialism would first prevail in Europe and then spread to the other parts of the world. He added that British imperialism must cease in Egypt as well as in India, and that it was our duty, our first patriotic duty in Egypt, to turn out the English, after which we should bring about social reforms."[4] These ideas made a great impression on Musa who, upon his return to Egypt, began to expound socialism and other liberal ideals in the Egyptian press.

In 1913 Musa published a booklet on socialism in which he sought to enlighten the public on a subject about which he thought there had been much confusion and lack of under-

[2] Farah Antun, *Ibn Rushd wa Falsafatuh* (Cairo, 1903).

[3] See Salama Musa, *The Education of Salama Musa*, tr. L. Schuman (Leiden, 1961), pp. 37–38.

[4] *Ibid.*, pp. 58, 71, 135.

standing. "I do not intend," he stated in the preface, "that this tract would be an invitation to the public to adopt socialism, much less a program for a political party or an association; it is merely intended to initiate mental fermentation until the public is ready for socialism." [5] Musa begins his discussion of socialism with a short introduction on the rise and development of capitalism, a summary of early socialist thinkers, and the basic ideas of Karl Marx. He then explains the meaning and the fundamental principles of socialism. Socialism, he says, aims at achieving economic liberty for the individual. Property and inheritance rights should be abolished so that the individual, born free from economic shackles, can earn his income on the basis of equality. In a socialist society only the state owns property—that is, the means of production—and the individual derives his income from work. But socialism, he went on to explain, does not provide equal incomes for all individuals; it provides equal opportunities for work, and the individual's income necessarily varies because the natural abilities of men vary. Socialism, Musa points out, recognizes these natural differences and the socialist state encourages men to exploit their natural abilities for the good of society by allowing each to gain a higher income in accordance with his physical and mental abilities. However, the state prohibits the individual, regardless of how high his income is, from bequeathing his wealth to his children who must earn their incomes in accordance with their own abilities.[6]

Musa's socialism is obviously a mixture of utopian and Marxian socialism, since he combines the principle of the abolition of private property with that which recognizes the variation of individual incomes. The latter is inconsistent with the Marxian doctrine which discourages disparity of incomes on the strength of the principle "from those who can to those who need," while the former expresses an extreme Marxist view. Musa also adopted some Fabian ideas, like democracy and peaceful change, while he rejected Fabian

[5] Salama Musa, *al-Ishtirakiya* (Cairo, 1913, 1962), p. 5.
[6] *Ibid.*, pp. 19–20.

concepts of private property. Needless to say though he derived his inspiration from European thinkers, he belonged to no particular school of socialism.

The brand of socialism that Musa wanted for Egypt seemed to be a combination of parliamentary democracy and state socialism. Democracy, he contended, should precede socialism. It should start at the lowest administrative level in the village, where a self-governing unit was to be established, and public services should gradually be socialized until society would be completely remodelled on a socialist basis. The central government should own the larger units of public services, each to be directed by a council composed of local representatives. In turn, a parliamentary government, based on the universal electoral system, would supervise all public agencies and conduct the foreign relations of the nation. A nucleus for the socialization of public services in Egypt, Musa notes, already existed in government ownership of the railway system. This type of ownership, he thought, might be extended to other public services as the basis of a future socialist order. The only criticism he leveled against the railway system was its undemocratic character and the unjust method of distributing compensations between officials and employees. But these shortcomings, he contended, were incidental, stemming mainly from traditional bureaucratic practices which would be eliminated if democracy and socialism were established.[7]

The three Christian thinkers, especially Shumayyil and Antun, whose socialism was essentially a protest against religious exclusiveness, were joined by a socialist thinker whose call for socialism was prompted by a great concern over poverty and deprivation. Mustafa Hasanayn al-Mansuri, a Muslim, resorted to socialism in voicing the grievances of the poor whose desperate conditions he came to share. He was born in Cairo in 1890 to a well-to-do family, but his

[7] *Ibid.*, pp. 20–22. No critical study of Musa's life and thought has yet been made, but a number of essays dealing with some aspects of his thought have been published in Arabic recently. See Ghali Shukri, *Salama Musa wa Azamat al-Damir al-'Arabi* (Bayrut, 2nd ed., 1965); and Mahmud al-Sharqawi, *Salama Musa: al-Mufakkir wa al-Insan* (Bayrut, 1965).

father lost his wealth before Mustafa was born and spent the rest of his life in poverty. From the time Mustafa began to attend school, he felt keenly the disparity between the rich and the poor and thus poverty was a theme of his writings. In 1911, when he graduated from college, he was chosen to pursue further study in Europe, but he failed his physical examination, and was deprived from attaining a high government post to which he was entitled upon graduation. After a short period of teaching in a primary school, he became schoolmaster and devoted his life to study and writing. He found in socialism the answer to the problem of poverty and began diligently to read Karl Marx, Tolstoy, Anatole France, and other Western authors. In 1913, he published his first work on *The History of Socialist Doctrines,* based on the material which he had collected from diverse readings.[8] Between 1913 and 1920, he published several other books and articles, mainly translations from Western writers, including *Progress and Poverty* by Henry George.[9] These writings, as well as his attendance of a public lecture on socialism given by a foreign visitor in 1920, led to his dismissal from his post; for the rest of his life, he lived in abject poverty in a small village near Fayyum, but he continued to take an interest in public affairs, and to write occasional letters to friends and to officials on questions of the day, especially after Nasir issued the socialist decrees of 1961.

Mansuri's socialism, like Shibli Shumayyil's, did not call for the abolition of private property, but for the providing of work and equal opportunities for all. His interest in socialism was confined to the material aspects of life, because he, unlike non-Muslims, did not suffer from any social discrimination. Since he had grown up in Egypt and had no first-hand knowledge of European social life, he advanced only a rudimentary socialism and, at the same time, stressed traditional views about the family and other social questions. He was perhaps the first Muslim socialist in the Arab world to voice

[8] *Ta'rikh al-Madhahib al-Ishtirakiya* (Cairo, 1913).
[9] *al-Taqaddum wa al-Faqr* (Cairo, 1920).

the grievances of the poor and to hold that socialism would repair the situation.[10]

No constructive criticism of early socialist thought was made in the Arab countries since most writers were then concerned with religious and nationalist issues. It devolved therefore upon Zia Gökalp, a Turkish nationalist thinker to write what might be regarded as the classic reply to socialist thought before World War I. Since before World War I, the Arab world was still part of the Ottoman empire, Turkish thinkers had an influence on Arab writers and often the thoughts of Turkish writers were reported and summarized in the Arabic press. Zia Gökalp was one of the intellectuals who had supported the Turkish Revolution of 1908 and whose writings Arab thinkers held in high esteem.

In 1908 Zia Gökalp joined a mixed group of young intellectuals in Salonika who were interested in "materialism." In their meetings they often discussed such subjects as liberalism, dialectical materialism, and positivist philosophy. No agreements on fundamentals seem to have emerged, but Gökalp came to see more clearly the inadequacy of materialism and became critical of socialist thought. In an article entitled "The New Life and New Values," [11] published in 1911, Gökalp remarked that a political revolution had been achieved—referring to the revolution of 1908—and that the nation was ready for a "social revolution." He examined various systems of values and ideas such as socialism, cosmopolitanism, and humanism, but he rejected them either because they were inconsistent with Islam's social morality or inadequate to transform the old into a new one. He advocated nationalism which, he thought, would create a new life, based on new values, not on utopias. His concern about national solidarity and cultural unity induced him to reject class struggle and to see in social-

[10] For a brief account of Mansuri's life, see 'Ali al-Din Hilal, "Mustafa Hasanayn al-Mansuri," *al-Musawwar* (December 17, 1965), pp. 40–41; *ibid.*, (December 21, 1965), pp. 28–29.

[11] Zia Gökalp, "Yeni Hayat ve Yeni Kaymetter," *Gene Kalember* (Salonika, 1911); English translation in Niazi Berkes, *Turkish Nationalism and Western Civilization* (New York, 1959), pp. 55–60.

ism certain elements opposed to national unity. He also saw a certain vagueness in the socialist ideal and the inability of socialists to advance society toward realization of their utopias, although he conceded that socialist thought may have contributed to progress, social justice, and freedom. "We do not want," he said emphatically, "the change which the socialists seek to produce, because we believe that they are mere utopias and will remain utopias." He maintained that the "new life" should emerge from the nation's "social consciousness." In the past, religion—one form of social consciousness—played a major role, but now "the ideals directing all nations are national ideals." Thus, Gökalp rejected socialism in favor of nationalism. "This," he said, "is the ideal which we hope the youth will follow." Gökalp lived long enough to see the realization of some of his ideals in the early Kamalist regime.

Before World War I, the call of the early socialist prophets aroused little or no enthusiasm since society was not yet prepared for such liberal ideas and most thinkers were either concerned with religious or with national issues rather than with social inequalities. These thinkers, few in number, were indeed ahead of their time; but their ideas marked the beginning of socialist thought which became the preoccupation of the succeeding generation. The thread of socialist thought was interrupted during the war, but it was not completely dropped. After the war, it was taken up by others, when the new conditions called for the reconsideration of national issues from a different perspective.

The Socialist Movement

Utopian socialism was given practical expression when, after World War I, political parties were established in which intellectuals and liberal reformers took an active part. European socialist parties provided the initial inspiration, and native leaders tried to adapt socialist theories to local demands. These parties, however, followed neither a coherent pattern, nor were their activities coordinated. At the outset, not even the name "Socialist Party" was used, because the idea of socialism was then looked upon with disfavor and suspicion. In a word, a socialist movement did exist, but its various adherents failed to establish a united party with a definite socialist program. A little background on the major parties is perhaps necessary for an understanding of the socialist movement.

Turkey and Persia took the lead in organizing socialist parties in the Islamic world, but their effect on the Arab world was limited, since Arab socialists established all their contacts with European socialists. One of the reasons why socialist parties appeared much later in Arab lands than in Turkey and Persia is that Arab leaders were too preoccupied in the struggle for independence to pay attention to social and economic problems. World War I brought new changes in its wake and some of the Arab leaders who were active in public life sought a new approach to political freedom. Most of the leaders held that their principal task was to achieve national freedom, but few saw any need to pay attention also to social problems. There were likewise a few thinkers who advocated socialist ideas before World War I and called for social reforms on the basis of socialist doctrines. Salama Musa, who resumed his writing on social problems after the war, was joined by others. The most impressive treatise on socialism published immediately after the war came from the incisive pen of Nicola Haddad, a Lebanese Christian domiciled in Egypt. The theme of his work on socialism was that the socialist movement in Europe had arisen as the inevitable result of the industrialization of society and the concentration of capital, and that the rise of industry was itself the necessary result of earlier stages of social development. He maintained that the triumph of socialism was inevitable not only in Europe but also throughout the world, regardless as to how long it might take. Implied in his theme was the thought that Islamic society could not escape such a destiny.[12]

[12] Nicola Haddad, *Socialism* (Cairo, 1920).

The first politician to introduce socialist ideas into the program of a political party after World War I was 'Aziz Mirhum. Like many other Egyptian thinkers, Mirhum received his education in France and was influenced by French socialist thought. After the war, when Egypt rose in revolt against the British occupation, a few enthusiastic intellectuals—Mustafa 'Abd al-Raziq, Husayn Haykal, 'Aziz Mirhum, Mansur Fahmi, and others—gathered to form a political party advocating liberal ideas. Zaghlul, leader of the nationalist movement, had organized the Wafd, the leading political party, and it was now the turn of younger men to play their role in political life. It did not take long to agree on the political objectives of the party, such as the achievement of independence and the protection of constitutional liberties, nor to call it the Democratic Party. But when the leaders began to discuss the social and economic goals, they found themselves divided into two schools of thought. One, represented by Mirhum, tried to adopt a socialist program. The other, led by Haykal, insisted on free enterprise. The task of reconciling the two conflicting views fell on Mustafa 'Abd al-Raziq, a moderate thinker and a member of an influential family. Haykal said that he was not opposed to measures which would provide minimum wages, free education, and free hospital services; and Mirhum conceded that he would not demand the abolition of private property nor the socialization of all public services. It was agreed that, when the principal objectives of the party were achieved, revision of the program would be considered.[13] For a short while the Democratic Party played an active role in politics, though its appeal was essentially confined to the intellectuals. Mirhum, who had labor connections, left the party to join the Wafd, hoping that his socialist views might have greater appeal among Zaghlul's followers. Haykal and other members dissolved the party to join the newly organized Liberal Constitutional Party, composed of Egypt's upper classes. Mirhum must have

[13] See Muhammad Husayn Haykal, *Mudhakkirat fi al-Siyasa al-Misriya* (Cairo, 1951), I, 80–81.

been disappointed with Wafdist leadership, for the party proved no less opposed to socialist ideas than others.[14]

More outspoken in its socialist views was another group which formed a bona-fide socialist party. In 1920, the Egyptian Socialist Party was organized by 'Abd-Allah 'Inani, Husni al-'Arabi, and Salama Musa. Musa, as already noted, was a Christian utopian socialist, but the other two, native Muslims, stood for radical socialism. The activities of the party proved to be limited, although Musa claims that the public responded with great enthusiasm; Husni al-'Arabi left it to organize a more militant Socialist Party.[15] It was formed in Alexandria by Husni al-'Arabi in cooperation with Joseph Rosenthal, a jeweller, and Antun Marun, a lawyer. Apart from its acceptance of socialism, the party had no clearly defined aims, and its members seem to have held varied views of socialism. The extremists favored an association with the Comintern and the party's name was changed in 1922 to the Communist Party of Egypt. Rosenthal, who objected to this change, was expelled from the party. Owing to agitation among workers, Husni al-'Arabi was arrested and expelled from the country. A decree depriving him of Egyptian nationality was later issued. He went first to Moscow, but later, after the rise of Hitler, went to teach Arabic in Germany. Marun's activities, regarded as anti-government, led to his arrest and subsequent death in prison in 1924.[16] It may seem strange that a country like Egypt, stricken with poverty and other social deprivations, should fail to respond to socialist propaganda. It was, however, the nationalist leaders (the Wafd leaders in particular) claiming to champion the cause of the common man, who opposed the socialist movement on the ground that national unity was absolutely necessary to oppose foreign domination and that their program was designed to

[14] Mirhum served as a Senator during the 1930s and 1940s, and often spoke on labor problems in Parliament, but no longer identified himself with left-wing groups.

[15] See Salama Musa, *The Education of Salama Musa*, p. 136.

[16] Alias Marqus, *Ta'rikh al-Ahzab al-Shuyu'iya fi al-Watan al-'Arabi* (Bayrut, 1964), pp. 14–15; and W. Z. Laqueur, *Communism and Nationalism in the Middle East* (London, 1956), pp. 31, 33–34.

serve the interests of workers and peasants. Small wonder, therefore, that socialist propaganda appeared like a voice in the wilderness.

Syria and Lebanon were, like Egypt, exposed to socialist thought. Before World War I, Christian thinkers who advocated socialist doctrines went to Egypt to express their ideas, because free expression of opinion was denied them in Syria and Lebanon; but after the war they became less inhibited and began to talk more freely. Some who had left Lebanon for Egypt began to return after the war when Lebanon proved to be more tolerant of liberal ideas than Egypt, and it was from there that socialist thought spread into Syria, 'Iraq, and other Arab countries.

Among the first attracted to socialist thought was Yusuf Ibrahim Yazbuk. His social background and the conditions in which he had grown up were largely responsible for the appeal that socialism held for him. He was born in Hadath, a suburb of Bayrut, at the turn of the century and was brought up as a poor orphan in the house of the Shidiaq family because he lost both parents early in life. One of the prominent members of the Shidiaq family who had become a protestant was alleged to have been killed by the instigations of native clergymen, and his brother, in protest, became a Muslim.[17] From tender youth, Yazbuk heard about the bigotry of the priesthood, the oppression of Ottoman rule, and the poverty of the majority of people like himself. The war years, during which Lebanon suffered starvation, inflamed his feelings about social injustices and stirred his affection for the poor and the oppressed. He had already learned French and was well read in literature when the war was over. He had read Rousseau, Voltaire, and Anatole France before he read Marx and the pronouncements of the Russian Revolution. Yet Yazbuk made no serious effort beyond his close friends to publicize his views on socialism until Riyashi began to publish a paper publicly declared in favor of socialism.

[17] This was Ahmad Faris al-Shidiaq (1804–87). He served under several Muslim rulers and published a number of literary works and edited, under the patronage of the Sultan, an Arabic newspaper *al-Jawa'ib*.

Iskandar al-Riyashi, a Christian journalist born in 1892 in Zahla, a Lebanese town near the Syro-Lebanese border, was a self-made man who became a journalist. He visited France briefly before starting his first newspaper in 1910 and distinguishing himself as a satirical writer. Like Yazbuk he felt a kinship with the poor, perhaps under the impact of the starvation days in Lebanon during World War I. After the war, he made another visit to France, renewing his prewar experiences with Parisian gay life; but he also fell under the influence of socialist writers.[18] "In France," he later wrote, "I detested everything, except the beauty of women and the oppressed. . . . I found in the land of Rousseau, Jauré, and Anatole France, capital is the basis of every material effort. So I rejected capitalism and its advocates, and I became a socialist."[19] On his way home he visited Germany and was influenced by the internationalist outlook of its Socialist Party. In 1922, he started publishing a new paper called *al-Sahafi al-Ta'ih* [the Wandering Journalist] which he announced he would devote to the cause of the workers and the oppressed.[20] In the first issue, Riyashi stated his fundamental socialist ideas and called for co-operation among classes and for helping the poor and the oppressed. He believed that there was no conflict between religion and socialism, since socialist ideals are explicitly mentioned in the sacred books of Christianity and Islam. He criticized monopoly rights which he held were inconsistent with the interests of the people, and called the attention of government officials to the fact that they were public servants and therefore ought to be just in the discharge of their responsibilities. Finally, he urged collaboration between Syria and Lebanon, because of their historical and geographical connections as well as their common interests.

[18] See Fu'ad Hubaysh, "Iskandar al-Riyashi, al-Sahafi al-Ta'ih," *al-Ma'rad*, vol. X, (February 7, 1931), pp. 2–3.

[19] See S. Ayyub [Sami al-Khuri], *al-Hizb al-Shuyu'i fi Suriya wa Lubnan* (Bayrut, 1959), p. 24.

[20] The first issue dated September 28, 1922.

No sooner had the first issue of *al-Sahafi al-Ta'ih* appeared than several thinkers began to write encouraging letters to Riyashi, expressing their socialist views. The first to respond, disguised under the pen-name of al-Shabah al-Baki [The Crying Shadow], was Yusuf Ibrahim Yazbuk. He first wrote a letter in support of Riyashi's socialist views and promised to be a contributor to his paper. In the issue dated October 10, 1922, Yazbuk published a short story about the plight of a poor woman and her two little children in the days of World War I. The woman was observed praying to Jesus Christ, the embodiment of love and poverty and the great protagonist of equality among men. She voiced her suffering and invoked the teachings of Christ who had sacrificed himself for the salvation of men but who remained silent about the prevalence of poverty and starvation in her country. She pointed to the rich who were corrupting the air with the odor of liquor and keeping the starving poor from picking up the leftovers thrown to the dogs. In her prayers, the woman cried for food and appealed to Christ for equality among men.

In this story, Yazbuk tried to stir sympathy with the poor and stress the principle of equality and also tacitly reproached the church for its silence about the rich and its neglect of the poor. In another literary piece, published on November 12, 1922, Yazbuk addressed himself to the worker. He held up that labor is the only source for earning a living in a socialist society, calling the attention to the Biblical story of Adam's expulsion from Paradise and how God commanded man to earn a living by the sweat of his brow. There are many, Yazbuk said, who exploit the efforts of workers and enjoy the fruit of their sweat by robbing them. He thus attacked capitalism and denounced those who earned their living at the workers' expense. Under socialism, he concluded, everybody should work in order to earn a living, he who did not work should have no place in such a community, and everyone should be compensated for his work in proportion to the amount of work contributed. Finally, Yazbuk stressed the principle of equality and called for co-operation among workers to achieve this goal. He rejected, however, the use of force in establishing a socialist order.[21]

But Yazbuk was not the only one who responded to Riyashi's call. There had already been a small circle of intellectuals organized by Yazbuk, and one of them, As'ad al-Mundhir, under the pen-name of a woman wrote a letter to Riyashi's paper, pointing out that not only men but also women were concerned about the condition of the poor and hoping that socialism might be adopted. Other members of the circle followed, and one of them went so far as to call for the organization of a communist party (although the majority wanted a socialist organization) and to bring into the open the activities of Yazbuk's socialist group. Among this circle was Fu'ad al-Shamali, the future communist leader, who was not an intellectual, but a worker whose labor activities in Egypt led to his expulsion in 1923.[22] He proved the most radical in the group and was able, in co-operation with Yazbuk, to form the Communist Party, as will be noted later. The socialists, growing in number, began to criticize the capitalist system, and to call on the government to enact laws for the protection of workers and for the nationalization of public services and industry. But except for Shamali, their activities remained essentially intellectual.

In 'Iraq, the socialist movement began almost a decade later, although collectivist ideas were not unknown to 'Iraqi intellectuals. Some had come under the influence of Arab socialists and others were influenced by European writers. Perhaps the first one to be attracted by socialist thought was Mahmud Ahmad, a literary writer who, under the influence of Yazbuk and other Arab socialists, began as early as 1924 to spread liberal and socialist ideas in 'Iraq. Ahmad published a number of novels and short stories, centering around the general theme of the poor and the wretched and the struggle

[21] As a literary writer, Yazbuk wrote with clarity and elegance. For a summary of these articles, see Khuri, *al-Hizb al-Shuyu'i*, pp. 20–23, 28–33, 38–40.

[22] Shamali, originally a Lebanese, had left Lebanon for Egypt before World War I (about 1912) and became a communist under the influence of Rosenthal; he returned to Lebanon in 1922 and died in 1940.

to liberate them from their desperate conditions. In a letter to Yazbuk, Ahmad stated that he had been spreading socialist thought in Baghdad since 1924 under the influence of the socialist writings of the Yazbuk group, and that in his novels *Jalal Khalid* and *Mujahidun* he described social conditions in 'Iraq and expressed the socialist aspirations of his fellow writers.[23] Ahmad served as a clerk in the secretariat of the 'Iraqi Parliament (later in the Municipality of Baghdad), but he was very active in literary circles and frequent contributor to journals. In one of his short stories about the condition of the 'Iraqi peasantry, published in a Baghdad daily newspaper and dedicated to Yusuf Yazbuk, he described the wretchedness of rural life and the spirit of perseverance in overcoming difficulties.[24] This literary approach, like Yazbuk's, was intended not so much to expound socialist theory as to stir the conscience of the people about the hardships of life in the country. Ahmad's hopes were apparently pinned on organizing trade unions rather than on active political agitations, for in his correspondence with Yazbuk he denied that the newly organized labour union had anything to do with the communist movement.

More outspoken about socialism were a few young men who had received their education abroad or in the Baghdad Law College. In 1930, they began to gather and organize an intellectuals' socialist band. This band came to be known as the Ahali group, after the name of a daily newspaper, which appeared in 1931. These young men were of a circle which felt keenly that political power had for a long time been in the hands of a small set of elderly men who paid little or no attention to social and economic problems. The group advocated essentially the principles of the French Revolution, stressing democracy and liberalism in particular.

Under the influence of 'Abd al-Fattah Ibrahim and Muhammad Hadid, the Ahali group adopted socialism as its

[23] Copy of the letter, dated April 19, 1929, was supplied to the writer by Yusuf Yazbuk.

[24] Mahmud Ahmad, "Baday al-Fayiz," *al-Watan*, Baghdad, May 27, 1929.

first article of faith. Ibrahim received his education in American institutions in Bayrut and New York, and Hadid at the London School of Economics in England. Having come from conservative families, both held moderate socialist views at the outset. Hadid indeed belonged to a family reputed for its wealth and conservatism. It was for this very reason that the group preferred to call its ideology Sha'biya (populism) rather than socialism. Ibrahim, with the aid of other Ahali thinkers, edited two little volumes in which the ideas and ideals of Sha'biya were expressed. The first volume, dealing with the history of political thought from the Greeks down to the Russian Revolution of 1917, was an introductory to the second volume which outlined the doctrine of Sha'biya and became the working program of the group.

The doctrine of Sha'biya, seeking "welfare for all the people" without distinction between individuals and classes on the basis of wealth, birth, or religion, advocated sweeping social reform in 'Iraq. It laid the main stress on the people as a whole rather than on the individual, but advocated in the meantime protection of essential human rights, such as liberty, equality of opportunity, and private property. The state, it was added, must pay proper attention to the health and education of the individual as well as recognizing his right to work. Thus Sha'biya comprised the principles of both democracy and socialism, yet it had to be differentiated from both since, in contrast with democracy, it advocated a kind of collectivism; and, in contrast with Marxist theory, it did not admit the existence of class struggle or revolutionary process of change. It also recognized, in contrast with Marxism, the institutions of family and religion. Sha'biya likewise recognized patriotism as an article of faith, but it repudiated nationalism, as the latter had often led to imperialism and the domination of society by one class, while the former merely inspired the individual with loyalty to his country. "The history of nationalism" reads the Ahali Manifesto, "is full of blood, tyranny, and hypocrisy," while the history of patriotism had shown that it advocates no aggression or social discrimination, and fully recognizes every citizen as equally important to his fatherland.[25]

In 1934, Kamil al-Chadirchi, a member of a nationalist party, joined the Ahali group. Chadirchi was a liberal whose ideas no longer fitted the nationalist mold and hence, under the influence of the Ahali group, he became a socialist. He proved to be the most outstanding leader of the group and expressed a passionate desire to combine democracy and socialism in one system. He became the editor of the Ahali paper and, after the National Democratic Party was formed, the leader of a moderate socialist party. Socialists who gradually moved toward the left to become communists did not weaken the Ahali group, because Chadirchi's strength of character and his insistence on a moderate socialist program kept the movement alive, although he agreed later to the nationalization of public services and industries. In principle, Chadirchi was in favor of a slow and evolutionary change toward socialism. In practice, however, he allowed his followers to participate in two revolutionary movements in 1936 and 1958, the first of which undermined his party and the second which completely destroyed it. Nevertheless, the ideas for which Chadirchi and his party stood remained, prior to the revolution of 1958, the watchwords of liberals and moderate groups.

These three separate, but not unrelated, socialist trends were but three typical manifestations of the mainstream of collectivist thought in Arab lands before that thought was transformed into a political movement. The Ahali was in a sense the logical culmination of the former two trends.

In line with earlier thinkers who tried to reform Islamic society under the impact of European ideas, the socialists sought to reform society by drawing on a different set of European ideals. They observed that European polity itself was under attack by liberal thinkers who desired to achieve a more equitable and just social order. Such reformers, regarded as protest thinkers, were not at all unknown to Islamic

[25] See *Mutala'at fi al-Sha'biya* [Reflections on Populism], (Baghdad, Ahali Press, 1932).

society. The founders of heterodox sects who were dissatisfied with the orthodox Sunni Islam belonged to the same category. In modern times, Arab socialists could be regarded as a modern sect—a protest group—in opposition to vested interest. They were radical social reformers who showed as much concern about the decadence of society as other reformers did and who sought a remedy in the adoption of a different set of ideas. These ideas were regarded as more progressive than nationalism and democracy because socialism appeared to repair systems based on nationalism and democracy. Both moderate and radical Arab reformers, however, derived their inspiration from European rather than Islamic thought and sought to transform society according to modern rather than traditional patterns.

Socialism as an ideology attracted few thinkers at the outset, but these were not in the forefront of the reform movement. Their thought reflected the idealism of penalized groups—social or religious—and it seemed either irrelevant or too abstract even to Westernized men who were concerned with national unity more than with social inequalities. From the beginning, minority groups were the first to be attracted by socialist preaching, and those in power looked at them with disfavor and suspicion: the Muslims showed no great enthusiasm for socialism because it was opposed to native traditions and inconsistent with the Islamic way of life. Above all, nationalist leaders opposed socialism because it weakened national unity by a class struggle while the nation was engaged in a struggle against foreign domination. Furthermore, these leaders could not be in sympathy with a movement directed against the upper classes to which most of them belonged.

The socialist movement proved to be transitory. Most of its radical followers were disappointed when the movement proved incapable of transforming society into the socialist utopia. Consequently, they began gradually to join the more militant revolutionary movement—communism. Most of them were intellectuals who failed to agree on fundamentals and addressed themselves to the common man. As a result, the communists succeeded where socialists failed. Meanwhile, moderate socialists, finding neo-nationalist circles willing to adopt socialist measures, often defected to nationalism. Small wonder that the early socialist movement spent itself so rapidly.

The Communist Movement

The communist movement in the Arab East, as elsewhere, may be regarded as the logical sequel to socialist preaching. Socialist leaders who used to confine their activities to the literate began to turn their attention to the masses, and their social philosophy was bound to be affected by proletarian interests. But the greatest impetus to communist activities was, of course, the Russian Revolution of 1917 that gave its theory a practical expression. To Muslim communists—indeed, to all others in the world—Moscow became another Makka, which provided a continuous inspiration and guidance the like of which socialist leaders had never known before.

A Soviet appeal to Islam seems to have been contemplated by Soviet leaders soon after the Revolution. They published the secret war treaties that the Tsarist regime had entered into with European Powers and renounced all rights and concessions which Russia had claimed under those treaties in Islamic and other Asian countries. Soviet leaders also declared that the Russian Revolution ushered in a new era, an era of anti-colonial uprisings wherein all "oppressed peoples" might rise and shake off Western domination. They appealed to their Muslim compatriots—in Central Asia and elsewhere—offering to respect their "mosques and shrines" and seeking their support in an effort to influence Muslim opinion outside Soviet Russia.[26] Believing that the "new era" would be favorable to

[26] For texts of proclamations to the Muslims of Russia and the East, see Ivor Spector, *The Soviet Union and the Muslim World* (University of Washington Press, 1958), pp. 21–22.

Islam, the Muslims of Russia spread the word to their co-religionists in the world that the Soviet regime was in complete harmony with the Qur'an and the Shari'a, and went so far as to compare Lenin with Muhammad and the communist creed with Islamic teachings.

Nor had Soviet leaders confined their appeal to words. In 1920, they held a conference in Baku, to which all non-Western peoples were invited. The Third International—the Comintern—issued the invitations, sponsored the conference, and supervised its work. In that conference, Muslim peasants and workers were called upon to join the peasants and workers of Soviet Russia in their struggle against "colonialism and capitalism." The Manifesto of the conference states:

> Arise . . . . peoples of the East! The Third International calls upon you to join a sacred war against the capitalist rabble. Comrade delegates, develop the class-consciousness of the masses; organize them into peasant soviets, soviets of toilers; call all the toilers to union with Soviet Russia; propagate the idea of the federation of the oppressed nations; and finally, create a union of the proletarians and peasants of all countries, religions and languages!

The proposals put forth to Muslims were essentially the same as those formulated for other "oppressed" peoples of Asia. It consisted of creating peasant and worker proletariats in Islamic countries, uniting them with the proletariats of other countries in a world republic, and proclaiming a war to overthrow "colonialism and capitalism" in co-operation with toilers of other peoples. The essential teachings of Islam were declared to be compatible with Soviety doctrines. But it was the concept of the *jihad*—an Islamic crusade or holy war—which Islam considers as one of the pillars of faith, that seems to have attracted Soviet leaders who saw in it an instrument which they could employ against European powers. Muslims were told in the Manifesto that they had often been called to "march under the green banner of the Prophet," but all such "holy wars" were "deceitful and false." "Now," the Manifesto added, "we summon you to the first genuine holy war under the red banner of the Communist International." [27] In order to give practical expression to these slogans, Soviet leaders offered to support the claims of independence and territorial integrity of Islamic countries that had still been struggling against European domination. Never before, since Napoleon made his proclamation to the Egyptians after his descent upon Egypt in 1798, had Muslims heard such flattering words from Europeans.

Communist Activities

For an understanding of the theory and practice of communism in the Arab world, an inquiry into its spread in Islamic lands as a whole might be illuminating. Five stages so far can be delineated. The first stage may be characterized as a dashing overture by Soviet leaders to the Islamic countries bordering on the Soviet homeland, presumably on the assumption that these would be stepping stones for communist penetration into other Islamic lands. These countries, especially Turkey and Persia, had shown remarkable resistance to Western encroachments and seemed logically ripe for communist activities, since their governments were ready to receive Soviet support against European intervention. Both on popular and official levels, communist infiltration gave the impression that Persia and Turkey would, sooner or later, become Sovietized outposts for further penetration into Islamic lands.

In both Turkey and Persia, leftist leaders tried to adapt communist doctrines to local needs and traditions, and the nationalists seem to have given them initial encouragement while they were still struggling against foreign intervention. However, no sooner did Turkey and Persia win national freedom than they began to restrict communist activities, and

[27] It is reported that when references to *Jihad* were made at the Baku Conference, the Muslim delegates, in a frenzy of excitement, rose from their seats to a man and, brandishing swords and daggers, swore to fulfill their duty of holy war (see Spector, *The Soviet Union and the Muslim World*, p. 30).

communist leaders were either exiled or thrown into prison. Nationalism rather than communism reigned supreme as symbol of identity, and during the years between the two wars communist activities, especially in Turkey, were confined to a handful of leaders. It became clear to Soviet leaders that, contrary to their expectations, Persia and Turkey were not ripe for communism and the Soviet Union came to terms with these countries rather than opposed them. Thus, separate agreements were signed with them, recognizing their independence and territorial integrity.[28]

The second stage, lasting almost two decades, may be described as a period of "withdrawal" from the region. Soviet leaders, realizing that the bordering countries were not ready for a communist drive, decided to wait for more favorable circumstances. Turkey and Persia were able to hold their own against European intervention, and their regimes seemed in Soviet eyes more "progressive" than the bourgeois regimes of other Islamic lands.

The Arab world, though potentially opposed to colonialism, had succumbed to European control, and Soviet leaders saw no hope in direct intervention. However, some Soviet agents penetrated deep into Arab lands and three centers for clandestine activities were soon to be known. The first two—Egypt and Palestine—were established independently; under their influence, a third center was set up in Lebanon. From these three points communist activities spread to other Arab countries.

The communist movement in the Arab world was the product of World War I; as a step toward the organization of a communist party, its leaders began to organize trade unions in the principal towns and cities. Socialist and intellectual sympathizers (the latter in particular) were urged to co-operate and pay attention to agrarian and labor problems

[28] Since it is deemed outside the scope of this work to discuss the communist movement save in so far as it relates to the Arab world, the reader may be referred for a discussion of communism in Turkey and Iran to the following works: George Harris, *The Origins of Communism in Turkey* (Stanford, 1967); S. Zabir, *The Communist Movement in Iran* (Berkeley, 1966).

in order to counterbalance the influence of the "bourgeoisie." After a communist party had formally been established in each of these countries (Egypt and Palestine in 1919 and Lebanon in 1924), the three joined the Comintern and intensified their efforts among workers. Except in Palestine, the activities of these parties were essentially clandestine. Their platforms called for labor legislation to improve conditions of workers (such as limiting working hours to eight, equal wages for foreign and native workers, and the right to factory inspection), freedom to organize trade unions, and the right to organize co-operatives. The Egyptian Communist Party paid attention to agrarian problems in particular and called for the limitation of land ownership to 100 faddans.[29] The media for disseminating these ideas were the press and underground communist circulars, although perhaps the most effective means were strikes and street demonstrations which revealed deep-rooted social unrest and mass dissatisfaction. Some of these demonstrations, it is true, were encouraged and exploited by nationalist leaders, but the masses were on the whole motivated by the wretchedness of their own social conditions which were usually expressed in nationalist slogans. Nationalist leaders, however, tried to restrict the right of strikes and demonstrations, and offered no constructive measures to improve social conditions or cope with recurring outbursts.

The Egyptian and Palestine communist parties seem to have received direct but not constant guidance and assistance from Moscow. The Lebanese party received an indirect support through Palestine. After the establishment of a Syrian Communist Party in the early thirties, both the Syrian and Lebanese parties turned toward the French Communist Party for guidance and assistance. The activities of the Palestine Communist Party suffered restrictions from local conflict between Arabs and Zionists, and the spread of communism was confined to the Jewish community for almost a decade. It was

[29] This measure was adopted by Egypt after the Revolution of 1952, fixing the limitation at first to 200 and later to 100 faddans (see p. 165, below).

not until the early thirties, when communist activities began to spread into other Arab lands, especially in Syria, that Arabs of Palestine began to respond to the communist appeal. The Palestine Communist Party, separating communist from Zionist aspirations, was gradually Arabicized as its leadership passed to Arab hands. Arab communist leaders in Palestine remained active until the establishment of Israel, when leadership reverted again to Jewish hands, and many Arabs were disappointed by Soviet support of the partition of their country.

Communist activities in the Arab world continued to depend heavily on the support of the literate strata—intellectuals, students, and minority groups—and could hardly be characterized as a *bona fide* proletarian movement. Small wonder, therefore, that constant quarrels on procedural and personal grounds weakened the whole movement. However, many liberal Arabs sympathized with the communists because of their opposition to European influence in the Arab world. Shortly before World War II, when Nazi propaganda began to attack Zionism and British and French imperialism, Arab opinion swayed toward Germany, and the Soviet Union was no longer looked upon as a possible "liberator" from Zionism and imperialism. For this reason, the communist movement in Arab countries suffered a setback from which it recovered only after the entry of the Soviet Union into the war in 1941.

A third stage in the progress of the communist movement may be marked by the re-entry of the Soviet Union into the Islamic world. The attack on the Soviet Union by Nazi Germany in 1941 and the subsequent occupation of Persia by Soviet and British forces rendered the area more receptive to communist propaganda. The victory of the Red Army against Nazi forces enhanced the prestige of communist leaders who resumed their activities among the labor and the masses. In Persia a communist party was formally organized, but in Turkey and Arab lands the communists continued to work underground. Turkey took a more restrictive attitude toward the resumption of communist activities because of her traditional fear of Russian encroachment; in the Arab countries,

British and French need of native support during the war prompted them to relax restrictions on communist activities.

Arab Communist Parties

Communist activities in Arab lands, receiving a fresh impetus during World War II, may be regarded as the fourth stage of the development of the communist movement in Islamic lands. Unlike the Turkish communist movement, which was arrested though not completely superseded by a nationalist one, the Arab communist movement made a headway because its leaders adopted nationalistic symbols and entered into an alliance with nationalists to achieve common ends.

The Lebanese Communist Party came into existence by the indirect support of the Palestine Communist Party, and was thus not directly influenced by Soviet leaders. Owing to suspicion of Zionism, the Lebanese leaders turned to the French Communist Party for assistance. Yusuf Yazbuk, it will be recalled, who began as a socialist, took an active part in the founding of this Communist Party in Lebanon. In 1926 he went to Paris to prepare the way for the eventual association of his party with the French Communist Party. From Yazbuk, who was thrown into prison upon his return from Paris, the leadership of the Communist Party passed to Fu'ad al-Shimali.[30] Despite government restrictions, the Party became very active under a new leadership and spread into Syria primarily through Armenian and other minority groups.

In 1930, the Communist Party of Syria underwent a significant change. Khalid Bakdash, a young Kurd who had just graduated from college, joined the party. Bakdash was a restless young man who had taken part in the activities of the

[30] Upon his release from prison, Yazbuk resumed his communist activities on his own as the editor of *al-Yasar* (The Left), but he was no longer a member of the Communist Party. Dissension among the leaders seemed to have led to his dismissal from the party. He told me that he was not interested in a movement which was gradually becoming less and less an intellectual enterprise. From that time on Yazbuk turned to literary and historical writings.

Syrian National Bloc against French control of Syria. His leftist ideas rendered his presence in national circles uncongenial and he decided to join the Communist Party. His enthusiasm for communism induced him to visit Moscow, where for two years he received training in communist discipline and leadership. No sooner had he returned to Damascus in 1935 than he assumed the leadership of the party. Nicola al-Shawi and Faraj-Allah al-Hilu were recruited from Lebanon—the latter became the deputy leader of the party in Bayrut. Qadri Qal'achi, an able writer from Aleppo and for long a member of the National Bloc, joined the party in 1935. He headed a branch of the party in Tripoli and was followed by Rida Tawfiq, from that city. Artin Madoyan, an Armenian, enlisted Armenian support for the party. Under Bakdash's able leadership, these and several others formed the Central Executive Committee. The center of gravity obviously shifted from Bayrut to Damascus when Bakdash and other Syrian leaders joined the party.

From the mid-thirties to the outbreak of World War II, the Syrian Communist Party played a significant role first in consolidating the communist movement and then in radiating communist ideas to other Arab countries. In one notable instance, an 'Iraqi communist group under the leadership of 'Abd al-Qadir Isma'il came into being and received inspiration and guidance from the Syrian Communist Party. By their co-operation with national parties at a time when liberal nationalists sympathized with left-wing groups both the Syrian and 'Iraqi leaders were influential in bringing to the attention of the public communist measures of reform. Changes in strategy helped the Arab communist leaders to play a significant role in internal Arab politics, notwithstanding the fact that co-operation with nationalist leaders proved shortlived before World War II. What was that strategy?

Changing Aims and Methods

It is evident from Soviet proclamations that the aim of the "appeal to Islam" was to persuade Muslim countries to adopt a system of government that would ultimately form,

together with other parts of the world, a World Federation of Soviet Republics, presumably under Russian leadership. These Sovietized republics, designed to serve the interests of the proletariats, would ultimately be established in accordance with a process of development dictated by historical laws. In order to speed up this historical process, the Soviet leaders called upon the proletariats of the rest of the world to unite and overthrow capitalist societies by joining the Russian proletariat in carrying out a "permanent revolution." In Islamic lands this call was considered to be the more appealing because the owners of the means of production were not native capitalists but foreigners who oppressed both the masses and other classes. Colonialism and oppression were the two slogans which Soviet leaders expected to work like magic in the spread of revolutionary propaganda in Islamic lands.

But Muslims, while applauding the anti-colonial call, failed to rally to the Soviet appeal. This situation aroused the curiosity of Soviet theorists, because the results ran contrary to expectations: in other instances, colonialist oppression had proved to be a catalyst capable of fomenting nationalist as well as proletarian revolutions. The explanation for the failure of their formula was in the communist theory of social development, which stipulates that the so-called backward societies should achieve a high stage of capitalism to become ripe for communism. Since most Muslim countries have either been in the feudal or primitive stage of development—even more backward than that of the Czarist Russia—they were, in the eyes of Soviet strategists, not yet ready for communism. The official Soviet withdrawal from the Islamic world during the inter-war years can be explained by this rationalization.

However, Soviet theorists tried to look at the colonial problem from a different perspective. Could a country in the colonial stage, it was asked, jump into the communist stage of development? The need to answer such a question had faced Soviet leaders in their dealings with the Asiatic provinces of the Soviet Union long before their attention turned to other Islamic lands. Stalin, who made a study of Marxism and colonial questions, tried to solve the problem by suggesting

that countries still in the pre-capitalist stage may skip the capitalist phase and establish socialism. He expressed such ideas as early as 1921 in one of the Communist Party's congresses and his suggestion was applied to the Central Asian communities which had been brought under the communist system.

In 1928, the problem of colonial countries not yet ripe for communism was formally discussed at the Sixth Congress of the Comintern held in Moscow. The European and Muslim representatives had an opportunity to express their opinion of the problem and they urged the immediate adoption of a positive policy toward their countries. There seems to have been no disagreement on the focal point that the "toiling masses" in the colonies represented the most powerful "auxiliary force" of the world revolutionary movement and that Soviet leaders should support it. But there were reservations on the possibility of "skipping" the capitalist stage which qualified the proposal put before the congress for immediate adoption. Because of their peculiar economy and of world conditions, it was agreed that the colonies might pass from "a non-capitalist path" of development into a socialist revolution. This "skipping," nevertheless, would not take place without experiencing first a bourgeois-democratic revolution which would prepare the colonies for the ultimate proletarian revolution. This transitional stage was regarded as not only necessary, but inevitable. Once this stage would be set, the strategy and methods of communist parties in colonial lands would be fully employed, augmented by Soviet moral and material support. Communist method, though varying from one colony to another, would consist essentially of disseminating propaganda among the poor and dissatisfied elements of society. The methods should include the promotion of trade unionism, co-operative societies (i.e., consumer unions, mutual aid societies, etc.), and "front" organizations. Communists were urged to co-operate with nationalist organizations struggling against ruling classes and seeking national and revolutionary aims. After 1933, when the Nazis seized power in Germany, communist parties were instructed to co-operate with democratic

organizations in order to oppose the rising tide of fascism which threatened the ultimate victory of socialism.

Muslim representatives, participating in the Sixth Congress, returned home to carry out these new methods. In Turkey and Persia, these methods made no appreciable change in the position of communist groups, because of the repressive measures of the Kamalist and Pahlevi regimes and of the overriding appeal of nationalism.

In Arab lands, especially in the countries lying between the Euphrates and Nile valleys, the new strategy, though not directly guided by Soviet leaders, helped to create a climate of opinion favorable for the influx of communist ideas when the Soviet Union resumed its offensive after World War II. Owing to a happy combination of favorable circumstances, Syria became the dynamic center of the new communist approach to the Arab world. The leadership of the Syrian Communist Party, which had just passed from benign to aggressive hands, proved instrumental in reviving communist activities in Syria and in coordinating them in other countries. More important indeed was the coming into power of Leon Blum's socialist government in France and the agreement of Syrian nationalist leaders to co-operate with it in the hope that Syria might achieve ultimate independence from French control. This step gave the Syrian Communist Party an opportunity both to demonstrate the possibility of co-operation with nationalist groups in accordance with new communist methods and to secure the relaxation of repressive measures against communists. In 1936, the Syrian nationalists came to an understanding with France and assumed power after a long period of struggle; the Syrian Communist Party gave them its blessing and full support. Khalid Bakdash, who now emerged as an influential communist leader, carried out this new communist policy of co-operation with Arab nationalists. Previously, communist leaders had stressed the international outlook of the communist movement and they spoke on behalf of "the toilers and the oppressed" and demanded for them "freedom and bread." After Bakdash's return from Moscow in 1935, Syrians began to hear him speaking on behalf of the Syrian "nation"—not just her proletariat—and he called for a struggle to achieve freedom from colonialism, feudalism, and capitalism. In 1936, he supported with great enthusiasm Syrian nationalist leaders who had come to terms with Leon Blum's government which promised to grant Syria and Lebanon independence. Bakdash became a *persona grata* to the French authorities and a great patriot in Syro-Lebanese nationalist circles. Never before had the communists in Arab lands enjoyed so much freedom as in the years between 1936 and the outbreak of World War II. Communist agitation radiated from Damascus into other Arab lands, especially to 'Iraq, where a so-called Reformist (Populist) regime was established in Baghdad after the *coup d'état* of 1936.[31] After the fall of Leon Blum and the 'Iraqi Reformists, communists fell in disgrace in nationalist eyes: neither did France, which Bakdash so eloquently praised as the great democratic and liberal nation, relax her control over Syria and Lebanon, nor did communist support of "national fronts" bring but momentary progress. When World War II broke out, communist leaders had already been driven underground. However, this short-lived communist agitation had far-reaching effects in preparing the public for a more forward renewal of communist activities after World War II.

The entry of the Soviet Union into the war and its collaboration with Western democracies opened a new chapter in communist activities. Its significance may be summed up as follows: (1) It resulted in the relaxation of restrictions over communists in Persia and Arab lands; (2) it gave an impetus to communist leaders to renew their activities; and (3) Soviet victories over the Nazi forces fired the imagination of the masses who responded favorably to communist propaganda.

In 1943 Arab communist leaders held conferences in Bayrut and Baghdad to review the situation and lay down new programs. A "national convention" was formulated which provided that communist parties follow national lines. They decided to support the independence and parliamentary gov-

[31] See my *Independent 'Iraq*, chaps. 5–6.

ernments of Arab countries and to promote inter-Arab cultural and economic ties. Communist leaders declared that their aim was not to overthrow national regimes, but to achieve power through democratic and peaceful methods. In Syria and Lebanon, the communists were given permission by the newly established national regimes to form recognized political parties, but no such permission was given to the 'Iraqi communists whose activities remained clandestine. Thus, while the Syrian and Lebanese communists could spread their propaganda with relative freedom, their 'Iraqi comrades were subjected to strict censorship and arrest whenever their agitation found an outlet in strikes and street demonstrations. In 1947, Comrade Fahd (Yusuf Salman Yusuf), leader of the unlicensed 'Iraqi Communist Party, and some of his collaborators were brought to trial and thrown into prison despite their denial of revolutionary pretentions.[32] In 1949, their clandestine contacts having been discovered, four of the leaders including Fahd, were sentenced to death and hung in public. Nonetheless, communist agitation continued in 'Iraq and the harsh measures against them aroused the sympathy of the public which the communists fully exploited after the Revolution of 1958.

In Syria and Lebanon, where relatively free expression of political opinion was permitted, the communists took an active part in politics and participated in general elections. Khalid Bakdash, though defeated in earlier elections, won a lone communist seat in Parliament in 1954. From 1949, when the military seized power, the communists have been able, like other civilian politicians, to solicit the support of army officers receptive of their ideology. In the mid-1950s, Syria appeared as if it were falling into communist hands. This prompted the leaders of other political parties to appeal to Nasir to unite Syria with Egypt ostensibly on nationalist grounds but in reality to reduce communist influence. After the merger (February 1958), Bakdash left Syria only to return

[32] The number of communists who were imprisoned exceeded 350. They remained in prison till the revolution of 1958, though some had been released earlier (see my *Independent 'Iraq*, pp. 362–63).

in 1966. In 'Iraq, the communists played a significant role in politics following the Revolution of 1958 and came very near to seizing power. At this time the nationalist-communist honeymoon came to an end, and the nationalists suddenly became aware that communist victory would lead to the complete subordination of national to communist aims. As a result, the 'Iraqi communist movement suffered a setback from which it has not yet recovered.[33] The communist movement in Arab lands, however, has not yet exhausted itself, although Arab nationalists are trying to arrest it by the partial incorporation of socialist measures in their programs. This is a new trend in Arab nationalism, reminiscent of early socialist thought in the Arab world.[34]

Rival Ideologies

Opposition to communism in the Arab world calls for an examination of the forces working against it. In Turkey, communist infiltration came almost to a standstill, while in Persia and the Arab countries it subsided, but it did not completely disappear. In such traditional regions as Arabia, it hardly existed, because of the almost complete absence of an intellectual elite and class consciousness.

From the time when they launched their "appeal to Islam," Soviet leaders seemed to have suspected that Islam, which had a strong hold over the masses, might stand as a barrier to communist infiltration. They therefore declared that communist doctrines were compatible with Islam and tried to alienate the masses from their religious leaders (who had shown initial hostility to communism) and to picture them as "parasites" and "oppressors" who deprived the masses of their lands and who had departed from the true teachings of

[33] For a discussion of communist aims and methods and their conflict with nationalists in 'Iraq, see my *Republican 'Iraq* (London, 1969), chap. 6.

[34] For an analysis of the conflict between communist and Arab ideologies, see al-Hakam Darwaza, *al-Shuyu'iya al-Mahilliya wa Ma'rakat al-'Arab al-Qawmiya* (Bayrut, 3rd ed., 1963).

Islam.[35] They asserted that only the communist system, designed to serve the interests of the proletariat and the oppressed, would give practical expression to Islamic principles. Soviet hostility to religious leaders prompted these leaders to denounce communism as ungodly and its doctrine as incompatible with the Qur'an and the teachings of the Prophet. There was of course ample evidence in Soviet literature to demonstrate communism's opposition to religion. Moreover, not all Soviet statements about Islam were flattering; Islam was often described by Soviet writers as a reactionary religion. The Muslim religious leaders exploited these derogatory remarks and proved to be far more serious opponents to communist infiltration than Soviet leaders had initially thought.

At the outset, communism was not interpreted by Muslim intellectuals to be in harmony with Islam. In the early interwar years, Muslim thinkers were still debating the compatibility of nationalism and Islam and paid little or no attention to the relevance of communist doctrines to Islam. Indeed it was taken for granted by many a Muslim thinker—just as by many a Christian thinker in the West—that communism was incompatible with the ethical-religious values.

Realizing an underlying doctrinal discrepancy between Islam and communism, Soviet leaders keenly felt the need for reinterpreting Islam from a communist viewpoint. Perhaps the first constructive interpretation on a materialist basis was undertaken by a Christian Arab from Palestine who taught Islamic history at the University of Baku after World War I. Pindali Juzi, in a work the first volume of which is devoted to a study of social movements in classical Islam, tried to provide a materialist interpretation for these movements. The underlying theme of the work is that Islam, in the last analysis, was hardly anything more than a religious rationalization of the economic factors at work in society. The leaders spoke in the name of religion, but the masses, desperately struggling to survive, followed their leaders in the hope that

[35] See a statement to this effect made at the Baku Congress by Zionomen, supported by a Muslim delegate, cited by Spector, *The Soviet Union and the Muslim World,* p. 40.

acceptance of religious doctrines might improve their conditions.[36] At first the book attracted little or no attention, and my recollection is that when the book was published while I was still in college it had been read by only a few classmates. Toward the latter part of the inter-war years the book was reprinted and more widely read throughout the Arab world.[37] Juzi's work on Islamic history provided Muslim Marxists with a rationale for a materialist interpretation of Islamic society, but it could hardly be regarded as a doctrinal justification of Islam's compatibility with communism.

Perhaps the most effective means of counteracting the opposition of Muslim religious leaders was the liberal step taken by Soviet leaders during the last war in permitting religious freedom in the Soviet empire. Ever since that time Soviet leaders have paid particular attention to Muslims in Central Asia and tried to improve their social and economic conditions. In order to demonstrate how Islamic life can be adapted to the Soviet system—perhaps for the purpose of giving an exemplary lesson, no less than for publicity—Muslim dignitaries from other lands have been invited to visit and converse with their co-religionists in Soviet lands to see for themselves what communism can do to improve conditions in an Islamic society, although the reports on these trips have not all been flattering. To an educated Muslim, the mode of life of young Muslims in the Soviet Union seemed to be an example of "reformed" Islamic life. The campaign against illiteracy, including the building of new schools, libraries, universities, and theatres, was just what his country needed in its present emergence from the traditional life.[38] However, no serious attempt has yet been made to modernize religious in-

[36] Pindali Juzi (José), *Some of the Intellectual Movements in the History of Islam*, vol. I: *Some of the Social Movements* (Jerusalem, 1928) (Arabic).

[37] Juzi contributed several articles to *al-Muqtataf*, one of the leading Arabic reviews in Cairo, and took an issue with some Arab scholars on matters relating to the interpretation of Islamic history (see *al-Muqtataf*, vol. LXXV [1929], *passim*).

[38] See George Hanna, *Ana 'A'id Min Moscow* (1947); *Fi Moscow Marra Thaniya* (1955); 'Abd al-Salam Dhihni, *al-Ittihad al-Sovieti*, (1955); M. Majdhub, *'Arabi fi Moscow* (1958).

struction nor to raise the intellectual level of religious leaders in Islamic institutions. Since he has praised Soviet authorities in his Friday sermons, it would appear that the Grand Mufti (jurisconsult) of the Soviet Union was satisfied (at least outwardly) with this kind of progress. Traditional Islam does not tolerate submission to non-Islamic rule, but the Muslims of the Soviet Union are of the opinion that Islam permits submission to non-Muslim rulers if they are just. This new Soviet rapprochement with Islam had a profound influence on lay Muslim attitude toward the Soviet Union and stirred a lively discussion among thinkers re-evaluating communism's compatibility with Islam.

Muslim thinkers were divided into two schools of thought on this issue. Witnessing the present plight of the poor and the exploitation by landlords, one school held that Islam, like communism, is opposed to the great disparity between rich and poor and asserted that it is the duty of the community to regulate its economic life on an equitable basis. At bottom, they argued, Islam and communism have an identical aim of trying to lay the foundation of society on a sound and equitable basis.[39]

The other school of thought, representing the traditional Islamic viewpoint, was opposed to communism. On purely doctrinal grounds Islam, probably more than any other religious system, is difficult to reconcile with communism. As a system which assesses all values of life in terms of divine revelations, it is opposed to Marxian materialism and, of course, to atheism. To the confirmed believer who follows the precepts of religion and law, communism appears to reduce life to a mere mechanical process, stressing worldly rather than spiritual values. Further, Islam recognizes the institution of private property and free enterprise, and the sacred law regulates all kinds of possession and disposal of property, includ-

[39] As 'Abd al-Majid Rizq-Allah, a Tunisian member of Parliament who visited Soviet Central Asia in 1962, remarked that it was not Islam's incompatibility with communism that attracted his attention but the degree of progress achieved in a Muslim country under the communist system (see 'Abd al-Majid Rizq-Allah, *'Ashrat Ayyam Bayn Moscow wa Tashkand* [Tunis, 1963]).

ing its transmission by inheritance to the owner's children and the near kin. Even the rights of the state to own or to dispose of property are limited by Islamic law.

These two extreme views, which resulted in a heated controversy, gave an opening to the rise of a third school of thought which tried to combine moderate socialist and Islamic views. This is the so-called school of "Islamic socialism." Its advocates maintain that Islam, if not compatible with communism, is not opposed to socialism. They also mixed nationalism with Islamic socialist thought, but to this school we shall presently return.

Communists who showed no willingness to compromise with Islam tried to argue that doctrinal incompatibility could equally be advanced against Christianity, Judaism, and Confucianism. But this doctrinal incompatibility has not prevented Christians, Jews, and Chinese from becoming communists, accepting the teachings of Marx and Lenin, and repudiating all national and religious institutions as the bulwark of the reactionary classes. A few extremists, who argued with Marx that religion is the opiate of the people, attacked Islam and its practices with anti-religious religiosity. Their program, advocating a complete reorganization of society based on the doctrine of world communism, appeared to be probably the most constructive among those offered by opposition groups and, in the meantime, may be regarded as the most destructive in its revolt against existing institutions. Its appeal to the masses and malcontents, who have not grasped the most elementary principles of communism, was due to the persuasive ability of local leaders, who presented communism as the panacea for all social ills. The discipline and solidarity displayed by the communists (though they often quarrel on procedural matters) and their tenacity in resisting repression have enhanced their prestige among their sympathizers. However, repressive communist measures and the appeal of nationalism have considerably affected the movement, despite the continued outcry of its leaders against feudalism, corruption, and colonialism. Communism's opposition to religion, overt or disguised, and its disdain for other national symbols and values, to say nothing of its affiliation with foreign elements, are but a few of the factors which make many hesitate to accept the communist creed.[40]

Nationalism is no less a rival to communist infiltration than Islam. For a long while the idea of nationalism was confined to the literate, but after World War I it began to infiltrate the lower strata of society and became a mass movement. Nationalists asserted the principles of self-determination and independence as the basis of the newly established regimes and were not prepared to tolerate foreign intervention. It is to be noted that this nationalist outlook was the manifestation of a movement to break away from the traditional ecumenical society and therefore it was incompatible with the new Soviet ecumenical system. Thus, the Soviet drive to regroup the Islamic nations under a Sovietized system ran contrary to the emerging pattern of the new Islamic state-system; for each state proved to be quite jealous of its newly acquired sovereign attributes.

At the outset the nationalists had not taken enough interest in social problems to appreciate a reform program such as that provided by communism. Nationalist leaders proved more interested in national solidarity and political independence than in class struggle. In Islamic lands, they may be divided at present into two camps, depending on their attitude toward the Soviet Union. In the "belt countries"—Turkey, Persia, and Afghanistan—they received Soviet moral and material support in their struggle against foreign intervention, but they resisted communist infiltration. Soviet leaders, on the other hand, fearful of Western influence in the belt countries, came to terms with nationalist leaders, even though their action undermined local communist activities. In the Arab world, where foreign influence persisted, nationalist leaders tried to suppress communist activities by force. Separated from Soviet territory by the "belt countries," Arab leaders felt at first secure to deal with communists harshly, and

[40] For a discussion of this point of view, see 'Abbas Hafiz, *al-Shuyu'iya* al-Siba'i, *Ishtirakiyat al-Islam* (Damascus, 2nd ed., 1960); cf. Muhammad *al-Thawrawiya* [Revolutionary Bases] (Damascus, 1958); Fu'ad al-Rikabi, al-Siba'i, *Ishtirakiyat al-Islam* (Damascus, 2nd ed., 1960); cf. Muhammad al-Hamid, *Nazarat fi Kitab Ishtirakiyat al-Islam* (Damascus, 1963).

their action reflected the influence of vested interest. To strengthen their position among the masses, this state of affairs prompted communists to denounce Arab nationalist leaders as reactionaries and stooges of colonialism. As a result, communist agitation after independence found a favorable response; but communist penetration after World War II, though it achieved considerable success during a short period of collaboration with nationalist agitators, aroused the suspicion of both nationalist and religious elements. Religion and nationalism proved to be the strongest deterrents to communist activities in Arab lands; the two may well remain as operative opponents for a long time to come.[41]

However, it is possible that the tide of communist activities might be reactivated, because religion and nationalism are essentially negative barriers that might be weakened. If circumstances should permit the Soviet Union or Communist China to intervene in, or extend their influence to Arab lands, such as the recent Israeli attacks on her neighbors, communist agitations would be bound to flourish. A more positive factor for arresting communist agitation would therefore lie in the rise of a new enlightened and progressive movement which might combine some ingredients of communism and nationalism and thus disarm the communist movement. The partial incorporation of moderate communist principles in the new Arab nationalism, especially as embodied in the Ba'th program, in Egypt's Arab socialism or in other variants of contemporary Arab nationalism, seems to be in the long run a greater deterring factor than traditional values. The incorporation of socialist principles in nationalist programs may be regarded as a healthy approach to social reform without the need of adopting a fully communist or capitalist system. Thus, if the Arabs could absorb ideas from foreign systems and adapt them to their needs and aspirations, the experiment might well be worth attempting, for it might save them from domination by any one type of ideology.[42]

[41] See 'Abd al-Mun'im al-Namr, *al-Islam wa al-Shuyu'iya* (Cairo, 1954); Muhammad 'Abd-Allah al-'Arabi, *Nazarat Bayn al-Shuyu'iya wa al-Islam* (Bagdad, 1955).

[42] See chap. 10.

Chapter 6

REVOLUTIONARY PROCESSES

Louis XVI:
C'est une révolte?
La Rochefoucauld-Liancourt:
Non, Sire c'est une révolution!

In countries undergoing rapid social change, the ruling elites must try to reconcile traditional practices and values with imported ideas and innovations, if the renovated political systems are to endure. Before independence, the rulers of the Arab countries were too preoccupied with the task of achieving independence to pay attention to social reform. When, after independence, social change did not measure up to popular expectations, these countries began to search for new and enlightened leadership capable of achieving long-needed progress. Since the old rulers had failed to provide such leadership, a conflict between the rulers and the ruled ensued, which created a climate of opinion favorable to revolutionary change.

New vs. *Old Generation*

Political power had long been in the hands of a ruling elite representing essentially an old generation which increasingly showed an unwillingness to take into its ranks young men who did not accept its leadership. These ruling classes were themselves the generation that was young after World War I, when it advocated nationalism and those liberal institutions in the name of which it began to rule after independence. But this generation had failed to prepare the succeeding generation to share its responsibility, although the latter tried to enhance its position in the political system through participation in parliamentary processes. However, young men found that the parliamentary system had become so completely dominated by an older generation that it despaired of any hope of co-operation. After independence, democratic institutions began to appear meaningless, and the Arab peoples soon learned how scandalously misused democratic procedures could be by unscrupulous leaders. Small wonder that the Arabs lost confidence in their leaders who appeared to subordinate public to private interests. The crisis of legitimacy necessarily became acute because governing elites failed to obtain popular consent for public policies and the people began to look elsewhere for leadership.

After World War II, a new generation, consisting essentially of intellectuals and professionals (lawyers, physicians, teachers, etc.), the majority of which came from the lower classes, began to grow up. They received their education in Western or national institutions organized on Western models. As they rendered services urgently needed in Arab countries undergoing rapid social change, their influence increased. Since the old generation failed to recognize adequately these services, young men increasingly fell under various ideological influences and participated in the upheavals that the Arab countries experienced shortly after World War II.

The new generation has been characterized by some as intellectuals and by others as a new middle class.[1] Neither term seems to define accurately these young men because they had diverse professions and social origins: the only aggregate term to apply is their belonging to a "new generation" aspiring to assume their share of public responsibility in contradistinction to an "old generation" resisting social change. In

[1] See Edward Shils, "The Intellectuals in the Political Development of the New States," *Political Change in Underdeveloped Countries* ed. J. H. Kautsky (New York, 1962), pp. 195 ff.; Manfred Halpern "Middle Eastern Armies and the New Middle Class." *The Role of the Military in Underdeveloped Countries* ed. J. J. Johnson (Princeton, 1962), pp. 277 ff.

terms of their status in society, the present writer has described them as follows: [2]

> Most of them have come from lower classes and some who came from an upper class preferred to identify themselves with this generation. Most of them, especially the civil servants and army officers, received fixed salaries; but the majority, especially the professionals had fairly good incomes. Nevertheless, very few may be counted as wealthy, unless they had inherited wealth from upper-class parents, and therefore they could hardly be compared to a European middle-class counterpart. Nor should their aspirations be regarded as bourgeois or middle class, in the modern sense, for their objective was not to champion the interest of only one class—their own—but the people as a whole, and the lower class in particular. In other words, they adopted the concept of a classless society rather than three-class society in which they would be the intermediary. Their economic thought was therefore based on some form of collectivism rather than on free enterprise, although certain liberal political and economic principles were acceptable to them. Neither in aspiration nor in vested interest can the new generation be identified as a middle class, old or new.
>
> Nor are the terms intelligentsia or intellectuals broad enough to apply to such varied groups as writers and thinkers, teachers and students, physicians and engineers, civil and military functionaries and the like. While some have the intellectual qualifications entitling them to be called intelligentsia; most have neither the intellectual aptitude nor the desire to be intellectuals. Most, especially doctors and engineers, are professional men and may be said to form a class of technocrats rather than intellectuals. They consider that illiteracy is a state of deprivation which they wish to abolish and that literacy should no longer remain a characteristic distinguishing one class from another.
>
> As a modernizing class, the new generation, both intellectuals and professionals, has displayed a passionate desire for development along one ideological line or another and was determined to resist the monopoly of power by the ruling oligarchy. This situation could not have lasted very

[2] See my *Republican 'Iraq* (London, 1969), pp. 6–7.

long, for in reality talent, vigour, and confidence in the future passed largely to this generation.

We have already noted that democratic institutions failed to measure up to expectations and rival revolutionary systems have been proposed by radical groups as a substitute for them; but no group had been able to achieve power and carry out its proposed plan. As a result, the crisis of legitimacy continued to grow into a malaise which often prompted the ruling oligarchy to use force pretending to maintain public order and suppress violence. These methods reinforced the prevailing impression that the old generation was not prepared to accommodate to the new social conditions.

The Need for Social Revolution

The failure of the new generation to influence the old and to undertake peacefully social reform raises the whole question whether rapid social reform can be carried out through democratic procedures in traditional societies or "developing countries." In Western societies—the "developed countries"—democratic institutions have been prized and considered as relatively advanced political systems, owing to the freedom enjoyed by groups and individuals alike. In the so-called developing countries, including the Arab world, democratic institutions have been considered, as noted before, a barrier to rather than an instrument of progress. Why, it may be asked, should democracy work in favor of progress in the developed but not in the developing countries?

Democracy, like other systems of government, cannot operate in a vacuum: it functions in accordance with the social milieu in which it has grown. In the West, it evolved in social conditions favoring progress and development, because it was the product of social forces that demanded such a trend. In the developing countries, where traditional patterns of authority persist, the newly adopted democratic institutions could not be expected to operate irrespective of existing conditions which necessarily reflect those traditional patterns. If the transplanted institutions operate in a manner which recognizes the traditional patterns, the political system is likely to improve and mature through the interacting synthesis of form and substance, as the experiment of Japan has demonstrated. If, however, the ruling elite, including the elements most active in society, endeavor to change the very basis of traditional society regarded as no longer compatible with modern conditions of life, the modernized political system has to develop new traditions and patterns of authority to supersede the traditional ones. A conflict between the elite adhering to the old patterns—the status quo—and the new, who press for progress and development, is perhaps inevitable and often this is manifested in some kind of violent social or political upheaval.

In Arab lands, where the emerging leadership aspires to achieve the sort of progress resulting in sweeping social reforms, the very basis of society must be changed to allow the development of new patterns of authority. Such a change is bound to threaten the position of the ruling elite whose interests are best protected by traditional practices and who are likely, therefore, to resist by force if necessary. Political or military uprisings—*coups d'état*—may replace one set of rulers with another, but if the revolutionary change is ever to be meaningful, no real progress and development can be expected until a social revolution is achieved. Not until the very basis of society has undergone complete change can one expect the new elite to play its proper role in society without resort to violence. The new generation that challenged the position of the old one tacitly came to the conclusion that they would not be able to play their role in achieving progress and development unless a social revolution was carried out. To what extent the revolutionary processes have achieved the cherished progress will be revealed by an examination of the theory and practice of political regimes created by the new generation in power in the revolutionary Arab countries.[3]

[3] See chap. 7.

Military Revolutions

The young Arab army officers watched for a long time with a keen eye the political struggle between the new elite and old rulers, and their sympathy with the generation to which they belonged was well known. The failure of the new civilian generation to replace the older rulers and achieve a social revolution prompted the young officers to overthrow the old regimes by force of arms. In Western democratic countries, traditions have developed which tend to keep the military isolated from politics, although persons whose careers have been in the military service are not infrequently elected, or appointed, to high political posts. This is quite a different matter, however, from the military's choosing to occupy high political office by means of the weapons of its own profession. Relieving themselves of official restraints, young Arab officers began to engage in underground activities as Free Officers—free from military and civil rules of conduct to which they never prescribed—in order to achieve, by military methods, the aims which the young civilian leaders were unable to reach by political processes.

The military's intervention in politics is not unprecedented in Arab history. From antiquity, the power of rulers was dependent on two pillars—the army and the clergy. The ruler, combining spiritual as well as secular authority, was the military chief and often took the field as the actual commander of the army. This tradition of the close association of rulers with the military persisted down through the centuries. Relations between rulers and army chiefs were not always harmonious, despite frequent matrimonial connections between military chiefs and reigning dynasties. When the army chiefs became more powerful than their masters, they often at will deposed one ruler after another. Just as the Praetorian Guard dethroned one Roman emperor after another, so the Arab legions and Ottoman Janissaries put to death one sovereign after another, replacing them by their own nominees. The struggle between the military and sovereigns degenerated to the throat-cutting level, so that either the military or the dynasty had to be liquidated. When society was subjected to this kind of fratricidal struggle, the very foundation of its political system shook, and a radical change in the system became inevitable. Against this background, the recurrence of military revolutions in the contemporary Arab world should not be surprising.

The contemporary military which has engaged in politics belonged to what we have called "the new generation." Before they entered military academies, the officers had received the same education as the civilians, which indoctrinated them with a spirit of intense nationalism. This nationalist indoctrination was continued in military training. The younger officers showed an intense interest in political activities and shared many ideas and aspirations with younger civilians rather than the older officers. Most of the officers were drawn from lower classes, but some older officers of higher ranks and from the upper class identified themselves with that class. The rank-and-file, as a rule, were drawn from peasants and workers, and most of them were recruited on the basis of national conscription. The majority of the common soldiers were illiterate, but many of them, while in the service, received elementary education mixed with nationalist indoctrination. It was, however, the younger officers who engaged the army in revolutionary activities while the vast majority of older officers tried to keep the army loyal to the regime in power.[4]

The number of officers who took an active part in clandestine activities and called themselves Free Officers was relatively small. They organized themselves in cells and tried to spread indirectly their revolutionary ideas among other officers in hopes of gaining potential supporters for the day when the Free Officers would rise up in arms against authority. At the top of the secret web of cells there was a central organization which directed the Free Officers movement and finally

[4] See Mohammed Neguib, *Egypt's Destiny* (London, 1955), chap. I; Colonel Anwar al-Sadat, *Revolt on the Nile* (London, 1957).

carried out the coup. The central organization laid down the general plan of the revolution, its aims and methods; but these thoughts were always expressed in broad principles rather than in detail, because of the inadequacy of their preparedness for the task they had undertaken and their preoccupation with the ways and means of carrying out the revolution.

In all Arab countries that have experienced military rule, the officers declared at the outset that their aim was to oust from power the ruling oligarchy whose peaceful removal had become impossible, and to entrust power to younger leaders. In almost all cases such an objective met universal approval since the old rulers had often disgraced themselves by corruption and misuse of democratic procedures. It was this initial favorable response of the public that often misled the military to conclude that the people desired the perpetuation of military rule after the task of overthrowing an unpopular leadership had been accomplished. Moreover, the military, habituated to obey orders and carry out quick action, installed at the outset a new spirit of order and efficiency in carrying out the business of government which tended to reduce corruption and bureaucratic red tape. The military's lack of experience may have led to many a mistaken judgment, but the public appreciated the celerity with which the military fulfilled their functions and the relative lack of nepotism and other corrupt practices which the public had witnessed under civilian rule. However, very soon some officers developed their own corrupt practices which in turn affected the army's image.

The military was not slow to bring to trial "traitors" who had betrayed the nation or committed gross injustices. Revolutionary tribunals, presided over by an army officer, proceeded to try a host of older leaders who had been arrested on the morrow of the military revolution. Same treatment was given to other beneficiaries of the old regimes who were reputed to have been corrupt or to have betrayed the national interest. Many of those brought to trial were given fair judgments, but in several cases, especially when the court dealt with "political crimes," its judgments were often harsh and reflected a vindictive attitude towards older leaders.[5]

More spectacular, perhaps, was the military's decision to carry out reform programs that had become popular among the people but that the older leaders, under the alleged influence of vested interest, failed to implement. There have been widespread criticism of corrupt practices and the wretched condition of the peasantry which kept the country poor and backward. Social reformers and outspoken young ideological groups had long called for the abolition of large land-ownership and the distribution of land to the peasants, but no leader under the old regimes was able to carry out any important measure of social reform or improve the deplorable condition of the poor. The military, believing that it had the power as well as the people's support to carry out such a program, declared immediately after they achieved power their readiness to carry out those reforms without careful study of the measures or the plans necessary for their implementation. Land reform laws were issued by decrees first in Egypt and Syria (1953) and later in 'Iraq (1959), but very soon it became clear that the improvement of economic conditions would depend primarily on finding new means of agricultural production, not on merely distributing state land or redistributing privately-owned land among a larger number of people. Thus, before they began to formulate their own ideological programs, the military learned by trial and error the pitfalls of carrying out social reform.[6]

The Patterns of Military Rule

Eight Arab countries—Egypt, Syria, Jordan, 'Iraq, the Yaman, the Sudan, Algeria and Libya—containing the largest portion of Arab lands, have experienced military revolutions,

[5] The revolutionary tribunals proved to be of such questionable value that the military in Egypt soon ended them, but the trials in Syria and 'Iraq lasted longer and the military engaged in retaliations against their own dissident groups.

[6] See chap. 7. For a background of the various military regimes in the Arab countries, see J. C. Hurewitz, *Middle East Politics: The Military Dimension* (New York, 1969).

and some of the others have not been entirely immune from military pressures. Three military coups took place in Egypt (1881, 1952, 1954); a dozen in 'Iraq (1936–1941, 1958–1968); more than a dozen in Syria since 1949; three in the Sudan (1958, 1964, 1969); three in the Yaman (1949, 1955, 1962); two in Algeria (1962, 1965); and one in Libya (1969). These thirty or more military coups by no means exhaust the list. They have been selected as instances where the army has consciously moved to overthrow an established regime and take control of authority.

The military, as noted before, has long been watching the political development of Arab lands with a keen eye. It has witnessed Arab countries dominated by foreign influence while their leaders engaged in a struggle for power. It has also seen young civilians try and fail to achieve power. Why should not the army itself, the officers concluded, put an end to the quarrels and vices of older politicians and rule their country through a military government? Thinking along these lines prompted the military to seize power and to seek the initial co-operation of civil groups in order to create strong regimes and realize national goals.

All these military revolutions took place either with the avowed purpose of establishing (as in Algeria, Libya, and the Yaman) or re-establishing truly democratic systems ('Iraq, Syria, and Egypt). The military sought the active co-operation of nationalist ('Iraq and Syria) and religious (Egypt) elements, and at the outset their rule was conducted in close co-operation with liberals. Later on, the military dominated the scene and the liberals (if not the nationalists) were either pushed to the background or deprived of power. The religious groups have, as a rule, been reluctant to support military governments (except in Egypt where the Muslim Brotherhood gave them initial blessing), either because they had come to terms with former regimes (as in Egypt and 'Iraq), or because the religious ideas of some of them proved to be too reactionary to be acceptable to the army (especially in 'Iraq). In Syria, the Muslim Brotherhood, even though it opposed the premilitary regime, failed to give support to the military because of their co-operation with liberal and radical elements; that same Brotherhood turned later against the military in Egypt.

Once in power, the military declared in almost all cases that it intended either to prepare the way for social reform or to carry out reforms themselves. In reality, the military seized power without having been prepared for it. Its move to clean the Augean stables met with universal approval; but the Herculean task of carrying out real reforms in a manner satisfactory to all remained in most cases unfulfilled. Nasir may be regarded as the army officer who came nearest to grips with the problem of social reform. At best, the reform program of the military was eclectic; it included various ideas that had become popular among the people, but these have rarely been studied in terms of their relevance to the real needs and aspirations of the people or in terms of their implementation.

At the outset the military pretended that it would let rule those civilian leaders who were known for their integrity and clean record and give them support from behind the scene to carry out reforms; but very soon, whether because they were tempted to govern themselves or because they found the civilian politicians unable to govern in a satisfactory manner, the officers took over the machinery of government to rule the country directly. In 'Iraq (1936), Syria (1949), Egypt (1952), and Algeria (1962), the military ruled through civilian government before taking over complete rule.

However, in most cases, the military is by no means in agreement about whether it should rule the country directly and what policy it should implement. Power achieved, a split in the army corps necessarily follows, and the faction that supported a civilian regime—in almost all cases the smaller one—is replaced by the faction that determined to rule directly through military dictatorship. This faction entrusts its leadership to a strong army officer who rules in a high-handed manner and eliminates from army ranks rival officers by putting on the retired list or by liquidating those suspected of disobedience. The split may lead to more than two or three rival factions, and the resulting struggle for power within the army may take the form of several coups and counter-coups until one faction emerges victorious. With a strong man ruling over the destiny of the country, the military regime is gradually transformed from military rule under a Revolutionary Council to the rule of a single man—military dictatorship. Only in Egypt has the military tried to legitimize its rule by obtaining popular support.

The suspension of civil in favor of military rule, although greeted with almost universal approval as heralding an eventual stable political system, carries with it its own weaknesses and evil influences. Dissatisfied with the slow progress through democratic procedures, the people are often reminded of the wisdom of Jamal al-Din al-Afghani's saying that Islamic lands could not possibly be reformed save by a benevolent despot.[7] The one-man rule, though often efficient and just, tends to be oppressive, and the military dominates the political scene and tends to perpetuate its own rule. Over a period of time, military rule itself becomes an objective, and the military ruler adopts repressive measures in order to maintain his regime. One of the first difficulties for the civilian population, once the initial task of over-hauling the government is accomplished, is how to persuade the army to withdraw from politics and relinquish power. In spite of initial assurances by officers that their intervention is only temporary, the lessons of history are not reassuring. For a while, military rule can continue with popular approval, so long as public opinion remins dissatisfied with old regimes and the army can maintain a good reputation as the advocate of revolutionary principles. But very soon the public becomes tired of military rule and desires a return to civilian government. The well-entrenched military shows no desire to give up its power. Hence the rift between the rulers and the ruled ensues and the crisis of legitimacy continues as long as the military fails to solve one of the problems perennial in Arab lands—stability of the political system on the basis of popular support rather than of coercion.

[7] See Muhammad al-Makhzumi, *Khatirat Jamal al-Din al-Afghani* (Bayrut, 1931), p. 90.

The effect of politics on the military is not a happy one. "A general has only one aim," said one military expert, "a general who is also a sovereign must have two; his actions as a soldier will always be subordinate to politics." [8] Politics impose certain restraints upon sovereigns who, in their careers as generals, should not submit to political forces in order to achieve the highest military success. If the general ever proves to be a successful sovereign, he must have submitted to restraints which no successful general would tolerate. Sudden rise to power seldom permits its victims, except perhaps in exceptional instances, to adjust themselves to the new positions they occupy. The all-powerful leader assumes a charisma which tends to make him withdraw within a smaller circle and alienates his supporters and admirers. Arab experience with military rule demonstrates again the truth of Lord Acton's saying that "Power tends to corrupt and absolute power corrupts absolutely." New leaders who are swept into power to rid their people of arbitrary rule and corruption often cannot avoid themselves developing the same traits that they hated in their enemies. Arab experience with military rule—indeed the experience of other nations as well—has demonstrated that the military liberators may become oppressors.

Most dangerous of all seems to be the difficulty in persuading the military to delegate power to a wider circle of supporters. By its very nature, military training requires obedience and lack of responsibility are the very negation of democracy—but not of authoritarianism. Obedience discourages responsibility, creativity, and free expression of opinion and leads to submission and servility—qualities inconsistent with the ways of bringing up a new generation. As a result, the military's ultimate purpose of serving the people's interest—improving their morale and preparing them to govern themselves—is defeated by depriving the people of the opportunity to learn how to assume responsibility. Obedience and lack of responsibility are the very negation of the

[8] Müffling, *Die Feldzüge der Schlesischen Armee*, p. 52; cited by Yorck von Wartenburg, *Napoleon as a General*, tr. W. G. James, I, 151.

qualities requisite for democratic procedure, and the people may remain deprived of these qualities as long as they live under military rule.

Ideological Parties

Once the military decides to govern alone, it is confronted with the problem of obtaining the consent of the governed, since popular enthusiasm is likely to cool off soon after the overthrow of the old regime. The military's initial support naturally depends on the army, but if it is to remain in power and carry out revolutionary aims, the legitimacy of its exercizing authority has to be established.

The military in Arab countries tried first to govern indirectly through existing party systems, but it pointed out to the parties that they must purge themselves of corrupt elements and adopt revolutionary aims. In both Syria (1949) and Egypt (1953) Husni al-Za'im, Muhammad Najib and later Nasir tried to co-operate with national parties—the People's Party of Syria and the Wafd of Egypt—but these parties refused to accommodate to revolutionary demands and were soon liquidated. In 'Iraq (1958) and Algeria (1962), the new leadership paid little attention to existing political parties and they soon disbanded.

The problem of legitimacy proved to be more difficult and complex than the military had anticipated, for the new rulers seized power by military force and tried to carry out social reform from the top of the social pyramid down rather than from the bottom up. Despairing of the co-operation of existing party-systems, the military tried to govern by a direct appeal to the people for support without the intermediary of political parties. Najib (Egypt), Qasim ('Iraq), and Bin Balla (Algeria), aroused public enthusiasm in their direct appeal to the masses; but it soon became clear that public support without political organizations was not a guarantee against rival leaders. Najib, Qasim, and Bin Balla were without much difficulty overthrown by rival military leaders.

Nasir, believing in the possibility of obtaining public support without political parties, organized the Liberation Rally. The Liberation Rally, without being called a political party, was designed to bind the people to the Revolution. Every citizen who believed in the aims of the Revolution was entitled to membership and asked to preach "unity, discipline, and work," in order to teach the people how to elect their representatives when elections would take place. It is clear that this organization was designed to legitimize military rule by creating an appearance of consent of the governed.

The Liberation Rally was not, however, a real political party; this fact was clearly stated by Nasir and by the organization's officers on more than one occasion. The Rally was not a structure through which the demands of the people were channeled to its rulers, but a device to enlist the support of influential interest groups for the military. In the final analysis, the Rally was an earnest effort by the revolutionary leaders to teach or indoctrinate the masses with the Revolution's aims and to secure support for them.

The Rally, however, failed to provide popular support, despite efforts to educate members in public participation. The Rally gave the military the appearance, though not the reality, of popular support. In 1958 it was dissolved in favor of the National Union.

The National Union was the nearest approximation to a political party. Article 192 of the Constitution of 1956 stipulated:

> The citizens constitute a National Union with a view to realizing the aims of the Revolution and to coordinating the efforts to build a nation healthy politically, socially and economically. The National Union will nominate candidates for membership of the National Assembly.

Still averse to political parties, Nasir tried to mobilize public support through the National Union without allowing the Union to become a party, although as a political organization it was more sophisticated than the Rally. In 1958, the National Union was dissolved on the occasion of the establishment of the United Arab Republic and was replaced by another National Union to include Syria. Although political parties in Syria were dissolved, the Union could hardly play the role of a political party. It was not until 1960 that it was completely reorganized. Like its predecessor, its function seems to have been to be a "school" to nurture popular participation. At this stage of the Revolution it was soon realized that issuing slogans without actual popular participation the regime could not rapidly mobilize society. Nasir seems to have been more concerned with holding the Syro-Egyptian union together than rebuilding the nation. His hope was pinned on modernizing society before it could provide a basis for a new nation. The gap between the new elite and the people—peasants, workers, and middle class—was not sufficiently bridged so that a true national unity could be achieved. Indeed, there was evidence that opposition to the new leaders continued even within the National Union. Thus the new leaders were, on the one hand, working to build the new society and, on the other hand, eliminating opponents by military methods. The National Union, though giving the semblance of legitimacy, could not provide a substitute for military support.

In July 1961, when the socialist decrees had been issued, the need for an organization designed to play the role of a political party became evident. Such an organization, constructed for the new society, was proclaimed: it was aptly named the Arab Socialist Union. This Union, based on the newly established socialist regime, was an organization based on "popular forces" considered to represent the corporate structure of society.

Nasir seems to have come nearer to what might be considered as a political party for the legitimization of his socialist regime. A Draft Charter for National Action was laid down which formulated the basic principles of the new socialist society. This charter is the major statement of the Egyptian Revolution and the basis of the new society and its social, political, and economic policies. Popularity and progressiveness are given as the two basic attributes of the revolutionary process. "The value of the true Revolution," states the Charter, "lies in its degree of popularity, in the extent to which it is an expression of the vast masses, in the extent to which it mobilizes their forces to rebuild the future, and also in the extent to which it enables these masses to impose their will on life." [9]

The function of the Socialist Union is to provide the conditions necessary for a truly democratic system. These conditions include the emancipation of the citizen from exploitation, equal opportunity to have a fair share of the national wealth, and guaranteed security for the future. "Only when a citizen possesses these three guarantees can he be said to have political freedom, and take part by means of his vote, in shaping the authority of the state he aspires to have." The Socialist Union was also to achieve national unity and a classless society. Finally, the Socialist Union was to provide the new leadership that would genuinely represent the nation. This leadership will be a collective leadership and should not be challenged by an opposition, although self-criticism was allowed within the organization in order to guarantee freedom.

The Socialist Union, though not formally called a political party, operated for all intents and purposes as a political party. But its purpose in practice proved less to mobilize popular support for the ruling elite than to persuade a reluctant public to accept new socialist principles just proclaimed by the military leaders. Nasir, in the last analysis, has still to rely on the armed forces for support, because he has not yet created that new society which would provide a new elite.

Egypt's Socialist Union was designed to be a model for other Arab revolutionary regimes, especially those that desired to join her in an Arab union.[10] A prototype of the Egyptian Socialist Union was adopted by the 'Iraqi military rulers in 1965, to remodel the 'Iraqi regime after the Egyptian

[9] See U.A.R., *The Charter* (Cairo, 1963).

[10] For a study of the structure and role of the Socialist Union, see Mahmud Mutawalli, *al-Ittihad al-Ishtiraki* (Cairo, 1964). See also P. J. Vatikiotis, "Some Political Consequences of the 1952 Revolution in Egypt," in P. M. Holt (ed.) *Political and Social Change in Modern Egypt* (London, 1968), pp. 362–87.

pattern before 'Iraq could unite with Egypt in an Arab union. Any Arab country which wishes to join this union must first adopt Arab socialism by revolutionary methods and establish a Socialist Union as a prerequisite to the achievement of Arab unity.

The Revolutionary Ideology

The revolutionary ideal, the essence of the new generation's protest against the monopoly of power by the old oligarchy, began gradually to spread after World War II. Apart from the Communist Party, the Ba'th was the first organized ideological group to include in its platform revolutionary reform. The military, prompted by civilian failure to implement revolutionary reforms, intervened first to overthrow the old elite and then to assume the leadership of the revolutionary movement. The civilian elite, as noted above, was divided on the issue whether the leadership of the revolutionary movement should remain in the hands of the military or the civilians. President Nasir proved to be the only officer who possessed the charisma and commanded sufficient public respect in both civil and military ranks to lead the revolutionary reform movement. But the revolutionary countries have not yet decided whether they would follow a revolutionary procedure individually, each under its own local leadership, or collectively under a unified command. At bottom lies the issue of Arab unity—whether the Arab countries should develop as separate modern nation-states or as an Arab United State, federal or unitary.[11] Both civilian and military revolutionary leaders have adopted a set of nationalist principles which may be summed up as follows:

First, the Arab revolutionary movement is not a class but a popular (mass) movement, striving to achieve a progressive society by means of social and economic reforms.

Second, it is a liberating movement, representing an awak-

[11] See pp. 262–65, below.

ened national consciousness and aiming at achieving full national freedom.

Third, the movement aims eventually at emancipating the individual from social fetters and inspiring him with a new spirit of freedom and full opportunity in life, but the nation as a whole must be freed first from foreign and domestic oppression by social and political revolutions.

Fourth, though it represents the entire Arab people, the revolutionary process must be carried out by a small group in each country dedicated to the revolutionary ideology until it becomes a mass movement.

Fifth, as a mass movement, it has to enlist widespread support for a popular system of government, with the nation as a whole participating in the exercise of its collective will. Under this system, no individual's economic needs should be a barrier to his political participation. Rather, the system should aim at liberating the individual from deprivations in order to be free for exercise of his political freedom. The ultimate objective of this system is social justice and individual freedom.

Sixth, the revolutionary process aims at the elimination of artificial barriers separating one Arab country from another, since these barriers have prevented the full exploitation of Arab resources and weakened the popular forces from concerted action. Thus, the achievement of Arab unity, leading to the coordination of popular forces in all Arab countries, is an integral part of the Arab revolutionary process.

Seventh, in a broader sense, the Arab revolutionary process is regarded as part of a world revolutionary movement aiming at national liberation and human progress. While co-operation might be sought with other revolutionary movements, the Arab revolutionary movement stresses its Arab national character and claims to achieve Arab national interests and aspirations.[12]

[12] See Muta' Safadi, *Masir al-Idulujiyat al-Thawrawiya* [Aims of Revolutionary Ideologies] (Bayrut, 1963), 2 vols.; Ahmad al-Shaybani, *al-Usus al-Thawrawiya* [Revolutionary Bases] (Damascus, 1958); Fu'ad al-Rikabi, *'Ala Tariq al-Thawra* [The Road to Revolution] (Cairo, n.d.); and Naji 'Alwash, *al-Thawra wa al-Jamahir* (Bayrut, 1962), pp. 177ff.

These basic principles are acceptable to all Arab revolutionary groups, including radical socialist leaders; even Pan-Arabs, often reluctant to identify their movement with world revolutionary movements, are not hesitant to admit the existence of certain common aims. Some radical revolutionary thinkers, especially the communists, while stressing the Arab character of their movement, have sought to identify it with the world communist movement and a few seem to stress in particular its identification with the Chinese communist movement.[13]

Recent trends in the revolutionary movement, especially after the June war of 1967, seem to identify Arab irredentism—a movement embodying aspirations to recover lost territory [14]—with the revolutionary process. The Arab Liberation Movement, having been given full expression in the Algerian war of independence, is now taking the form of a guerilla warfare in an attempt to recover Arab territory from Israel. Once it gathers momentum, the resistance movement will then be gradually transformed into a full-fledged war of liberation with the ultimate objective of recovering the whole of Palestine from Jewish domination and incorporating it in a future Arab union.[15]

The major point of difference among revolutionary leaders seems to be on the question of leadership; some stress individual military or civilian leadership and others advocate collective leadership. The first school, considered more realistic, has maintained that anyone who proved to be able to achieve Arab national aims should be acknowledged as the supreme leader. Other revolutionary groups have stressed the principle of collective leadership and held that decisions should be made by consultation in national "command councils," representing various shades of opinion, and should be carried out by one supreme leader or by collective action.

[13] Fu'ad al-Rikabi, *Fusul fi al-Thawra wa al-'Amal al-Ishtiraki* [chapters on Revolution and Socialist Action] (Cairo, 1960).

[14] See pp. 207–209, below.

[15] See Nadim al-Baytar, *Min al-Naksa Ila al-Thawra* [From the Setback to the Revolution] (Bayrut, 1968).

Leadership of the Arab revolutionary movement today has proven to be a bone of contention among the various revolutionary groups, as indeed it was in past Arab history. The caliphate, the embodiment of supreme leadership in Islam, was the rock on which Islamic unity was wrecked and this traditional rivalry over leadership has been inherited by Arabs in modern times. Yet the mass of the Arab people yearn for strong leadership and are prepared to follow the leader who wields power and possesses strength of character to achieve national goals.[16]

[16] As stated before (see Preface), a fuller discussion of leadership will be the subject of a forthcoming volume, entitled *Arab Contemporaries: The Role of Personalities in Politics*.

Chapter 7

ARAB SOCIALISM

The undeveloped state of the class struggle ... causes socialists of this kind to consider themselves far superior to all class antagonisms. They want to improve the condition of every member of society, even that of the most favored. Hence, they habitually appeal to society at large, without distinction to class. For how can people, when once they understand their system, fail to see in it the best possible plan of the best possible state of society?
The Communist Manifesto

The Soviet Union's new propaganda techniques for the spread of communism after the dissolution of the Comintern gave communist parties in the Arab world greater freedom to support nationalist movements and to co-operate with genuine nationalist parties as a step toward the ultimate victory of communist ideology. Arab nationalist parties, especially those in whose activities the new generation participated, welcomed the co-operation of the communists as it became increasingly apparent that both nationalists and communists would be confronted with the threat of cold-war defense measures designed to reassert foreign influence in the Arab world. The initial Soviet support for Arab nationalism enhanced the position of communist leaders and caused the public to take note of the tenacity and endurance with which they defied authority. The activities of local communists came to be regarded as forms of national struggle and personal heroism. Some nationalist leaders had certain mental reservations about becoming too closely associated with communist objectives, but most sought by co-operation with the communists to strengthen their position against vested interest. Naturally, they expected that communism would eventually be superseded by nationalism. Thus communist and nationalist leaders often found themselves speaking the same language, although their goals were far from being identical.

Because communist appeal appeared to be gaining ground at the expense of the nationalists, nationalist leaders were concerned that their newly won independence might be exposed to danger by communist activities. Nationalist apprehensions appeared well grounded when in 1947 the Soviet Union supported the United Nations' Partition Plan of Palestine; her subsequent recognition of Israel in 1948 marked the first open conflict between nationalist and communist aims. These Soviet acts threw Arab communist parties into a moral crisis. Utter confusion followed: some local communists supported Soviet policy out of party allegiance, but others who did not allow Arab national interest to be superseded by Soviet interest, revolted, and either followed an independent communist policy or became extreme nationalists. Ten years later, when the United Arab Republic was established, an equally sharp disagreement occurred on the question of Arab unity. Initially, Syrian communists showed a lack of enthusiasm for unity with Egypt and after the 'Iraqi communists opposed the union of their country with Egypt, nationalists and communists began to clash with one another.[1]

The short-lived nationalist-communist honeymoon, artificially brought about by post-war events, was further ruptured by deep-seated differences in basic principles. Arab nationalists maintained that their ideology was based on the assumption that each nation possesses its own unique national character. The ultimate goal of any nationalist movement, they asserted, was to unify people who possess a common national character and to form a state within the national homeland. Each national unit—the nation-state—should be composed of essentially one nation, and each nation should consist of citizens enjoying freedom, equality of status, security, and prosperity. The people should determine their form of government, the embodiment of the national will.

[1] See my *Republican 'Iraq* (London, 1969), chaps. 5–6.

In contrast, the communist ideology is based on international rather than national ideals. The proletariat of each nation should join an international proletarian movement so as to achieve the victory of the working class. Each country should become a unit in a grand Soviet Union. It follows that Arab national aims, including Arab unity, would be achieved by the Arab proletariat and that the future United Arab State—or States—would become one or more units in a larger Soviet Union. Arab nationalists, seeking the independence and unity of the Arab world, thought that an association with the communist movement would bring about their cherished goals. Nationalist leaders were prepared to support a communist bloc only so far as it opposed colonialism and did not involve their countries in cold-war issues.

As early as 1945 some Arab nationalists and socialists began to co-operate and formulate nationalist-socialist platforms. The socialists, believing in the gospel of democracy, found themselves concerned with the same social problems as the nationalists. Both agreed on a neutralist foreign policy, based essentially on the belief that the Arabs were not prepared to be drawn into international conflicts involving issues of no concern to them. The initiative to correlate socialist with nationalist aims was taken by Arab Socialist parties in March 1950 at a conference held in Bayrut to discuss foreign policy.[2] It was then, long before the Ba'th Party had played a significant role in the Arab socialist movement, that the Arab socialist parties agreed to co-operate with nationalist parties and laid down the principle of a neutralist policy, a principle which later became the official policy of many an Arab country. Radical socialists who objected to this co-operation either resigned from their parties, as in the case of those in Lebanon, or were expelled, like those in 'Iraq and Syria. Meanwhile, Arab liberal nationalist parties, especially those representing the new generation, began to adopt socialist ideas and co-operate

[2] The Arab socialists who attended the conference represented the Lebanese Progressive Social Party (Lebanon), the Arab Socialist Party (Syria), the Egyptian Socialist Party (Egypt), and the National Democratic Party ('Iraq).

with socialist parties. It was, however, the Ba'th Party, consisting essentially of young men favoring a marriage between Arab nationalism and socialism which exploited this developing climate of opinion. What helped the Ba'th emerge as the most active Arab socialist party was, first, its appeal to the new generation, and second, its stress on Arab unity at a time when dissension in the Arab world and rivalries among Arab rulers were regarded as the principal reason for the Arab defeat in the Palestine wars. In its platform of the "One Arab Destiny," combining Arab unity, socialism and democracy, the Ba'th seemingly offered the Arab world a panacea for all its ills.

The Ba'th Socialism

Several intellectual groups toyed with the idea of blending socialism with Arab nationalism, but only one proved capable of giving it an articulate expression and presenting it to the public with greater vigor and deeper sense of conviction than others. This group, under the dual leadership of Michel Aflaq and Salah al-Din al-Baytar, was able to embark on a new departure in politics because it was both mentally and emotionally prepared to break with older leaders, with whom it had experienced dissatisfaction and bitter frustrations and also because it received the support of younger men.

'Aflaq and Baytar were both born in Damascus; 'Aflaq in 1910, the son of a Greek Orthodox grain merchant, and Baytar in 1911, a member of a Muslim family reputed for its conservatism and attachment to religious learning. Both studied in government schools and in 1928 went to the University of Paris for further study, the first one specializing in history and philosophy and the second one in physical sciences. Back in Damascus in 1932, they taught in high schools and met often to discuss important questions of the day. While in Paris, they were lured by communists to attend party meetings; they thus learned at first hand communist discipline, an experience which proved to be useful for the building up of the Ba'th Party. But 'Aflaq went deeper in his study of communist literature and discussed with Baytar Arab national questions in the light of his readings. Eventually they came to the conclusion that Marxism could not offer all answers to Arab national questions. After they returned home and discovered the readiness of Syrian communist leaders to subordinate national to international objectives, their apprehensions of communism increased. Like other young men, they were disillusioned by the conduct of older leaders who appeared to put vested before national interests. Moreover, no sooner had the French authorities begun to hand power over to national leadership than national leaders began to slip into corrupt practices and show a lack of respect for liberal institutions.

In 1940 'Aflaq and Baytar resigned their teaching positions to enter politics. They began to impress young men with new ideas and urge them to adopt a puritanical attitude toward life, disdaining material comforts; the public looked with respect on leaders who led spartan lives. 'Aflaq and Baytar did not distinguish themselves as public orators, but they were able to inspire students, and 'Aflaq in particular, though often verbose and vague by Western standards, made a great impression upon young men. These very traits as well as his elegant literary style proved to be his great assets. Long before he became the philosopher of the Ba'th Party, 'Aflaq had become known as an Arab thinker and man of letters.[3] In 1943, he delivered speeches attacking Marxism and materialism and stressing the cultural and spirtual values of Arab nationalism, but the Ba'th remained an intellectual movement until 1946 when it became a licensed political party. One year later, at the first Party Congress, the basic principles, the platform, and the constitution of the party were adopted.[4] In 1950, the Ba'th began to play an influential role in politics

[3] For 'Aflaq's early literary writings, see Shakir Mustafa, *Muhadarat 'An al-Qissa fi Suriya* [Lectures on the Arabic Novel] (Cairo, 1958), pp. 301–27.

[4] 'Aflaq was elected Secretary-General of the Party, and Baytar, with a few other prominent members, as the Executive Committee. The name of the party—The Arab Ba'th (Resurrection) Party—was officially adopted.

and adopted the name of the Ba'th Socialist Party when Akram al-Hawrani's Arab Socialist Party merged with the Ba'th in 1954. The Ba'th had already established branches in a number of Arab countries: in Jordan in 1948, under the leadership of Munif al-Razzaz; in 'Iraq in 1952, led by Fu'ad al-Rikabi; and still another in Lebanon, led by Jibran Majdalani. Other branches, of lesser significance, were later established in parts of Arabia, the Nile valley, and North Africa.[5]

The Ba'th ideology, though essentially the product of 'Aflaq's ideas, developed gradually and some of its fundamental principles were adopted in annual congresses after careful study. Since he has not yet written a cohesive work expounding his social and political thought, most of 'Aflaq's ideas must be found in public lectures and speeches;[6] other members, like Razzaz, have recently contributed a number of studies.[7]

The Ba'th ideology is a blend of ideas and ideals derived partly from Arab culture and partly from Western thought. Its formulation has evolved from contemporary Arab experience as well as from immediate Arab needs and aspirations to form a modern nation-state and occupy a respected position among the community of nations. Although the Ba'th is essentially an Arab nationalist party advocating ideas familiar to

[5] For a brief history of the Ba'th Party, see Gebran Majdalany, "The Arab Socialist Movements," *The Middle East in Transition*, ed. W. Z. Laqueur (London, 1958), pp. 337–50; Ibrahim Barjawi, "A Brief Account of the Ba'th Arab Socialist Party: Its Origins and ideas," *al-Hadaf*, Bayrut, March 26, 1963; K. S. Abu Jaber, *The Arab Ba'th Socialist Party* (Syracuse, 1966), chaps. 1–2; Muta' Safadi, *Hizb al-Ba'th* (Bayrut, 1964), Part 3; Gordon H. Torrey and John F. Devlin, "Arab Socialism," *Modernization of the Arab World*, eds. J. H. Thompson and R. D. Reischauer (Princeton, 1966), pp. 178–96.

[6] For a compilation of 'Aflaq's speeches and articles, see his *Fi Sabil al-Ba'th* (Damascus and Bayrut, 1959 and 1962); and *Ma'rakat al-Masir al-Wahid* (Damascus and Bayrut, 1958, 1959, and 1963). For a translation of some of his writings see S. G. Haïm, *Arab Nationalism: An Anthology* (Berkeley, 1962), pp. 242–49; and Kamal H. Karpat, *Political and Social Thought in the Contemporary Middle East* (New York, 1968), pp. 189–97.

[7] Munif al-Razzaz, *Ma'alim al-Hayat al-'Arabiya al-Jadida* (Cairo and Bayrut, 1953; 4th ed., 1960); *al-Tajriba al-Murra* (Bayrut, 1967); 'Abd Allah 'Abd al-Da'im, *Durub al-Qawmiya al-'Arabiya* (Bayrut, 1959).

other nationalist parties, some of its ideals, viewed in different perspectives, appear radically different from others.[8]

The Ba'th went a step further in blending socialism with Arab nationalism without explicitly associating the concepts "socialism" and "nationalism." 'Aflaq, as noted above, had espoused socialism for a long time—some say that he was once a Marxist—but after he discovered certain weaknesses in Marxism, he and other leaders came to the conclusion that non-Marxist socialism would meet the demands of Arab society.

'Aflaq saw socialism not merely as an economic system but, perhaps more important, as a combination of values designed to achieve dignity for man through his participation in the activities of society and by means of insuring a minimum standard of living. This socialism is based on the concept of justice and co-operation among individuals and not on class struggle or class warfare. War, if to be waged, should be waged against poverty, disease, ignorance, and vested interest. This socialism is Arab in the sense that it is a system suitable to Arab society, and the path toward the realization of national aims. Socialism, by liberating the individual from the fetters of deprivation, by preventing exploitation, and by providing a minimum standard of living, removes obstacles to the development of individual abilities, the realization of the aspirations and the sense of mission of the Arab nation. This type of socialism should be championed by the state which represents the will of the people—a general will which should include the will of the poor, workers, peasants, intellectuals, and all the enlightened elements of society. The achievement of socialism can be furthered by its inclusion in a program supported by popular organizations such as trade unions, social organizations, political parties, and professional associations. It is evident that this brand of socialism is different from European socialism and communism, since it is not envisaged as the final outcome of class struggle, but the product of co-operation among classes; it is an internal move-

[8] For a discussion of the Ba'th views of Arab nationalism, see chap. 8.

ment, it is not tied up in any way to an international movement, and it does not deny individual liberty or private property. It is, in a word, a special kind of socialism which meets the demands of Arab society.[9]

The Ba'th maintains that the depth in the prevailing decadence is the principal feature in Arab society today. The causes of this weakness are not limited to external factors or confined to internal organization, but include the weakness of Arabs as individuals. Decadence has penetrated into the inner core of the individual and has affected his social morality, his education, his thought, and his views of as well as his attitudes toward society. The solution to this problem demands a revolutionary change—a complete transformation—both in the spirit, outlook on life, and social values of the Arab individual and in the social, economic, political, and cultural organizations of Arab society. After the transformation of the prevalent outlook, the Ba'th seeks to establish a democratic and socialist Arab society by revolutionary means. When this society is established, its free government is to represent the will of the people.[10]

Closely connected with the Ba'th's struggle for freedom is its call for an over-all Arab union. This call for unity is more than a demand for political unity: it seeks the creation of a single Arab state based on Arab nationalism and seeking to achieve freedom, democracy, and socialism. Arab unity provides the framework for the Arab nation to realize its free will and resume its course of progress. Freedom, whether individual or national, cannot be attained unless Arab unity is achieved, for each part cannot alone withstand foreign demands, but all together are strong enough to resist such pressures.[11]

These ideas and ideals have been gradually embodied in the Ba'th's constitution, its internal rules and regulations, and in circulars issued to members and sympathizers. Ever

[9] 'Aflaq, *Fi Sabil al-Ba'th*, pp. 193–97, 198–206, 207–11, 219–23.

[10] 'Aflaq, *Fi Sabil al-Ba'th*, 159–63, 167–69, 170–74, 175–80, 181–84, 185–90.

[11] 'Aflaq, *Fi Sabil al-Ba'th*, 227–37, 238–43, 265–73. See also chap. 10, below.

since the first congress met in 1947, the constitution has been revised to reflect new methods for the implementation of the platform, but basic principles have remained unaltered.[12]

The constitution defines the Arab homeland as including all Arab countries from the Atlantic to the Arab (Persian) Gulf, and from Turkey and the Taurus Mountains to the Arabian Sea and the Great Sahara of Africa. In achieving its goals, the Ba'th Party, while having headquarters in Damascus and branches in other Arab capitals, "does not concern itself with regional policy except from the point of view of overall Arab interests." Parliamentary democracy based on direct representation would be the constitutional system of the Arab homeland. "Arab foreign policy," the constitution provides, "will aim at giving a true picture of the Arab will to live as free men and of their sincere desire to see all nations enjoy freedom alike." Arab sovereignty should be complete and not infringed by any foreign powers. It follows that "all treaties, agreements, or bonds concluded by Governments which infringe on the Arab's complete sovereignty will be abrogated." The social and economic princples of the party embodied in comprehensive programs drawn up in the light of recent Arab experiences and supervised directly by the state. "The Party's educational policy," the constitution suggests, "aims at creating a new Arab generation believing in the unity and eternal mission of its nation, taking to scientific thinking, freedom from the bonds of supervision and reactionary traditions, infused with the spirit of optimism, struggle, and national solidarity among all citizens in realizing the total Arab revolution and serving the cause of human progress." The state undertakes to achieve these aims by setting up and supervising educational institutions.[13]

In each Arab country, the branch of the Ba'th undertakes to achieve the goals of the party in accordance with the internal

[12] For text of the constitution, see *Constitution of the Ba'th Arab Socialist Party* (Damascus, 1947); translation in Haim, *Arab Nationalism*, pp. 233–41.

[13] *Ibid.* For the above points given in the Ba'th *Constitution*, see Articles 1, 24, 25, 26ff., and 44–48.

conditions of that region. A Regional Command assumes the executive power of the party in that region and a Regional Convention, to be convened annually, discusses and approves party programs. A National Command, composed of the representatives in various regions, exercises the executive powers of the party, and a National Convention, to be convened annually and attended by official representatives of each region, formulates the general policy of the party. Decisions and instructions of the party are issued by the National as well as the Regional Commands. These, regardless whether made available to the public or not, are to be circulated among the party's members.[14]

The Ba'th and Nasirite Leadership

Despite the fascination and the enthusiasm the Ba'th ideology aroused among young men, the party failed to provide effective leadership and win the support of the public. On the contrary, the struggle for power among Syrian political parties, especially the conflict between Ba'thists and communists, became so acute that the Ba'th leaders became afraid of an impending communist seizure of power by force. No less concerned about the intensity of this struggle were elderly nationalist leaders whose power was in danger of slipping from their hands to younger leaders. Ever since the Suez crisis of 1956—a crisis in which the Arab countries supported Egypt—Nasir had shown an interest in and acceptance of the principle of Arab unity and readiness to offer leadership to Arab countries. The Syrian leaders, with the possible exception of the communists, seized this opportunity and pleaded for the immediate union with Egypt under Nasir's leadership.

Since the Ba'th leaders attach so much importance to Arab unity and they were ready to accept Nasir's leadership, they

[14] See *Internal Regulations of the Ba'th Party.* The party's official organ, *al-Ba'th,* was issued in Damascus, but other regional organs, licensed or unlicensed, were issued under different names. See also Munif al-Razzaz, *al-Hurriya* [Freedom] (Bayrut, 1965); and *al-Tajriba al-Murra* [The Bitter Experience] (Bayrut, 1967); Tarif Khalidi, "A Critical Study of the Political Ideas of Michel 'Aflaq," *Middle East Forum,* Vol. XL (1966), pp. 55–68; Leonard Binder, *The Ideological Revolution in the Middle East* (New York, 1964), pp. 182–87.

led the drive of unity with Egypt. Having himself called for Arab unity, Nasir could not possibly turn down such an appeal. However, the Ba'th's motives were not all altruistic devoid of political ambition. Since the appeal was based largely on Nasir's charisma and strength of character, the Ba'th leaders concluded that a union under Nasir's leadership would be mutually advantageous to both sides: Egypt's doors would be thrown open to the Ba'th Party and Nasir's power would be enhanced by Ba'th support.

Even though he tacitly approved of Ba'th principles, Nasir was not interested in the Ba'th as a political party and suggested, after the union, the self-liquidation of all political parties, including the Ba'th. Moreover, he showed no inclination to allow the Ba'th leaders to continue their activities, although two Ba'thists were included in his Cabinet. It became evident that Nasir had no desire to embrace any particular ideology: he preferred to adopt reform measures based on tested principles rather than on abstract assumptions. The Ba'th leaders, especially 'Aflaq, who excelled in abstract formulations, were not unaware of the vagueness of their principles, and thought that Nasir would give their concepts practical expression through his machinery of government. Since Nasir and the Ba'th had radically different outlooks, disagreement necessarily appeared and eventually led to Ba'thist support of Syria's secession from the United Arab Republic in 1961.

The "setback"—to borrow Nasir's own words in describing the collapse of the Syro-Egyptian unity—gave both Nasir and the Ba'th leaders an impetus to revise their aims and methods. It is not an unhealthy sign to look back at one's own record, whether to put to rest certain mental reservations or to gather momentum for further advances. The lesson Nasir had learned from this experience (to mention but one relevant reason) led him to maintain that any Arab country desiring to join the United Arab Republic must adopt Arab socialism before unity is considered.

The Ba'th leaders, after several meetings of the regional and national commands, reaffirmed their belief in Arab unity, but they began to evolve some new principles. For example, they declared that their differences with Nasir stemmed from the Ba'th insistence on democratic processes; they also urged collective leadership instead of personal rule. Before the Syro-Egyptian unity, they often talked about democracy and socialism, but the relative priority of the two was not clear since 'Aflaq too often pointed out that all basic principles should be achieved together. The Ba'th acceptance of unification with Egypt, however, indicated that it was ready to subordinate democracy to socialism and Arab unity. In the light of short-lived union experience, the Ba'th leaders began to emphasize collective leadership as a necessary step toward a truly democratic system. Thus, when the opportunity to consider the renewal of Syria's unity with Egypt presented itself in 1963, the proposed plan of unity was wrecked on the rock of collective leadership; Nasir was not prepared to share authority with the Ba'th leaders.

This was not all. The Ba'th leaders began to review their position on the regional level and ideological and procedural conflicts with rival groups following their effort to assert their leadership in Syria. This internal conflict invited the intervention of army officers who, having seized power in 'Iraq and Syria in February and March 1963, began to impose their ideas and methods on Ba'thist leadership. Neither the frequent call of the national and regional commands to a discussion nor the intervention of 'Aflaq and Baytar could bring about harmony and cohesion for the differences among political leaders were reflected in the army. One military faction strived to overthrow or liquidate another, each trying to impose its version of the Ba'th ideology on others. As a result the Ba'th no longer remained as a single party but became a set of groups and individuals, each claiming to represent the needs and shifting aspirations of a divided Arab nation.

Nasirite Socialism

Nasirite socialism, unlike Ba'thist socialism, is a reform program derived largely from Egypt's own experience with problems of social and economic development and not a set of abstract principles. Before the Syro-Egyptian union, Nasir introduced certain social measures like the agrarian reform law, but the Revolution's fundamental achievements were essentially political, such as the overhauling of the political-administrative system, the elimination of foreign influence, and the reorganization of the army. No less significant was Nasir's adopting Arab unity as a means of asserting Arab leadership and positive neutrality as a principle of foreign policy. His experience with Syria, however, led him to conclude that a social revolution must be carried out in each Arab country before an over-all Arab unity is achieved. Thus, in Nasir's eyes, Arab socialism had priority over Arab unity and also represented the final form of Egypt's system.[15]

Nasir was well aware of the need for social reform and kept stressing the necessity of "two revolutions"—one "political, in which [the nation] recovers its right for self-government," and the second "social, in which the classes of society would struggle against each other until justice for all countrymen has been gained and conditions have become stable." [16] But the nature of this "social revolution" was still vague; his ideas on it had not yet crystalized. Nasir had approached leaders of various political opinions and parties for guidance, but found little that might illuminate the way. The reason, however, is not that they were lacking in "ideas" or "theories," but that Nasir himself had no interest in theories. As a pragmatist—one who always depended on "trial and error," as Nasir described himself—he would not accept a ready-made formulation of abstract theory. He would rather experiment with specific reform measures and proceed logically from one step to another. It was this practical approach that prompted him at the outset not to abolish free enterprise but to restrict it. However, when restrictions of free enterprise are introduced in a country

[15] See Nasir's speech at the Preparatory Committee for the National Congress of Social Forces on November 25, 1961, in "The Proceedings of the Preparatory Committee," entitled *al-Tariq Ila al-Dimuqratiya*, p. 69.

[16] Nasir, *Philosophy of the Revolution* (Cairo, [1954], pp. 23–24; Nasir's speech in *The Path Towards Democracy: Proceedings of the Preparatory Committee for the Congress of Popular Forces* (Cairo, 1961), p. 9 (hereafter cited as *Proceedings of the Preparatory Committee*).

that needs large amounts of capital and rapid increase in production, private capital tends to leave the country and the government is bound to increase restrictions against the flight of capital. "In 1957," said Nasir, "we began to talk about socialism, and felt the need for the establishment of socialist, democratic, and cooperative society. . . ." [17] In 1961, socialist decrees were issued for Syria and Egypt; Syria's secession prompted Nasir to seek enforcing them more effectively in his own native land, thereby trying to show what socialism could accomplish in a single Arab country. Thus, the set of principles embodied in Egypt's socialist program must be seen as the product of experience and not merely of an abstract formulation by politicians.[18]

Egypt's pressing economic difficulties were the underlying motive for the adoption of socialism. In a country suffering a rapid growth of population, its leaders naturally would keenly feel the need for economic development to cope with this and other problems. Having achieved some progress in agrarian reform and industrialization, the one further logical step was to experiment with socialism. Since the public had certain reservations about socialism, the Egyptian leaders gave both social and economic reasons as justification for the adoption of socialism. Egypt, as an "underdeveloped" country, it was argued, had been closely tied up with Western capitalism. Its economy, molded by foreign influence to provide Western industry with raw materials, had been essentially agricultural and completely dependent upon demand in capitalist markets; thereby it had become abundantly clear that the rate of increase in national income was likely to remain limited. These economic ties had their social effects. Egypt's social structure had become very rigid and composed

[17] *Proceedings of the Preparatory Committee*, pp. 21–22.

[18] In 1961 Nasir's socialist program was thrown open for public debate. First, a Preparatory Committee met and formulated proposals which were later submitted for discussion to a congress representing various sections of the people (called the popular forces) held in 1962. For proceedings of the Preparatory Committee, see *ibid.*; for proceedings of the popular forces, see *Mahadir Jalsat al-Mu'tamar al-Watani li al-Quwa al-Sha'biya* [Proceedings of the Conference of Popular Forces] (Cairo, 1962).

of two extremes: poor peasantry and rich landowners. The small nascent middle class had been enriched at the expense of the poorer classes and hence the gap between the poor and the rich had necessarily widened, leading to tension and social unrest.

The Egyptian Revolution was to repair this situation by the redistribution of agricultural lands among the peasants, thus emancipating the peasantry from the bondage of big landownership and stimulating increased agricultural production. However, the emancipation of the peasantry did not result in an immediate increase in production; on the contrary, there was an initial drop in production. To increase national income, experts urged industrialization of the country without abandonment of agrarian reform. In a relatively short time, a number of factories, including heavy steel and iron plants, were established. Like agrarian reform, industrialization proved to be an expensive enterprise. Many of the manufactured commodities could have been purchased more cheaply in foreign markets, even though the newly built factories provided new jobs for an increasing number of Egyptian workers.

Since these reforms did not measure up to the expectations of Egyptian leaders, the abolition of free enterprise and the experimentation with socialism was the next logical step. Not only social and economic reasons but also political factors were given to justify this new economic policy. Syria's secession from the United Arab Republic in 1961 had been prompted by vested interest; the Syrian move is said to have encouraged private owners in Egypt to seek salvation in surreptitious acts. Private enterprise thus appeared as the perennial enemy of revolutionary leadership and Nasir seems to have decided on delivering it the final death blow. Despite industrialization and agrarian reform, the conditions of workers and peasants did not show any sign of improvement and popular dissatisfaction caused Nasir's concern. Free enterprise was made to bear the blame for these consequences and transformation from capitalism to socialism was declared necessary—indeed inevitable—to solve domestic economic problems.

What are the essential elements of Nasirite socialism? The basic principle is that the state rather than the individual determines the kind and quantity of the commodities to be produced for the welfare of society. Since the state controls all production—it leaves a relatively small private sector for free enterprise—private ownership must be subordinate to public ownership. The purpose of public ownership of the means of production is eliminating individual profit as the ultimate determining factor in the production process and giving precedence to society's social and economic needs. The state endeavors to formulate the economic plan on the strength of the advice of experts.

The social aspects of Nasir's socialism are manifested in the manner in which goods and services are to be distributed on an equitable basis. The state rather than the individual determines equal distribution on the basis of the welfare of society as a whole. Under this system no one can exploit another since the instruments of production in public and private sectors are both under state supervision. Although this system has obviously drawn on European socialist experiences, Egyptian experts have tried to work out its details on the basis of Egypt's experiences and immediate needs.[19]

Landownership under the revised agrarian reform law was limited to a maximum of 100 faddans, one-half of the limit under the law of 1953. This step was intended to liquidate feudalism which persisted despite earlier agrarian reforms. It meant both that the land taken from previous owners was redistributed and that the increasing capital at the disposal of the state would be employed to bring new lands under cultivation (i.e., Aswan Dam and New Valley projects, etc.). Co-operative societies were established to insure justice and to help regularize the peasant's relationships with the producer and consumer. Moreover, state supervision was designed to provide guidance and ensure the maximum benefit from agricultural production.

Under this system both public and private sectors operate to benefit society as a whole. The public sector consists not

[19] Cf. *Proceedings of the Preparatory Committee*, pp. 231–33; 272–79; 520–24.

only of nationalized industries but also of new industries to be created by the state. It also includes wholesale commercial activities and certain public utilities (banks, export and import trade, insurance companies, etc.) which affect the entire public. All other types of economic enterprise remain within the private sector.

The relationship between employers in both sectors are also regulated by the state. In order to insure justice, workers are represented in the companies' boards and councils and share in profits. Provisions regulating labor affairs, minimum wages, and limited working hours are specified. To reduce disparities in income, a progressive income tax affects not only individual incomes in private investment but also incomes in public service.

One of the merits of this system is to maintain a certain balance between public and private interests. Under Egypt's free enterprise system, the individual enjoyed full freedom which often proved harmful to public interest. The communist system tends, in distributing the national income on the basis of need, to subordinate individual to public welfare and to ignore completely individual's interests. Nasir's Arab socialism, while stressing public welfare and without subordinating public to private interests, leaves a degree of free enterprise for the private sector, but if conflict were ever to develop between the two, public interest would prevail.

In the matter of private property Nasir's socialism can be distinguished from other brands of collectivism. While communism abolishes private property in principle and socialism abolishes only the ownership of capital, Arab socialism permits not only private property but also limited private capital for employment. Arab socialist thinkers maintain that this system achieves a higher level of social justice than other systems on the grounds that the individual receives a reward in accordance with capitalist societies' law of supply and demand or in accordance with communist societies' stress on the individual need. The individual's reward under Arab socialism is determined by the state to insure just compensation in accordance with certain periodically adjustable rules.

Like the Ba'thist socialism, the Nasirite socialism tries to reduce disparities between classes and to achieve the ultimate classless society. Classes, although accepted as a social fact, are not necessarily, as Marxist theories assert, in a state of struggle among themselves. Since classes are the product of socio-economic factors, Arab socialism tries to reconcile social conflicts not just by reducing disparities in income but by abolishing privilege and other social differentials. Social differences can be reduced by the elimination of exploitation and the extension of social services and cultural opportunities to all.

When Nasir has been asked whether Arab socialism might be implemented through democratic procedures, he has invariably replied that democracy is the ultimate goal of socialism, but if democracy were prematurely established before feudal and reactionary elements were liquidated, vested interests would be the primary beneficiary and socialism would not endure. Socialism, Nasir maintained, is more important than democracy and therefore has a greater claim on his resources.[20]

Nasir and the Ba'th appear to agree on a transitional revolutionary period before democracy is established. The essential weakness in this argument is the vagueness concerning how long revolutionary and authoritarian methods must continue: the transitional process may be endless, since each transitional period might lead to another in which new aims may develop as the process of change continues. Thus democracy remains more like a mirage—a pious aspiration which may never be reached—than an immediate objective to be achieved.

Nasir's socialism, in contrast with Ba'thist socialism, stresses distributive justice and society's basic economic rather than cultural and spiritual values: Nasir's goal is to achieve a welfare state. This state, however, is mainly concerned with the

[20] See *ibid.*, pp. 69–204; during the debate of the Preparatory Committee, Khalid Muhammad Khalid put the question of democracy to Nasir, as the present writer did a few years earlier, but Nasir seemed to have made no significant change in his views about democracy (see *ibid.*, p. 617ff.).

conditions of workers and peasants; the principle of distributive justice is to be achieved at the expense of other classes. In a country whose annual rate of growth of population is 2.8 per cent (an increase of more than 750,000 annually), social reform requires either drastic birth control measures or a far more rapid rate of increase in per capita income.[21] But a stress on the principle of equitable distribution of income can hardly contribute to a maximum increase of production, if the ownership of the instruments of production are taken away from experienced private owners and given to state functionaries who operate industry with less efficiency. No less a drain on the national income were heavy expenditures on arms and armaments—expenditures designed partly to achieve some of Nasir's nationalist goals of Pan-Arabism, support of revolutionary movements in other Arab countries, participation in Afro-Asian activities, and primarily defense of Egypt against Israel's periodic attacks. While defense preparedness is regarded as absolutely essential, it means the diversion of a relatively high percentage of the annual income to armament and military services. Faced with a population explosion and an armament race with Israel, Nasir's domestic economic reforms are bound to be adversely affected.[22]

Prudent Socialism

Ever since Nasir declared the primacy of Arab socialism, Syrian and 'Iraqi leaders working for Arab unity began to call for the adoption of Arab socialism as a step toward ultimate Arab union. In 1963, when the Ba'th came to power in

[21] The national income has risen from EL. 1285.2 million in 1959/1960 to EL. 1762.2 in 1964/1965.

[22] For a discussion of the theory and practice of Nasir's Arab socialism see my "Contemporary Arab Political Thought," *Hiwar* (1967), pp. 10ff; M. H. Kerr, "The Emergence of a Socialist Ideology in Egypt," *The Middle East Journal* (1962), pp. 127–44; Fayez Sayegh "The Theoretical Structure of Nasser's Socialism," *St. Antony's Papers: Middle Eastern Affairs*, No. 4 (London, 1965), pp. 9ff; Rif'at al-Mahjub, *al-Nizam al-Ishtiraki fi al-Jumhuriya al-'Arabiya al-Muttahida* [The Socialist System in the United Arab Republic] (Bayrut, 1967); Anouar Abdel-Malek,

'Iraq and Syria, the Syrian and 'Iraqi governments informed Nasir that they were ready to join with the United Arab Republic. This step seemed natural since Arab socialism was a principal article in the Ba'th program. Negotiations for Arab unity, however, broke down because Nasir was not prepared to share authority with the Ba'th. Neither Syria nor 'Iraq were ready to meet Nasir's prerequisites for Arab unity.

After the fall of the Ba'th from power in 'Iraq in November 1963, elements favoring Arab unity, known as the Nasirites, pressed for negotiations with Egypt and a unity agreement to undertake certain preparatory steps was signed. The machinery for unity was set up and steps to prepare 'Iraq for ultimate union were undertaken; the adoption of some socialist measures was the most important. Although there was a strong opposition to socialism, 'Iraq, on the occasion of the anniversary of the 'Iraqi Revolution in 1964, took the drastic step of issuing decrees nationalizing banks and industries.[23]

The immediate effects of nationalization were the flight of capital and noticeable decline in production which necessitated the importation of an increasing number of commodities. Since 'Iraq is an underpopulated country which had just begun to build an infant industry and since most of its resources had not yet been exploited, it was keenly felt that free enterprise would help to develop the country more rapidly than socialism. Nor were the religious groups happy with socialism since they believed that Islam in its material and spiritual values was opposed to socialism. These and other reasons of internal rather than ideological character led to the downfall of the Nasirite group. In 1965 a new govern-

---

Egypt: Société Militaire (Paris 1962), English translation, *Egypt: Military Society* (New York, 1968). For criticism of Arab Socialism, see Ma'ruf al-Dawalibi, *Nazarat fi al-Ishtirakiya al-Thawriya* [Inquiries into Revolutionary Socialism] (Bayrut, 1965); Salah al-Din al-Munajjid, *al-Tadlil al-Ishtiraki* [Socialist Falsehood] (Bayrut, 1965); Jibran Shamiya et al., *al-Ishtirakiya fi al-Tajarib al-'Arabiya* [Socialism in Arab Experience] (Bayrut, 1965).

[23] For a discussion of the steps taken by 'Iraq to adopt Arab socialism, see my *Republican 'Iraq* (London, 1969), chap. 9.

ment, headed by a civilian Premier, 'Abd al-Rahman al-Bazzaz, was formed.

Bazzaz has long been known in nationalist circles as a thinker who expounded the Islamic basis of Arab nationalism in an attempt to introduce religious and ethical values in Arab nationalism.[24] As a nationalist, he was bound to be influenced by Nasir's call for Arab socialism, especially during his exile in Egypt during 1959–63; but his experiences in Egypt persuaded him to accept only mild socialist views which were consistent with Islamic teachings concerning the welfare of the community. In several speeches, Bazzaz asserted that his socialist views were derived from Islamic rather than European socialist thinkers, but obviously he was well acquainted with Western socialist writings from which he derived some of his ideas. Once in power, however, he was convinced that the 'Iraqi socialists in following Nasir's footsteps had moved too fast and that the adverse effects of nationalization on 'Iraq's internal conditions called for a modification of the newly adopted socialist measures.

Bazzaz declared that he was in favor of "prudent" rather than Nasir's "Arab" socialism. Prudent socialism, a brand of Arab socialism that would "fit 'Iraq," aimed at raising the standard of living by an increase of production and just distribution of national wealth without abolishing free enterprise. The nationalization of banks and major industries, Bazzaz declared, was necessary to create the public sector, but the private sector was to remain intact and never to be encroached upon again. The private sector would be encouraged to participate in economic development and to establish new firms and factories. If necessary, he asserted, private capital may even be increased. A third "joint sector," correlating the public and private sectors and combining public and private investment, was to be established with adequate guarantees protecting the capital invested in it. Foreign capital might be encouraged to participate in the joint sector. The three sectors thus combine socialism and free enterprise

[24] For Bazzaz's ideas of nationalism, see chap. 8, below.

and are intended to exploit 'Iraq's natural resources for the maximum benefit of the people.

Prudent socialism is a special type of mixed economy, seeking to strike a balance between free enterprise and collectivism. It was designed to achieve production without abandoning the principle of equitable distribution of the national wealth advocated by Arab socialists. As a happy compromise, it proved to be satisfactory to the business community and Arab nationalists, even though it was criticized on ideological grounds because it put the principle of equitable distribution of national wealth on the same footing with the interests of so-called capitalist and reactionary elements. If ever socialism were to be a real blend of Arab and Western concepts adapted to an Arab country, prudent socialism proved to be indeed the most practical system responding to the needs and aspirations of Arabs. In the short period which Bazzaz tried to implement prudent socialism, a favorable public reaction indicated that the people were prepared to accept his mixed economy but not a fully collectivist system. After Bazzaz's fall from power, prudent socialism remained in force though not without certain modifications inspired by various ideological groups.[25]

"The One Arab Movement"

As an ideology, Arab socialism was intended to be a unifying rather than a disruptive factor in the movement toward Arab unity. But no sooner had the nucleus of an Arab union been achieved—the United Arab Republic—than several variants of Arab socialism began to develop, stemming partly from parochial and partly from personal and procedural differences. Many an Arab thinker who wanted unity on a socialist basis began to ask what went wrong in the implementation of a scheme which was acceptable to all in principle but failed in practice. Some critics held that the Ba'th leaders,

[25] For an account of the working of prudent socialism in 'Iraq, see my *Republican 'Iraq*, chap. 10.

who propounded the doctrine of Arab socialism long before Nasir, should have been given a role in the Arab socialist system of the United Arab Republic; others reproached both Nasir and the Ba'th for their failure to reconcile their differences in an effort to achieve a common national goal. To these critics, personal and procedural differences rightly appear as secondary matters which ought to have been subordinated to overriding principles.

Since Nasir is unmistakably committed to Pan-Arabism and since he possesses a charisma for Arab masses that no other leader can match, Arab nationalists tend to blame the Ba'th leaders for failure to recognize him as the leader of "The One Arab Movement." No other Arab movement dedicated to the cause of unity, it has been argued, should stand in the way of Nasir who proved to be the most effective leader to achieve national goals.[26] For this reason most nationalists appealed to all to rally behind Nasir.

The group which began to call for One Arab Movement was organized in Bayrut—a center with relative freedom for the expression of political opinion—following Nasir's speech on July 23, 1963, on the occasion of the anniversary of the Egyptian Revolution, in which he himself used the term "The One Arab Movement." [27] Arab nationalists, deeply disap-

[26] Before 1952, neither Arab nationalism nor Arab unity seems to have been in Nasir's mind as objectives of his revolutionary movement. But after Nasir took over leadership in 1954, he gradually began to identify the Egyptian Revolution with the Pan-Arab movement. There were several considerations which may well have influenced him in this decision. Egypt by herself, Nasir keenly felt, was weak and limited in resources; but if united with other Arab countries she would become strong and could lead a bloc of Arab states extending from Northwest Africa to the Indian Ocean. Nasir considered Egypt's central position so important that she would play a leading role in three overlapping, though not necessarily conflicting, circles—an inner Arab, an African, and a broader Islamic, embodying the greater part of the other two circles. "There is no doubt," Nasir said, "the Arab circle is the most important and the most closely connected with us—its history merges with us, and we have suffered the same hardships, lived the same crises and when we fell prostrate under the spikes of the horses of conquerors they lay with us" (Nasir, *Philosophy of the Revolution* [Cairo, 1955], p. 56). To Nasir, Egypt's interests appeared closely connected with Arab interests.

[27] In this speech Nasir attacked the Ba'th leaders for sowing dissension in the Arab nationalist movement.

pointed by Syria's secession from the United Arab Republic and thus frustrated in their most cherished national goal, responded immediately and favorably to this call.

The One Arab Movement avoided, perhaps consciously, controversial matters, stressed three major demands–Arab unity, Arab socialism, and Nasir's leadership–and advocated Nasir's revolutionary method. Arab unity, according to this movement, has to provide the political framework within which the Arab revolutionary forces could operate.[28] In some of the pronouncements, the movement has been described as one Arab nationalist, socialist, and revolutionary movement, aiming at the transformation of Arab society into a full-fledged socialist system within the framework of an over-all Arab union consisting of all Arab lands.[29] However, nothing is said about democracy, presumably leaving it to Nasir to decide on the matter. Indeed, there is even a reproach in some of the public statements of this movement to the Ba'th leaders for their insistence during this transitional stage on democratic procedure which could permit reactionary elements to obstruct the Arab revolutionary process.[30]

Some Arab thinkers sympathetic to the One Arab Movement began to criticize the Ba'th leaders sharply on democratic procedures and for their failure to accept Nasir's terms. One Arab writer suggested that the Ba'th, the Syrian Socialist Union, and the Algerian National Liberation Bloc should merge into one organization under Nasir to lead One Arab Movement in order to achieve an over-all Arab socialist union.[31] Another writer, 'Abd-Allah al-Rimawi, a dissident of the Ba'th Party, maintained that the Charter formulated by the Egyptian Congress of the Popular Forces in 1962 should be regarded as the program of the One Arab Movement, but he suggested that the Charter should be revised so as to stress

[28] See "Bayan Harakat al-Qawmiyyin al-'Arab fi Dhikra Infisal Suriya 'An al-Jumhuriya al-'Arabiya al-Muttahida," *al-Watha'iq al-'Arabiya*, 1963, pp. 703–6.

[29] "Bayan Harakat al-Qawmiyyin al-'Arab fi al-Dhikra al-Sadisa Li al-Wahda Bayn Suriya wa Misr," *al-Watha'iq al-'Arabiya*, 1964, pp. 62–75.

[30] *Ibid.*, p. 73.

[31] Naji 'Alwash, *Fi Sabil al-Haraka al-'Arabiya al-Thawriya al-Shamila* [Toward the General Arab Revolutionary Movement] (Bayrut, 1963).

Arab nationalism and Arab unity as well as the dynamic nature of the socialist and revolutionary principles enshrined in it. He also suggested the omission of transitional measures relating specifically to Egypt and the inclusion of articles relating to Palestine so that the Charter would become a truly ideological program for the Arab homeland.[32] In another volume, Rimawi, the most outspoken advocate, developed more fully his program consisting of Arab nationalism, Arab unity, and revolution by adding to it the principles of rational secularism and democracy. He went on to say that democratic procedures could not be applied to this movement and that a transitional authoritarian regime was necessary before democracy could be established.

There is nothing new in Rimawi's set of general principles which the Ba'th had not stated in its program, but he seems to stress emphatically the dynamic nature of the "Arab procession" based on a classless mass movement representing young men and assuming the leadership of the Arab nation rather than on a single party (i.e. the Ba'th). He hailed the One Arab Movement as the "inevitable historical process," produced by "forces long in the making" which will lead to the unity of the Arab homeland as well as to the assumption by the Arab nation of its "well-deserved position" in the world.[33]

The One Arab Movement, though essentially a protest movement against the Ba'th, expressed the feeling of many Arab nationalists who regarded Arab unity as their most cherished aspiration. It was supported not only by dissident Ba'th members, but also by other groups in favor of Arab socialism generally and Nasir's leadership in particular.[34]

[32] 'Abd-Allah al-Rimawi, *al-Haraka al-'Arabiya al-Wahida* [The One Arab Movement] (Bayrut, 1954), pp. 387–94.

[33] 'Abd-Allah al-Rimawi, *al-Bayan al-Qawmi al-Thawri* [The National Revolutionary Declaration] (Cairo, 1966).

[34] See "Bayan al-Ishtirakiyyin al-'Arab," *al-Watha'iq al-'Arabiya*, 1964, pp. 440–45; Fu'ad al-Rikabi, *al-Thawra al-'Arabiya al-Ishtirakiya wa al-Tanzim* [Organization and the Arab Socialist Revolution] (Cairo, 1964); *Fusul fi al-Thawra wa al-'Amal al-Ishtiraki* [Essays on Revolution and Socialist Action] (Cairo, 1964); *'Ala Tariq al-Thawra* [On the Way to Revolution].

Following the June War of 1967, however, Nasir's leadership has been weakened considerably and his image in Arab eyes tarnished, although his strength of character was never called into question. Popular refusal to accept his resignation when it was offered after military defeat reflected a genuine confidence in his leadership despite criticism by opponents.[35]

Until 1967, when war broke out, the Arab "revolutionary procession" appeared to be in the ascendency and might even have engulfed some of the more recalcitrant Arab countries; but the June War, resulting in military defeat, arrested the movement and turned Arab attention to the external threat away from controversy on social reform. The Arab revolutionary procession, without abandoning its social content, has now taken the form of a "liberation movement"—an irredentist aspect of the Arab nationalist movement.[36]

[35] Salah al-Din al-Munajjid's trenchant criticism of Arab Socialism before the June War and his attack on Nasir's leadership after the war represent the viewpoint of the anti-Nasirite groups (see his *al-Tadlil al-Ishtiraki* [Bayrut, 1965]; and *A'midat al-Nakba* [Bayrut, 1967]).

[36] See chap. 8, pp. 205 ff. below.

Chapter 8

CONTEMPORARY IDEAS OF NATIONALISM

You are the best nation ever brought forth to mankind.
Qur'an III, 106

We have already seen how Arab nationalism arose before World War I as a reaction to the Islamic mode of loyalty in whose name the Ottomans had ruled Arab lands. The full development of this nationalism might have led to the establishment of secular institutions and perhaps ultimately to the separation of civil from religious authorities—a concept of separation inspired by Europe. However, the upsurge of anti-European feeling resulting from the failure to achieve independence and national unity after World War I necessarily affected the positive character of nationalism and inspired it with a negative outlook. From the end of World War I to the early thirties, there was little substance in Arab nationalist thought, including even the works of articulate thinkers, amounting largely to rhetorical speeches and fiery statements demanding independence and Arab unity.[1] From the thirties to World War II, Arab nationalism began to fall under anti-liberal influences, Fascist and Nazi ideologies in particular, and tended, as a reaction to continued national frustrations,

[1] See Amin al-Rayhani [Rihani], *al-Qawmiyat* [On Nationalism] (Bayrut, 1956), II, 5–8, 49–56, 86–87, 142–46.

to become militant in character. Only after World War II, when most of the Arab countries had achieved independence, did Arab thinkers begin to reformulate Arab nationalism with a new outlook and to infuse it with positive elements.

Integral Nationalism

Of the Arab countries, the relatively more advanced were placed under foreign control and the more backward remained independent. For this reason Arab nationalism became highly emotional and negative and its leaders, preoccupied with foreign intervention, put forth the claims of independence and national unity before any other. The movement to achieve the dual goal of independence and unity came to be known as Pan-Arabism, often simply called "Arabism" (*'uruba*). The hotbed of the movement was in Syria, but the center of activities moved to 'Iraq when King Faysal, head of the new Arab regime, had ascended the throne in 1921 after the fall of his government in Damascus in 1920. Before 'Iraq became independent in 1932 each Arab country had to struggle for independence alone, although lip service to unity was often paid by many a nationalist.

After 'Iraq's independence, Pan-Arab leaders, especially Syrians and Palestinians, began to move to 'Iraq and to urge her people to achieve Arab nationalist goals and to inspire them with the idea that 'Iraq was the most promising country to play the role of an Arab Prussia in the achievement of Arab unity. "The existing regime in 'Iraq," said the Pan-Arabs, "was an artificial creation of Britain designed to maintain her own imperial interests and therefore unworthy of survival; the only truly Arab national regime would be that in which 'Iraq would form part of a United Arab State." [2] These ideas, widely disseminated in the country by nationalist societies and in schools by nationalist teachers, influenced the policy of 'Iraq and prompted her nationalist officers to use the armed forces for political purposes.

[2] See my *Independent 'Iraq* (London, 2nd ed., 1960), p. 162.

Pan-Arab ideas were widely discussed in civil and military circles and many books and articles were published. These ideas were perhaps best expounded in a volume entitled "These are Our [National] Aims: Those Who Believe in Them Are on Our Side," embodying speeches and articles on Arab nationalism which some members of the Muthanna Club, a nationalist organization founded in Baghdad in 1935, prepared and published in the name of Sami Shawkat, a prominent member of the Muthanna Club and then Director General of Education.[3] In this work, Arab nationalism is expressed in ideological and totalitarian terms. In a speech on the "Profession of Death," which Shawkat had given in Baghdad in 1933 and which was circulated and read in all Government high schools, he expounded in simple but forceful language his doctrine of power. In this speech, Shawkat played on the emotions of young men with his apparently cogent argument that countries like Egypt and India, though rich and culturally advanced, had not yet achieved independence. Countries like Afghanistan and the Yaman, on the other hand, though poor and backward, were independent. "Wealth and knowledge," Shawkat concluded, "were not the sole means of destroying the foundation of imperialism and shaking off the fetters of submission." There is, he added, another more important factor which "shields the honor of nations and prevents their submission to imperialism—power!" By power he meant "the perfection of the profession of death." If life were a right inherent to the individual, so was death in the defense of the life and honor of nations.[4] In another speech Shawkat developed the doctrine of the "Rugged Life," in an attempt to urge young men to follow the life of the Arabs in early Islam, which in his eyes was austere and simple. More interest was aroused by the essays which dwelt on Arab past glories and on the future possibility of Arab unity. In a speech given to high-school teachers of history, Shawkat called on the teachers to infuse with nationalism their teaching of

[3] Sami Shawkat, *Hadhihi Ahdafuna: Man Amana Biha Fahwa Minna* (Baghdad, 1939).

[4] *Ibid.*, pp. 1–3.

history and demanded glorification of the Arab nation. As to those books which discredit the Arabs, they should be burned, not excepting the work of Ibn Khaldun, the greatest Arab philosopher of history.[5]

Integral nationalism remained the predominating force in the Arab world until the independence of most Arab countries had been achieved following World War II, although some positive aspects, ideological or otherwise, began to appear before that war.[6]

Nationalism and Religion

The intellectual milieu of Istanbul in which many an Arab nationalist grew up was dominated by young Ottoman secular thought and most of the leaders who opposed Sultan 'Abd al-Hamid's Pan-Islamism tried to keep the nationalist movement immune from Islamic influences. Most Arab nationalists were not prepared to accept the young Ottoman view of Islam, because Islam was regarded as a product of the Arab cultural heritage from which they did not want to depart; indeed, most of them, including Christian thinkers, took pride in Islam because it laid special emphasis on the Arabic character of the Qur'an and on the Arabic language.

It is this significant cultural element which prompted Arab thinkers to regard Islam as a component of Arab nationalism just as Turkish thinkers regarded it as an alien element in their cultural heritage. To the Arabs, Islam came into being in Arabia, the cradle of the Arab race, and Muhammad was an Arab prophet and a national hero. The Qur'an was not

[5] *Ibid.*, p. 44. See also my *Independent 'Iraq*, pp. 166–67. Although Sati' al-Husri, who served as Director General of Education before Shawkat, was also of the opinion that history might be used for nationalist indoctrination, he criticized Shawkat in the press for his attack on Ibn Khaldun because Ibn Khaldun did not attack the Arab race and his use of the term Arab was applied to the Baduins (see Sati' al-Husri, *Dirasat 'An Muqaddimat Ibn Khaldun* [Cairo, 1953], pp. 151ff.).

[6] For a brief account of the ideas of nationalism expressed by the various political parties in the Arab world, see Sati' al-Husri, *al-'Uruba Bayn Du'atuha wa Mu'aridiha* [Arabism Between Its Advocates and Opponents] (Bayrut, 1952), pp. 139ff.

only revealed in the Arabic language but all believers, Arabs as well as non-Arabs, had it as their obligation to recite it in Arabic. The Arabs were the first believers of Islam and they struggled to spread it and establish the Islamic empire. It is true that Islam opposed Arab racial ascendency by stressing equality among all believers, but it was this equality which had attracted non-Arabs to learn the Arabic language and contribute to the Islamic and Arabic literary heritage. It was the Arabic language and Arab cultural heritage which superseded the racial bond and made possible the Arabization of people who adopted the Arab tongue and identified themselves as Arabs, especially the people of the Fertile Crescent. No one has expressed this feeling more finely than al-Biruni, a native of Khwarizm (Khiva) and a great scientist who displayed his preference for Arabic when he said:

> Our religion and our empire are Arab and twins, the one protected by the power of God, and the other by the hand of Heaven. How often have tribes of subjects congregated together, in order to impart a non-Arab character to the state. But they could not succeed in their aim, and as long as the call to worship continues to sound in their ears five times each day and the clear Arab Qur'an is recited among the rows of worshippers ranged behind the imam and its reforming message is preached to them in the mosques, they have got to submit, the bond of Islam is not broken, and its fortress not breached. Sciences from all countries of the world have been translated into the language of the Arabs, have been embellished and become attractive, and the beauties of the language have permeated their veins and arteries, even though each people considers beautiful its own language to which it is accustomed and which it uses in its daily business. I speak from experience because I was brought up in a language in which it would be strange indeed to find a science perpetuated. Then I went over to Arabic and Persian and am a guest in both languages, having made an effort to acquire them; but I would rather be reviled in Arabic than praised in Persian.[7]

[7] M. Meyerhof, *Das Vorwort zur Drogenkunde des Beruni* (Berlin, 1932), p. 39f; cited by J. Schacht, "The Islamic Background of the Idea of an Arab Nation," *The Arab Nation*, ed. William Sands (Washington, D.C., 1961), p. 23.

It was the Arabic language and culture which inspired Arab thinkers, Muslims and Christians alike, to develop Arab national consciousness and call for an Arab identity separate from Ottoman identity in the late nineteenth and early twentieth centuries. As a product of Arab heritage, Islam has been looked upon as a spiritual force and a set of moral values necessary for life. But if Islam is seen as a component of nationalism, it no longer remains the exclusive loyalty in the traditional sense.

Perhaps the representative thinker whose primary loyalty was to Islam but who accepted nationalism as a basis for the Islamic state was the reformer Rashid Rida. He infused his writings on Islam with Arab national feeling and often showed more concern about Arab problems than those of other Islamic countries. In the true traditional Arab view of Islam, Rida spoke of the founder of Islam as an Arab prophet, the Qur'an as revealed scripture in the Arab tongue, and the Arabs as the carriers of the message of Islam beyond the frontiers of Arabia. In this respect he was faithful to both Arab and Islamic loyalties and believed that the unity of one contributes to the other. He maintained with other Arab nationalists that Islam had been undermined by Ottoman rulers. He supported the Arab nationalist movement in order to free Arab lands from Ottoman rule and to bring back the caliphate even if the Turks failed to co-operate. He also joined Arab nationalist societies and took an active part in politics during and after World War I, as noted before; [8] but he was disappointed with the Arab nationalist movement because it brought foreign intervention in its train. Thus in the latter part of his life, he turned to reassert primary loyalty to Islam in its puritanical Wahhabi form in Arab lands that remained in his eyes immune from foreign influence.[9]

Like Rida, his life-long friend and collaborator Amir Shakib Arslan (1869–1946) professed primary loyalty to Islam

[8] See pp. 66–67, above.

[9] See Rashid Rida, *al-Wahhabiyun wa al-Hijaz* [The Wahhabis and the Hijaz] (Cairo, 1344/1926); Albert Hourani, *Arabic Thought in the Liberal Age* (London, 1962), pp. 299–306; Ibrahim Ahmad al-'Adawi, *Rashid Rida: al-Imam al-Mujahid* (Cairo, n.d.), chaps. 11–12.

but, following the collapse of the Ottoman empire after World War I, he supported Arab nationalist leaders more strongly than Rida, particularly because he was opposed to European occupation of Arab lands. His view of nationalism was, accordingly, negative; he remained at heart faithful to Islam and saw in nationalism a force which would strengthen Islam against Christian encroachments. Arslan, indulging more than Rida in political activities, was not a religious reformer; he was essentially a writer and chronicler of events, and spent the latter part of his life in Europe, engaged in the defence of Arab rights by journalistic activity.[10] He even toyed with the idea of an Arab alignment with Germany and Italy and went so far as to negotiate with them on behalf of some Arab leaders. Failure of his diplomatic gambles benefited neither Arab nationalism nor Islam, for he spent most of his career in political maneuvering rather than in constructive religious or social reform. His literary output, however, was prodigious and his Arabic style masterful.[11]

Rida and Arslan may seem to have held contradictory views concerning Islamic unity and Arab nationalism because they were faithful to two seemingly identical loyalties which had conflicting aims. It is true that their primary loyalty was to Islam, but they also asserted loyalty to Arab nationalism which proved instrumental in the destruction of Islamic unity. It was more obvious in Arslan's than in Rida's career that the claim of Islamic unity took priority over the claim of Arab unity; but to Rida the two were not necessarily irreconcilable. The intellectual life of these two men represented a transition in the life of Muslims from one mode of loyalty to another, although they were not always consistent in expressing their preference to one or the other.

In the early twenties the assertion of secular ideas alarmed

[10] He published, in co-operation with Ihsan al-Jabiri, *La Nation Arabe* in Geneva, Switzerland, during the inter-war years.

[11] For his life see: Sami al-Dahhan, *al-Amir Shakib Arslan* (Cairo, 1960); Ahmad al-Sharabasi, *Shakib Arslan: Da'iyat al-'Uruba wa al-Islam* (Cairo, 1963). See also Muhammad 'Ali al-Tahir, *Dhikra al-Amir Shakib Arslan* (Cairo, 1947).

religious circles, and nationalist leaders, who needed the support of religious groups in the struggle for independence, sought to conciliate religious leaders by paying lip service to Islam. Moreover, the growing interest in Arabic and Islamic studies both in native and foreign educational institutions, created an awareness of the overlapping elements of culture and religion and of the importance of Islam to Arab nationalism. No sooner had some writers begun to publish works on certain aspects of Islam than the favorable response to such publications encouraged other writers who had previously displayed liberal and secular tendencies to follow. In the thirties there was a noticeable output of works for which Islam supplied the literary raw materials; these books varied from historical novels to scholarly works. Muhammad Husayn Haykal, then known as a liberal writer in Egypt,[12] Ma'ruf al-Arnawut, a Syrian essayist and novelist,[13] and Darwish al-Miqdadi,[14] a Palestinian teacher who lived in 'Iraq—to mention but three representative examples—chose certain aspects of Islam as themes for their writings and established for the general public that Islam was a vital force that could be instrumental in the shaping of modern Arab life.[15]

At the outset this trend disturbed Christian Arab thinkers who feared that the association of religion with nationalism might arouse religious fanaticism and restore the social exclusiveness of Ottoman days. Meanwhile, secular thinkers regarded the trend as a step backward, construed to please religious and conservative quarters rather than to serve the

[12] See p. 219–20 below.

[13] Born in Bayrut in 1892 and worked in Damascus as a journalist (see Sami al-Kayyali, *al-Adab al-Mu'asir fi Suriya* [Cairo, 1959], pp. 98–101).

[14] Miqdadi served both in 'Iraq (1924–45) and Kuwayt (1945–57).

[15] The first wrote biographical studies of the Prophet and early caliphs, Muhammad Husayn Haykal, *Hayat Muhammad* (Cairo, 1935); *Fi Manzil al-Wahi* (Cairo, 1937); *al-Siddiq Abu Bakr* (Cairo, 1942); *al-Faruq 'Umar* (Cairo, 1945). The second wrote historical novels, Ma'ruf al-Arnawut, *Sayyid Quraysh* (Damascus, 1929); *'Umar Ibn al-Khattab* (Damascus, 1936); *Tariq Ibn Ziyad* (Damascus, 1941); *Fatima al-Batul* (Damascus, 1942). The third wrote the history of Islam as the "History of the Arab Nation," Darwish al-Miqdadi, *Ta'rikh al-Umma al-'Arabiya* (Baghdad, 1935).

cause of modernism and progress. Very soon, however, it was realized that the religious and ethical values of Islam were so ingrained in Arab society that they could not be ignored as a basic ingredient of nationalism. It was Christian thinkers, like Qustantin Zurayq, a well-known historian and educator at the American University of Bayrut, and Edmond Rabbath, a lawyer and once a member of parliament in Damascus, who began to explain the inescapable association of religion and nationalism, and sought to derive from Islam the same ethical values that were derived from other great religions. Zurayq often impressed young men with the need of spiritual values and pointed out that there was no inherent conflict between the true spirit of nationalism and religion; on the contrary, he said, "Arab nationalists should fall back on the sources of their religion and derive from it inspiration and spiritual guidance." [16] He saw in the life of the Prophet an Arab hero whose conviction led him to "found the basis of a new civilization." [17] Rabbath carried the idea of the religious basis of Arab nationalism a step further by arguing that Islam is in essence a national religion. True, he analyzed Arab nationalism essentially in terms of culture and language, but he attributed to Islam the basis of political unity.[18]

Perhaps the most forceful expression of this blend of Islam and nationalism by Muslim thinkers is to be found in the writings of 'Abd al-Rahman al-Bazzaz.[19] Belonging to a family well-known for its attachment to religion and Islamic learning, he was eminently fitted to appreciate the significance of religion and its ethical values, having combined in his training as a lawyer both Western and Islamic learning. He was

[16] Qustantin Zurayq, *al-Wa'i al-Qawmi* (Bayrut, 1939), pp. 112–13.

[17] *Ibid.*, p. 117.

[18] Edmond Rabbath, *Unité Syrienne et Devenir Arabe* (Paris, 1937). See a translation of a section of this work in S. G. Haim, *Arab Nationalism*, pp. 103–19. For a brief discussion of the ideas of Zurayq and Rabbath, see Hourani, *Arabic Thought*, pp. 309–11.

[19] Like Bazzaz ('Iraq), Muhammad al-Mubarak (Syria) has advocated almost similar views on the relationship between religion and Arab nationalism, but Bazzaz's writings are more liberal and original. For Mubarak's views, see his *al-Umma al-'Arabiya* (Damascus, 1959).

disturbed to find young men who claimed to be nationalists but who were lacking in spiritual values, and others who received traditional education but who were lacking an understanding of the concept of nationalism. Therefore, he addressed himself to the problem of reconciling Islam with nationalism. Bazzaz was reproached by some who suspected that he might arouse religious or sectarian controversy, especially in 'Iraq where confessional differences have been intimately connected with domestic politics, although in reality his aim, as I pointed out in another work, was "not to arouse traditional zeal, as some have suspected, but to temper the spirit of young men who advocated secular nationalism by the reintroduction of religion and ethical values into Arab nationalism." [20]

Like Rashid Rida's, Bazzaz's intellectual background stems from Islam, and thus he could see no contradiction between Islam and nationalism: all that was in Islam was in Arab nationalism. "So far," Hourani noted, "Rashid Rida would have agreed. . . . But there is an essential difference. Rida would have defined Arab culture in terms of Islam; Bazzaz does rather the opposite. Islam is a national religion: The real Islam was Arab Islam." [21] Rida may have accepted nationalism vaguely, but Bazzaz has been fully appreciative of the significance of nationalism in modern Arab life and has tried to reconcile Islam, which in his eyes is both a cultural and political force, with nationalism. Nor is nationalism, he contended, a sufficient force without spiritual and moral value. Thus Bazzaz has advanced the cause of reconciling Islam with nationalism a step further than Rida. In political thought as in practical politics, he has shown a remarkable flexibility and aptitude for tolerance and moderation.[22]

[20] See my *Republican 'Iraq* (London, 1969), p. 251. For Bazzaz's writings on Islam and nationalism, see *al-Bazzaz on Arab Nationalism* (London, 1965).

[21] Hourani, *Arabic Thought*, p. 308.

[22] See 'Abd al-Rahman al-Bazzaz, *Min Wahyi al-'Uruba* (Cairo, 2nd ed., 1963). For Bazzaz's career in politics, see my *Republican 'Iraq*, chap. 10.

Regional Nationalism

The division of geographical Syria into four political units after World War I was a great disappointment to Syrian as well as to Arab nationalists who sought a union of these segments, notwithstanding the fact there was some justification for the division while society was split into ethnic and confessional groups. Although the division of Syria was considered by nationalists to serve essentially foreign interests at the expense of national unity, there was no agreement among leaders that would reconcile local differences and unite the country against foreign intervention. On the contrary, Syrian nationalists were opposed to both the French and their protégés who accepted internal division; on the other hand, some Lebanese leaders began to advocate Phoenician or Mediterranean symbols of identity, such as the use of ancient non-Arab names of legendary heroes and ancient place names, in order to maintain their separate existence. If unity were ever to be achieved, the conflicting symbols of identity would have to be embodied in a movement capable of uniting the entire area known as geographical Syria. The Syrian National Party, later called the Social National Party, which Antun Sa'ada organized in the early thirties, was the first group to demand unity for which there was a certain mental readiness. The extent to which the party was capable of offering the type of ideology which would meet the challenge is worthy of study. Since the party was essentially the product of the thought and activities of its leader, especially in the initial stage, some knowledge of the background of his life might be useful.

Antun Sa'ada was born in Lebanon in 1904 of Christian parents; his father, a physician who had outspoken ideas about national affairs, migrated first to Egypt and then to Brazil shortly before World War I, leaving his son in Lebanon. It was not until 1920, when Antun had barely received primary education, that he joined his father. In São Paulo, the father distinguished himself as a social reformer and published a periodical advocating co-operation among the various Syrian confessional groups and calling for the unity of his mother country. While in Brazil, the son witnessed among Syrian settlers the same religious exclusiveness and factional rivalries which he had known in his native land, and he was impressed by his father's lofty ideas about national unity and religious tolerance.[23] It was in Brazil that young Sa'ada was inspired by the idea of national unity and began to inquire into the causes of disunity and confessional rivalry; his studies of the history and culture of his native land imbued him with the notion of Syrian unity and the compulsion that he had an obligation—almost a divine call—to return and initiate a movement that would overcome internal dissension and achieve the unity and independence of his mother country.

In 1929 Sa'ada returned to Lebanon and began at once to review the situation and choose the place where he should begin his preaching. After two years of exploration, he decided to start in Bayrut and to appeal to young men of his generation. He found the campus of the American University of Bayrut, where students from neighboring countries assembled, to be the most promising for recruiting followers. Since he had no formal college education, he could scarcely hope to obtain a lectureship; he therefore offered to teach German to students desiring to learn foreign languages in informal classes. During the academic year of 1931–32, his teaching brought him into direct contact with students, some of whom formed the nucleus of the party in 1932. Within four or five years, the number grew to nearly a thousand, and the party claimed membership of several thousands shortly before the war broke out. At the outset the party was a secret organization, which prompted the authorities to arrest him in 1935 on charges of founding an unlicensed organization and conspiring against the security of the state. After serving

[23] During my visit to South America in 1936, shortly before Sa'ada had left for Lebanon, I was impressed by the depth of confessional and local rivalry among Syrian settlers both in Brazil and Argentina despite efforts to reconcile them (see my "al-'Arab fi America al-Junubiya" [The Arabs in South America] *al-Mu'alim al-Jadid*, [1939], pp. 133–43).

six months in prison, he was released in 1936 only to be arrested again, imprisoned and released after short detainment. In 1937 Sa'ada obtained permission to establish a press for his party and the activities of his followers became visible and widely publicized in several Lebanese and Syrian cities. In 1938 he decided to extend his preaching to Syrian émigrés in the New World in order to secure their support for his work at home. On his way he visited Italy and Germany, whose leaders as well as their totalitarian regimes he admired. From Germany, he went to Brazil and Argentina to organize branches of his party among Syrian settlers. Shortly after his arrival, the war broke out and he found himself cut off from the headquarters of the party. The French authorities in Syria and Lebanon disbanded the party and detained some members on allegations of their secret contacts with the Axis Powers. It was not until 1944, when national regimes were re-established in Syria and Lebanon, that the party obtained permission to resume its activities. Sa'ada, however, was unable to return and assume actual leadership until 1947.[24]

Since Sa'ada's aim was to unite geographical Syria into one country, he formulated the doctrines of the party on premises which would supersede forces of disunity. He was also opposed to symbols of Arab nationalism because its advocates stressed Arab history, religion, and culture which were, in his views, the product of a decadent civilization and the cause of dissension and confessional conflicts. He saw in Syria's identification with Arab nationalism a surrender of its unique qualities and, in becoming part of a larger country that was less advanced or progressive than Syria, the acceptance of an inferior status. Sa'ada also denied the ethnic basis of Arab nationalism that became evident to him when he had witnessed some Arab leaders claiming their Arab tribal origin. On the strength of the evidence of science, he said, he was not prepared to accept

[24] For an account on the founding of the party and on Sa'ada's background, see Labib Z. Yamak, *The Syrian Social Nationalist Party: An Ideological Analysis* (Cambridge, Mass., 1966), chap. 4; Jamil Sawaya, "The Genesis of the Syrian Social Nationalist Party," in K. H. Karpat (ed.), *Political and Social Thought in the Contemporary Middle East* (New York, 1968), pp. 98–102.

the ethnic origin of nations because every nation is a commixture of races, generated by migrations and intermarriages.

The ingredients of Syrian nationalism as recognized by Sa'ada were three: geography, history, and population. To geography he attached the primary importance in the emergence of nations and the formation of national character, although he conceded that geography is not an absolute factor because its effects diminish as civilizations grow. He maintained that in the history of every nation, especially in the initial stage, geography plays the most important role; and, in support of his view, he quoted writers who stressed the geographical factor, such as: "A nation is the product of the marriage between a group of people and a tract of land." [25] The Syrian region, extending from the Mediterranean to the Persian Gulf, is a homeland ideally suited to create the Syrian nation: its natural boundaries, its fertile lands, and its location and climate which conspire to produce an unusually gifted people. Syria, however, is not only the small area confined between the Mediterranean and the Arabian Peninsula; it comprises, in his eyes, the whole region from the Taurus Mountains to the Arabian Peninsula and from the Mediterranean to the Zagros Mountains and the Persian borders. Thus, it includes Cilicia, Syria, Lebanon, Palestine (including Jordan and Israel), the Sinai Peninsula, and Cyprus. He almost adopted the term Fertile Crescent instead of Syria as a symbol of identity, since some had objected that certain parts of 'Iraq, Sinai, and Cyprus could hardly be regarded as parts of geographical Syria. However, the adoption of this term by some Arab nationalists as a means to unite Syria with 'Iraq prompted Sa'ada to reject it; very soon he also dropped the word Syria from the name of the party, and was satisfied by the qualifying terms "National" or "Social National."

The history of Syria, according to Sa'ada, was not merely the period of Arab "domination," which Arab nationalists have stressed, but the entire history from the Stone Age to the present. The Canaanites, in his view, were the first people to

[25] Sa'ada, *Nushu' al-Umam* [Evolution of Nations] (Damascus, 2nd. ed., 1951), p. 161.

stress an attachment to the land and create a nation which came to be known as the Phoenician nation.[26] The Arab period was but a chapter in Syrian history and Arab rule was influenced by the geography and indigenous character of the Syrians, which made it different from Arab rule in the Arabian Peninsula reflecting the national character of Arab rulers. The continuous history of Syria created the Syrian nation, and Syrian history influenced world history and contributed to world civilization. To identify Syrian nationalism with Arab nationalism, Sa'ada said, means that the former is subordinated to the latter. To Sa'ada this is neither historically true nor is it right to ignore the enduring national forces produced by Syrian history extending in time much longer than Arab history. The Syrian nation, as product of the interaction between Syria's geographical environment and its perpetual history, possesses a permanent national character of its own: it is one of the great nations of the world and has played its own role in history. Every Syrian should be proud of his nation's contributions to civilization, but the Syrians today, divided and dominated by foreigners, are unaware of this fact. It is then the duty of the Syrian National Party to make Syrians conscious of themselves in order to occupy their deserved place in the modern world.

From the beginning Sa'ada, unlike many contemporary leaders, displayed complete devotion to his task and spent all his time and energy spreading his doctrines and paying no attention to personal gain or convenience. Like ancient prophets, he conceived of himself as having a mission and he was determined to carry it out at any cost. Never before in Syria's modern history had a leader possessed such conviction, vigilance, strength of character, and charisma. In the eyes of many a critic he appeared as vain and ostentatious, but his earnestness and dedication commanded public respect.

After his return to Lebanon in 1947, Sa'ada embarked at once on preaching his doctrines with renewed vigor. This brought him once again into conflict not with the French,

[26] Sa'ada, *Nushu' al-Umam*, chap. 7.

since French control had come to an end, but with native authorities. He began to reformulate the concept of Syrian nationalism, giving it more positive content. The name of the party, changed in his absence to the Nationalist Party, was formally adopted as the Social Nationalist Party, reflecting the stress on social and economic elements in the program of the party.

In 1948 Sa'ada gave a series of talks to party members in which he reformulated the Syrian ideology to distinguish it from free enterprise which, he said, produced a capitalist society, and from communism, which subjected the individual to state servitude. He wanted to establish a corporate society based on "social nationalism," in which the individual is born and acquires rights corresponding to his services, as a constituent element of his ideology. "Society," he maintained, "is not a product of human will nor does it come into being when a number of individuals agree among themselves to enter into a social contract." [27] According to this view, the individual derives his status from society and, in contradistinction to the doctrine of natural rights, has no inherent rights—whatever rights he may enjoy are derived from his membership in society. Sa'ada maintained that the society which his ideology sought to establish would strike a balance between capitalist and communist societies; but his stress on the totality of the group left little or no room for the individual—or class—to enjoy a separate existence. Sa'ada's society seems to possess collectivist attributes, although emphasis is laid on spirtual rather than non-spiritual values. His stress on the corporate character of society is a reaction to the individualism of Arab society which often tends to subordinate group interests to the individual. To Sa'ada, Arab society seemed primitive.

On the basis of his general view of society Sa'ada proceeded to review the assumptions of the Syrian nation and social

[27] Sa'ada, "al-Majmu' wa al-Mujtama'," *al-Nizam al-Jadid*, vol. I (1948), 49 (Yamak's translation, *The Syrian Social Nationalist Party*, p. 101); see also Sa'ada's *Nushu' al-Umam*, pp. 143–44.

nationalism.[28] The basic principles of the party, reformulated after World War II, were as follows:

1. Syria is for the Syrians and the Syrians are a complete nation;
2. The Syrian national cause is an integral cause completely distinct from any other cause;
3. The Syrian cause is the cause of the Syrian nation and the Syrian homeland;
4. The Syrian nation is the product of the ethnic unity of the Syrian people which developed throughout history and goes back even to prehistoric times;
5. The Syrian homeland is the geographical environment in which the Syrian nation emerged. It has natural boundaries which separate it from other countries, extending from the Zagros Mountains in the northeast, to the Suez Canal and the Red Sea in the south, including the Sinai Peninsula and the Gulf of 'Aqaba; and from the Syrian [Mediterranean] Sea in the west, including the Island of Cyprus, to the arch of the Arabian Desert and the Persian Gulf in the east. This region is also called the Syrian Fertile Crescent, whose star is the Island of Cyprus;
6. The Syrian nation forms a single society;
7. The Syrian social national movement derives its inspiration from the talents of the Syrian nation and from its cultural, political, and national history;
8. The Syrian national interests are above all other interests.[29]

In order to establish the society which he envisaged, Sa'ada laid down five reform measures which he regarded as absolutely necessary for the implementation of basic principles. These were: the separation of church from state; the prevention of interference by the clergy in political and judicial affairs; the removal of all barriers separating one religious and

[28] Sa'ada, "Ta'alim wa Shuruh fi al-'Aqida al-Qawmiya al-Ijtima'iya," *al-Nizam al-Jaddid*, no. 8 (1950), pp. 84ff.

[29] For a discussion of these principles, see *ibid.*, pp. 11–33.

confessional group from another; the abolition of feudal rights and the reorganization of the national economy based on fair distribution of production among workers and due regard to the interests of the nation and the state; and the establishment of a strong national army which could play an effective role in the self-determination of the nation and the homeland.[30]

Sa'ada's ideology attracted many young men, both Christians and Muslims, in Lebanon and Syria, who saw in it not only a new symbol of identity that would supersede local and confessional jealousies, but a new way of life which would enable the new generation to take an active part and eventually to provide new leadership. These goals might have also attracted young men in other Arab countries, where there was need for a new ideology and leadership, if they did not have certain mental reservations about the validity of some of Sa'ada's basic principles, such as his claim that the Syrian homeland, consisting of the entire Fertile Crescent, is separate from the rest of the Arab world and that its history transcends Arab history. Sa'ada's ideas appeared unintelligible to almost all Arabs who had been brought up in the traditions of Arab history and culture, and his stress on the Syrian nation as distinct from the Arab nation was regarded as contrary to Arab national ideals. Most objectionable, of course, was his repudiation of Arab spiritual and cultural values which formed the very basis of Arab national consciousness not only to Arabs outside the frontiers of Sa'ada's national homeland but also to Arabs within the region in which he sought to establish the Syrian homeland.[31] Had he been will-

[30] *al-Nizam al-Jadid*, no. 8 (1948), pp. 36–47; Yamak, *The Syrian Social Nationalist Party*, chap. 6. For a translation of some of Sa'ada's writings on basic principles, see Karpat, *Political and Social Thought*, pp. 87–98.

[31] The most trenchant critic of Sa'ada on the ground of his opposition to Arab nationalism and disregard of Arab history and culture is Sati' al-Husri, see p. 205, below. For Husri's writings on Sa'ada and his party, see his *al-'Uruba Bayn Du'atuha wa Mu'aridiha* [Arabism Between Its Advocates and Opponents] (Bayrut, 1952), pp. 96ff: and *Difa'un 'An al-'Uruba* [In Defence of Arabism] (Bayrut, 1956), pp. 15ff. For a reply by a member of the Syrian National Party to Husri's criticism, see Sami al-Khuri, *Raddun 'Ala Sati' al-Husri* [A Reply to Sati' al-Husri] (Bayrut, 1956).

ing to identify Syrian with Arab nationalism and included the Arabic culture and language as integral elements of his nationalism, his ideology might have appealed to wider circles both within and outside Syria and Lebanon. Sa'ada was not satisfied to spread his ideology by peaceful methods; from the very beginning he came into conflict with the authorities and did not shrink from resorting to violence in order to achieve power despite his inadequate preparation for overthrowing the existing regime by force. After the execution of Sa'ada in 1949, his successors followed the same hazardous course of violence which gave the authorities the pretext to outlaw the party, notwithstanding that the ideology continued to appeal to certain elements in Syria and Lebanon. The inherent weaknesses of this ideology were primarily responsible for the collapse of the party and its demise was hastened by its many active and often violent opponents some of whom were Ba'thists.

Romantic Nationalism

In contradistinction to Syrian nationalism, the Ba'th Party has expounded a national ideology broader in scope and basic assumptions, and steeped in Arab culture and historical heritage. It is true, as Munif al-Razzaz, one of the Ba'th leaders, stated that Arab nationalism was based on several factors, including geography and culture, but the significance of each factor varied from one school of thought to another. Razzaz maintained that there is the broad concept of Arab nationalism, which the Ba'th Party advocated, and the narrow local nationalism, reflecting parochial feeling, which would be eventually superseded by Arab nationalism. He added:

> Because the matter [i.e. nationalism] defied exact definition, it is perhaps inevitable that there should be arguments between Arab Nationalists and those who identify themselves as Syrian Nationalists or those who identify with a pharaonic past. Are the people of Syria merely Syrians, or are they Arabs? The various spokesmen of these groups have tried to attack this question logically, but logic cannot

> solve such problems. If one confines oneself to very ancient history, to a limited geographic setting and to the accidents of modern history relegating to the background such factors as language and civilization, then the Syrians are Syrians and the Egyptians are Egyptians. But, if one also takes cognizance of such factors as common language, extended history, and 'broad' culture, then the Syrians and Egyptians alike must be classified as parts of the Arab nation.[32]

Arab nationalism, in Michel 'Aflaq's view, is the embodiment of the Arab spirit.[33] Language, history, and traditions, important as they are, are only external bonds. Nationalism means a striving toward the national goal and a will to progress which awakens whenever the nation's course of progress is retarded or existing conditions deteriorate and the nation lags behind the progress of the world. Arab nationalism is thus the "procession" of the Arab nation toward the realization of its needs and aspirations. These aspirations embody the views of the nation on life and society, now and in the future, and are the product of the nation's character and the values which it wants to realize. In other words, Arab nationalism now is an emanation of all the interacting inner forces, values, and ambitions held by the Arab nation: this nation has a mission which is the realization of its ideal. The process of this realization constitutes the Arab nation's experiences in the awakening of its people, solving their problems and raising their standard of living.

Arab nationalism is formulated as an ideology which would achieve its goals in two stages, each stage embodied in a movement intimately connected with the other. The first is the emancipation of Arab lands from imperialism, the second the unification of the Arab homeland. The first cannot completely disappear until the second one is realized. There seems to be nothing new in this formulation, for Arab thinkers have been

32 Munif al-Razzaz, *Tatawwur Ma'na al-Qawmiya* (Bayrut, 1960), pp. 18–19; tr., Ibrahim Abu Lughod, *The Evolution of the Meaning of Nationalism* (New York, 1963), pp. 7–8.

33 For a brief discussion on 'Aflaq's background and his views of Arab Socialism, see pp. 153 ff. above.

calling for independence and unity long before the Ba'th came into existence. But the Ba'th Party was perhaps the first ideological group to put forth Arab unity as a primary demand and to call for a revolutionary approach to achieve it. Even if some of the Arab countries have not yet achieved independence, the Ba'th leaders asserted, Arabs must work for unity so that they can continue to struggle for unity when independence is eventually achieved. The Ba'th's call for unity came indeed at a time when the Arabs were in greatest need for it, that is, when it became evident that the Arabs were unable to stand up to Israel as a result of disunity. The Ba'th expressed this point in its well-known slogan of "common Arab destiny," which was an apt cry against bickering Arab leaders who revealed their negativism, traditionalism, and vested interests.[34]

The Ba'th viewed independence and unity as two inseparable aspects of one national goal and asserted that, even before independence is achieved, the Arabs must prepare for unity—each unit perceiving itself as part of the Arab whole—so that when independence is achieved, unity could follow.

Arab nationalism is a process of evolution: it will never stop and it will never disappear. The values of Arab nationalism are truth, goodness, and justice. These are not the product of economic conditions because they do not represent the will and interest of a group of individuals, but, on the contrary, they are the manifestations of the nation's love for truth, goodness, tolerance, co-operation and progress.

This concept of nationalism is different from the European concept, because it is based on the doctrine of the nation's will to live, not on economic conditions. The will of the Arab nation to live is derived from the present Arab stage of development, the product of a historical process that has been in progress for generations. No one can reverse this process by a voluntary or arbitrary action. In the last analysis, Arab nationalism is "the predetermined heritage of the Arab individual which created his personality in the formation of which he had no choice."

[34] Michel 'Aflaq, *Ma'rakat al-Masir al-Wahid* [Struggle for the Common Destiny] (Bayrut, 1958), pp. 18–24.

The task of the Ba'th Party concerning Arab nationalism is to express the Arab spirit through a practical approach, but the ultimate goal is the realization of the Arab ideal. Idealism and pragmatism are not two opposed goals, but two stages in the process of development. For 'Aflaq, realism in politics is a preliminary form of idealism: it is the parade ground where the Party can exercise itself and then progress in an ascending manner to reveal ultimately the reality of the Arab spirit.[35]

Religion, and the Islamic religion in particular, is an important element in Arab nationalism as its spiritual manifestation. Islam is closely linked with the Arab spirit and it is a symbol of its identity. It offers an ideal form of existence to believers, and it was revealed originally to the Arabs because their virtues had made them fit to transmit its eternal message.

Islam and Arabism have always been used to express the inner spirit of the Arab nation. In the past, Islam represented the strength of the Arabs. In its modern manifestation, Islam appears in the form of Arab nationalism. Arab society lacked a spiritual message until Islam had provided one. Thus Islam is the embodiment of the spirit of the Arab nation, and through Islam this spirit can acquire the force to achieve the nation's goals of truth, faith, and goodness. Of all nations, according to 'Aflaq, the Arabs alone possess this spirtual element for their nationalist renaissance.

True, religion ideally always favors the good and sides with the oppressed; but it may also become an instrument of the oppressor and reactionary elements. The Ba'th interprets religion as meaning progress and rejects mythical beliefs which lead to dissension and petty jealousies. True religion is an important element of Arab nationalism, although Arab nationalism is not based on religion alone.[36]

Arab nationalism is not viewed as opposed to other

[35] Tarif Khalidi, "A Critical Study of the Political Ideas of Michel 'Aflaq," *Middle East Forum*, 42 (1966), 55–68.

[36] See 'Aflaq, *Fi Sabil al-Ba'th* (Bayrut, 2nd. ed., 1963), pp. 122–36. For the translation of one of 'Aflaq's articles on religion, see Karpat, *Political and Social Thought*, pp. 192–95.

nationalisms; it rather pays due respect to them. This is because Arab nationalism is humanistic in outlook and tries, like other nationalisms, to contribute to humanism the ideals of tolerance, love, co-operation, and peaceful relationships with other nations. History, in 'Aflaq's eyes, is viewed as the history of humanity in the form of each nation's striving to achieve its goals of freedom, unity, and socialism.[37]

'Aflaq also views Arab nationalism as an "eternal Arab idea," (*risala khalida*). It is a progressive manifestation of the Arab idea which assumes various forms at various historical periods. In this age, nationalism calls for unity, freedom, and socialism. Broadly speaking, nationalism is viewed as an eternal phenomenon manifested in various forms in various stages of history. History, according to 'Aflaq, is determined by two forces: humanism and nationalism. The latter is the force within each nation working in harmony with the former broader force. Thus, 'Aflaq's views of Arab nationalism form a particular part of his general view of nationalism as a universal phenomenon, and the role he assigns to the Arab nation in achieving its goals is an aspect of the role humanity plays in achieving the goals of the human race.

The significance of the Ba'th's philosophy of Arab nationalism lies in its comprehensive view of nationalism within which all other views are included: it is capable of embodying them all because it is both general and vague, romantic in character rather than realistic. One may even be tempted to call it mystical, in the sense of 'Aflaq's idea of nationalism being essentially love of one's own countrymen comparable to al-Hallaj's love of God.[38]

[37] 'Aflaq, *Ma'rakat al-Masir al-Wahid*, pp. 131–35. See also 'Abd-Allah 'Abd al-Da'im, *al-Qawmiya wa al-Insaniya* [Nationalism and Humanism] (Bayrut, 1957).

[38] 'Aflaq's ideas are expressed in a series of articles published on various occasions, but he has not yet formulated them into a coherent and systematic study. Such an attempt has been made by Munif al-Razzaz, one of the Ba'th leaders, but his words should not be taken to represent 'Aflaq's ideas specifically, since Razzaz often expresses his own ideas. For a translation of some of 'Aflaq's writings, see S. G. Haim, *Arab Nationalism*, pp. 242–49; K. H. Karpat, *Political and Social Thought*, pp. 189–97.

Secular Nationalism

Christian Arab thinkers who advocated Arab nationalism consciously tried to avoid identifying religion with nationalism and stressed the linguistic and cultural components of nationalism. Even Christian writers like Zurayq and Rabbath, who tried to regard Islam as an element of nationalism, made it clear that they spoke of the ethical and spiritual aspects of Islam rather than its strictly religious or doctrinal aspects. Only one Muslim thinker, making a sharp distinction between religion and nationalism, stressed the secular elements of nationalism and formulated perhaps more clearly and consistently than any other writer a systematic and coherent theory of Arab nationalism—Sati' al-Husri.

Growing up under the late Hamidian regime, Husri spoke Turkish as his native tongue and was thoroughly at home in Turkey, although he was born in the Yaman in 1880 and his parents were Arabs from Aleppo. He studied in Turkish schools and learned Turkish and French before he began to study Arabic after he settled in Arab lands following World War I. From the time of his graduation from school in 1900 until he left Turkey in 1919, he was in the service of the Ottoman government and taught in schools which he established in Istanbul. It was during his service in the Balkans that he developed his conception of secular nationalism. He came to the conclusion that what separated Greeks, Bulgars, and Serbs, though all Christians, from the Turks was not religion but their distinct linguistic and cultural background. He found the Balkan peoples quarrelling more fiercely among themselves on national issues than with the Turks, and he concluded that differences in language and culture were more deeply ingrained in nations than religious differences. No less significant was his attraction to positivist philosophy, then fashionable among young Ottoman thinkers. He once told this author that in school he had studied, among other subjects, Islamic law (*Shari'a*) and was struck by how antiquated the method used to teach it was then compared with the method of teaching physical sciences. The scientific method, which helped him to study social problems objectively, had attracted him from his early days and he remained faithful to this method and to positivist philosophy to the end of his life.

After World War I, Husri settled in the Arab world. In 1919 he went to Damascus to serve as Minister of Education in Faysal's Arab Government and reorganize its educational system. From 1921 to 1941, he served in 'Iraq as an educator, both in administrative and teaching capacities, and as head of the Department of Antiquities. For a short period during World War II, he served again in Damascus as an adviser on education, and then after the war he moved to Cairo where he was head of the newly established Institute of Arab Higher Studies of the Arab League until he retired in 1957. He died in 1968. His impressive literary output dealt almost exclusively with Arab nationalism, its theory and practice.[39]

Husri returned to the Arab world at a mature age; therefore he was able to approach Arab problems as an outsider who viewed them with a fresh and unbiased eye though not without sympathy. His past experiences in a foreign country and the absence of religious or social biases which often limit Arab thinkers brought up in their own social environment, helped him to give objective answers to Arab national questions, especially in the educational field. In this respect Husri was ahead of his time; in his ability to apply rational and naturalistic methods to social problems he surpassed even the new generation of Arab intellectuals.

However, the political conditions in the Arab world after World War I had a certain negative influence on some of Husri's premises of Arab nationalism. While in Turkey, he took no active part in politics and viewed national issues with a high degree of objectivity. After his return to the Arab world, where French and British control came into conflict with Arabs on national questions in which Husri's views were directly involved, his ideas of Arab nationalism were neces-

[39] For Husri's life, see two of his yet incomplete memoirs *Mudhakkirati fi al-'Iraq* (Bayrut, 1967–68).

sarily affected by political considerations, and the achievement of independence necessarily became the immediate goal of Arab nationalism in his eyes. After independence had been achieved, the next step was to achieve unity and thus the goals of nationalism remained in his eyes essentially political. Asked by the present writer as to what would be his preference for the system of government after unity is achieved, he replied that the form of government was of no great interest to him; it would be the responsibility of the generation after him. At the present, he added, public attention should focus on the problem of unity: it is the national duty of every Arab to support the leader who is capable of achieving Arab unity. In this respect, Husri's nationalist goals scarcely went beyond the aims of men of his generation.

Apart from the negative aspects of nationalism, reflecting essentially his personal experiences and frustrations, Husri's writings on the nature and components of nationalism are thorough and objective primarily because foreign intervention had no direct bearing on the positive elements of Arab nationalism or his formulation of a theory of nationalism. It is in this field that his writings are most significant.

Husri's theory of Arab nationalism is based on one fundamental assumption—his conception of "Arab" and "Arab people." Anyone who speaks the Arabic language is, in his eyes, an Arab and belongs to the Arab people. The full development of nationalism necessarily transforms the people into a "nation," and the nation into a single "state." "Lucky are the nations," he opined on the ultimate goal of nationalism, "that have achieved their national unity and completed their political personality, so that their international boundaries coincide with their national frontiers." [40] At such a stage patriotism *(al-wataniya)*, which means loyalty to the homeland, does not come into conflict with nationalism, which means loyalty to the nation. But if a nation is divided into more than one state, then patriotism necessarily becomes the subject of disagreement between those who want the unity

[40] Husri, *Ara' wa Ahadith fi al-Qawmiya al-'Arabiya* (Cairo, 1951), p. 44.

of the nation—the advocates of nationalism—and those who want to keep it divided—the advocates of patriotism. In the latter situation, the divided nation forms two or more states, and the form in which such states exist—an artificial political structure—does not conform to the true or complete political personality of the people: a single nation in a single state. For this reason, Husri maintains that the ultimate goal of the nationalism of a divided nation is to unite and form one state; and if one or more of these states have lost their independence the aim of nationalism will be to restore independence to them and then to unite them into a single state.

From this step Husri proceeds to the next logical one by inquiring into the elements constituting nationalism. He dismisses the theory of the common origin (i.e. ethnic unity) of a nation as contrary to scientific and historical evidence. There is no nation which can claim to be racially pure. He also refutes Renan's doctrine of the will of the group to form a nation, and argues that this will is not the cause but the consequence or the manifestation of other elements—language and history. True, he says, nationalism may exist in a dormant condition, and the need to awaken the national consciousness means to arouse the people's faith in the future of their nation and to realize its national goals. In the case of the Arabs, this awakening is manifest in the call for independence (if independence has not yet been achieved) and unity. The aim is for all Arab peoples to form a single nation and a single state. Husri's own intellectual message is to awaken the national consciousness of the Arabs for realization of this ultimate goal.

The bonds which form a nation are spiritual and intellectual rather than material. For this reason Husri attaches a secondary importance to geography and common economic interests, although he realizes how important a role material interests play in the life of individuals and groups. He maintains that these cannot be regarded as constituent elements of nationalism, and they may even run contrary to national unity. As to religion, which he admits to be significant as a social force, he maintains that it can be a unifying as well as divisive factor. A national religion, as Judaism, may become a basic element in nationalism; but universal religions, like Christianity and Islam, do not recognize national differences and therefore weaken national consciousness. For this reason Islam, stressing universal values, cannot become a constituent element of Arab nationalism.

The two pillars in the national foundation of a nation are history and language; the latter is the most important cohesive factor which distinguishes one nation from another. The functions of language, according to Husri, are the following:

> Language is, first of all, the avenue of communication between people; secondly, it is the vehicle of thought for the individual; and thirdly, it provides the medium for the transmission of ideas and the heritage of the fathers to succeeding sons [generations];
>
> Thus we find that unity of language produces a kind of community of feeling and thought, and binds individuals together with a long chain formed of ideational and emotional links;
>
> Since the language differs from group to group, it is natural that the aggregate of the individuals who share a language should manifest a mutual destiny, similarity and sympathy more than others do. Thus they constitute a nation separate from other nations. . . .[41]

Next to language, history is the other basic element in nationalism and is described, in Husri's words, as "the nation's expression of its memory and self-consciousness." History, according to Husri, creates a kind of "moral kinship" and it "brings people nearer to each other." If a nation were subjugated to foreign domination and lost its self-consciousness, "that self-consciousness will not be recovered until it recalls and goes back to that history." [42] Husri distinguished between the history of scholars, whose object is to investigate historical events, from the history which is alive in souls and minds of

[41] Husri, *Muhadarat fi Nushu' al-Fikra al-Qawmiya*, p. 20 (translation of the quotation by L. M. Kenny, in "Sati' al-Husri's Views on Arab nationalism," *The Middle East Journal*, 17 [1963], 238).

[42] *Ibid.*, p. 21.

the people. It is the latter which nations remember and represents glories of the past and creates hopes for the future. If a nation forgets its history it loses its feeling and self-consciousness, and it recovers national consciousness by going back to its history.

Husri discusses Arab nationalism not as a separate phenomenon but in the context of other nationalist movements. He traces the origins of modern nationalism in Western Europe, its spread into eastern Europe and the Balkans, and finally into the Ottoman empire. Arab nationalism emerged as a consequence of the awakening of the national consciousness of the other peoples of the Ottoman empire, despite the bond of religion which had united Turks and Arabs in the past.[43]

Husri advocates a secular type of Arab nationalism, completely divorced from religion. His argument is based partly on the nature of Islam, which stresses universal rather than national values; partly on the historical experiences of the Arabs among whom nationalism emerged as a reaction against Islamic unity; and party because of the existence of Christian Arabs in Arab lands, whose bonds of unity with other Arabs are language and history. Last, but not least, is Husri's own position toward the relationship between religion and the state. He is firmly committed to the doctrine of separation and believes that in the modern age religion should be a matter of individual conscience.[44]

Husri also discusses several obstacles that stand in the way of realizing Arab national goals: the most important are foreign pressures which run contrary to national unity and the consequential vested interest created to perpetuate foreign influence. He saw in parochial feelings, such as Egyptian and Lebanese regional patriotisms, barriers to national unity, but he maintained that these were ephemeral cross-currents which would be eventually superseded by Arab nationalism. Husri

[43] Husri gave a series of lectures in Cairo in 1948 in which he discussed the rise of nationalism in Europe and its spread to the Arab world (see *ibid.*, pp. 2–24, 116–56, 158–206).

[44] Husri, *al-'Uruba Awwalan* [Arab Nationalism First] (Bayrut, 1955), pp. 99–108.

criticized Sa'ada's Syrian nationalism on the ground of its local exclusiveness.[45] He was, however, at first attracted to the Ba'th ideology and its stress on Arab unity because he saw in it certain similarities to his conception of nationalism; but when the Ba'th supported Syria's secession from the United Arab Republic in 1961 contrary to its assertion of the principle of Arab unity, he denounced the Ba'th leaders as advocates of parochialism (*iqlimiya*) rather than of Arab unity.[46]

Husri's analysis of Arab nationalism reveals an appreciation of the social and cultural forces which determined its scope and character. He studied Arab history with a keen eye and concluded that essentially what brought the Arab nation to life in modern times were the Arabic language and Arab history. In addition to his scientific approach, he had a grasp of the universality of human phenomena and tried to study Arab problems in the context of the larger human problems. His secular views often helped him to study with detachment Arab problems, although he possessed his own political prejudices, such as stressing the overriding principles of Arab unity and the forming of a single nation-state; and he criticized others who preached other variants of Arab nationalism.[47]

Irredentist Nationalism

Pan-Arabism, as we have already had occasion to notice, tacitly embodied an element of irredentism because the Arabs had, by migration or acculturation, become closely intermingled with other peoples, especially Turks and Persians. Moreover, the political boundaries drawn up first between the Ottoman empire and Persia and then between Turkey and the Arab countries did not always follow "national" lines. However, irredentism was vague and scarcely perceptible in

[45] Husri, *al-'Uruba Bayn Du'atuha wa Mu'ariduha*, pp. 69ff.

[46] Husri, *al-Iqlimiya: Judhuruha wa Budhuruha* (Bayrut, 1963), pp. 49–116, 158–63, 213–97.

[47] Cf. Elias Marqus, *Naqd al-Fikr al-Qawmi: Sati' al-Husri* [A Critique of Arab National Thought: Sati' al-Husri] (Bayrut, 1966).

the early inter-war years because Arab nationalists were too much preoccupied with a struggle for independence to pay attention to such questions. Two incidents may be said to have had direct or indirect effect on irredentism. First, the overthrow of Shaykh Khaz'al, the hereditary Arab provincial governor of Arabistan (Khuzistan)—the area lying east to the Shatt al-'Arab and the Persian Gulf—and his replacement by a Persian over an essentially Arab population in 1924; the other was the annexation of the sanjak of Alexandretta (Iskenderun) by Turkey in 1939. The first incident, though it aroused the indignation of the native Arabs in Muhammara (Khorramshahr) and their closely connected Arab neighbors of 'Iraq, stirred no nationalist agitation in other Arab countries.[48] The second incident aroused greater agitation in the Levant than in other Arab countries, but it prompted the Alexandrettan Arabs who had the occasion to visit Arab countries to arouse nostalgic feelings among young nationalists and to identify irredentism with Pan-Arabism.[49]

Some of the Alexandrettans who settled in Damascus, like Zaki al-Arsuzi and some of his followers, proved instrumental in the dissemination of revolutionary ideas among young nationalists. Although Arsuzi preferred to work independently and to influence young men directly, some of his followers joined either the Ba'th or other radical ideological groups with which they shared revolutionary ideas. In Arsuzi's eyes, Turkey's annexation of Alexandretta was not merely the loss of an Arab territory but a serious blow to Pan-Arabism. To

[48] For centuries Arab tribes lived in the area of the Persian Gulf head, but only in recent times an Arab paramount shaykh ruled over his tribesmen and enjoyed a large measure of autonomy within the Persian political structure. Shaykh Khaz'al entered into treaty relations with Britain to strengthen his position, but this Arab enclave came into conflict with the revival of Persian nationalism under Riza Khan (see A. J. Toynbee, *Survey of International Affairs*, vol. I: *The Islamic World Since the Peace Settlement*, 1925 [London, 1927], pp. 539–43; and Qadri Qal'achi, *al-Khalij al-'Arabi* [The Arab Gulf] (Bayrut, 1965), pp. 605–13.

[49] For a discussion of the annexation of Alexandretta by Turkey and its impact on the Arabs, see my *Qadiyat al-Iskandaruna* (Damascus, 1953). For a summary of the legal and diplomatic aspects of this question, see my "The Alexandretta Dispute," *American Journal of International Law*, 39 (1945), 406–24.

achieve the goal of Pan-Arabism, he called for a social revolution which would create a new social order capable of uniting the Arabs and restoring to them their lost territories—Alexandretta and Palestine. The new social order, according to him, should be based on Arab nationalism, socialism, and opposition to imperialism, to be achieved through revolutionary processes. Arsuzi said nothing new which the Ba'th leaders had not expressed in their program but, significantly, he began to preach these ideas before the Ba'th Party had yet been organized. Some of the dissident Ba'th leaders who seized power in the mid-sixties claimed to have derived spiritual guidance from his teachings and hailed him after his death in 1968 as a national hero. Although an articulate and prolific writer, Arsuzi developed no special doctrine of irredentism; he believed that Pan-Arabism, in which irredentism was embodied, would be the sure way to restore Alexandretta to the Arabs.[50]

The cause which has given a clear expression to irredentist views is, of course, the loss of Palestine. From the days when this country was still under the Mandate, the Arabs of Palestine made it crystal clear to other Arab countries that their struggle against the establishment of the Jewish National Home was not merely a local opposition to the influx of Jewish immigration into Palestine but a general stand against Zionism—a threat to the Arab world as a whole. Only slowly did the other Arab countries begin to realize this threat, especially toward the end of World War II, and they collectively intervened to prevent by their armed forces the establishment of Israel in 1948–49. In the first two wars—the wars of 1948–49 and 1956—Arab rulers had reason to complain that foreign intervention handicapped their confrontation with Israel, but in the third war (1967) Arab rulers proved utterly

[50] Like 'Aflaq, Arsuzi received his education in France, but he displayed an aversion to the West because he believed that the European Powers, especially France, were responsible for the Arab loss of Alexandretta, his birthplace. For his political views, see his *Mashakiluna al-Qawmiya* [Our National Problems] (Damascus, 1958); *al-Jumhuriya al-Muthla* [The Ideal Republic] (Damascus, 1965); and *Sawt al-'Uruba fi Liwa' al-Iskandaruna* [Voice of Arabism in the Province of Alexandretta] (Damascus, n.d.).

incapable of standing up to Israel's challenge. As a result, Arab irredentist feelings ran very high, a feeling which, if Israeli threats and retaliations should continue, may well place irredentism above all Arab national goals and change the character of Pan-Arabism.

The June war demonstrated that neither revolutionary regimes of the new generation nor Nasir's leadership were strong enough to repulse Israel's attacks, much less to overcome this imminent threat to Arab nationalism. If Arab nationalism were ever to achieve its goals, Israel's attacks had to be first repulsed and then reduced. Irredentism began to dominate Arab thought and became the overriding aspect of Arab nationalism; the political manoeuvres and commando activities that have ensued since the June war were but instruments giving expression to this doctrine.

Another new generation is now slowly but vigorously coming to the fore and it may well eventually replace the generation that brought to power the rulers of existing regimes. This generation, born in the frustrations and difficult circumstances that followed the creation of Israel, is made up of essentially younger men who blame Israel for all the miseries that have befallen them and are therefore ready to embark on a war of attrition, regardless of how long and costly this war may be.

The Palestine Liberation Movement, as this new political trend is called, is essentially an irredentist movement. Its immediate aim is not to re-establish Arab rule in Palestine, since Israel is too formidable an enemy to be defeated at the present moment. Its immediate purpose is to impress upon all Arabs that the Palestine problem is the central issue in Arab nationalism, to remind them constantly that what they consider the greatest injustice ever committed in history was inflicted on them, and to focus the conscience of mankind on the Arab feeling of injustice and the necessity of bringing the Palestine question for discussion in all international conferences.

Thinking along these lines naturally began to develop first among young Palestinians and then other Arabs who realized that old concepts of Arab nationalism were no longer relevant to the consequences of the June war of 1967. Indeed, young Palestinians began to organize resistance movements of their own—Fath and other organizations—before the June war, but the activities of "freedom fighters" (*fida'iyyin*) were bound to increase after the defeat of the Arab states. Although Fath commanded wider public appeal, due mainly to publicity and to the effective leadership of Yasir 'Arafat, other commandos held essentially the same irredentist views and today Palestine is the central theme of Arab nationalism. Israel, they hold, will not resign herself to being liquidated as a state; this task must be accomplished by a "War of National Liberation." The war must be in the nature of a revolution and may take the form of a surprise *blitzkrieg* or guerrilla warfare, depending on future circumstances. The ultimate objective of the War of Liberation is to re-establish Arab rule in Palestine in which the Jews would be allowed to live as Palestinian citizens. Israel as a Jewish state is rejected and must disappear because it is inconsistent with Arab national goals. Once Palestine is re-established as an Arab state, Arab unity would become again the overriding objective of Arab nationalism. Today the Arabs cannot unite as long as Israel exists. In a word, the liquidation of Israel is considered but a step to the Pan-Arab goal expressed in the motto: Liberation of Palestine is the road to Arab unity.[51]

Retrospect

The assumptions of nationalism which we have just discussed deal essentially with the aims and components of nationalism but pay little or no attention to their relevance to existing social conditions which often run contrary to abstract theories. Even Husri's theoretical structure, based on social and historical analysis, ignores the strength of local or

[51] For a discussion of irredentist views, see Naji 'Alwash, *al-Tariq Ila Filastin* [The Road to Palestine] (Bayrut, 1968); Nadim al-Baytar, *Min al-Naksa Ila al-Thawra* [From Setback to Revolution] (Bayrut, 1968); Faud Qazan, *al-Thawra al-'Arabiya wa Isra'il* [The Arab Revolution and Israel] (Bayrut, 1968); 'Umar Abu al-Nasr, *Ya 'Arab: al-Fida'iyyun* [O Arabs: Freedom Fighters] (Bayrut, n.d.); see also Y. Harkabi, *Fedayeen Action and Arab Strategy* (London, 1969).

regional forces that cannot be dismissed as merely parochial feeling (*iqlimi*) just because they run contrary to Arab unity—the cherished objective of his national ideal. In Egypt, 'Iraq, and Lebanon there has always been a strong feeling favoring the development of local nationalism—Pharaonic, 'Iraqi, or Phoenician—but such local loyalties have neither been adequately recognized within nor reconciled to the broader context of Arab national identity. In order to formulate a realistic theory of nationalism, attention must be paid to the relationship between regionalism and nationalism; the former cannot be dismissed as contrary to national goals because the problem of regionalism exists regardless of theoretical assumptions. The desiderata of the Arab unity conversation of 1963 in Cairo amply demonstrated this fact.[52]

The evidence of the historical experiences of the Arabs, which demonstrates that the type of national unity demanded today has never existed in the past, has not yet been adequately pondered. As a result, the variants of Arab nationalism have vacillated from regional symbols stressing local interest, to broad national symbols stressing cultural values, but no realistic symbol of identity has yet evolved to meet both local and national claims.

No less significant is the absence of positive national objectives. It is true that Arab socialism has been specifically designed to provide such a positive content, but the socialism that President Nasir has proposed is based essentially on Egypt's own experience, as noted before, and cannot provide a positive goal for all the Arab countries, as the experiences of 'Iraq have also demonstrated. At best Nasir's Arab socialism provides a positive content to an Egyptian variant of Arab nationalism. The Ba'th's Arab socialism, reconciling in theory the concepts of democracy, socialism, and nationalism, might be regarded as the nearest approximation to a positive content of Arab nationalism, but this ideology is so vague and abstract that when the Ba'th leaders were entrusted with power it proved to be an impractical program for action.[53]

[52] See chap. 11, below.
[53] See p. 161, above.

Some Arab thinkers have criticized both the exclusive character of nationalism and its lack of positive content, and have demanded in no uncertain terms a reconsideration of national aims on both the regional and national levels. In a lecture given in 1956, George Tu'ma [Tomeh], a liberal thinker sympathetic to the Ba'th leaders, seriously questioned the lack of historical relevance to national goals and called for broader concepts of nationalism consistent with the national and international development of the Arab world.[54] Others, like Khalil Kanna, a liberal politician of 'Iraq's pre-revolutionary period, offered a specific program on the regional level within the framework of Arab nationalism.[55] But nonc of these constructive approaches has yet found wide acceptance, although they are likely to attract the attention of serious thinkers.

Finally, revolutionary principles seem to have been accepted as a means to achieve national goals by almost all Arab nationalists, including Husri, without adequate scrutiny. Indeed, the Arab nationalist movement, from its inception, sought by revolutionary means to achieve independence as well as other national objectives. Even after independence, Arab thinkers who formulated positive aims of nationalism like the Ba'th leaders, continue to stress the revolutionary procedures, although revolutionary processes have not yet proved more effective in achieving reforms than evolutionary procedures.

Contemporary writers on nationalism seem to be more interested in collectivist principles dealing with the welfare of the nation as a whole than with the welfare of the individual. Thus individual liberty and democratic procedures are relegated to a lower level than those principles which deal with national freedom, public security, and social justice. There are, of course, thinkers who regard liberty and democracy as having greater claims, but these are not essentially nationalist writers.[56]

[54] George Tu'ma, *Fi al-Mafhum al-Qawmi* (Bayrut, 1956).

[55] Khalil Kanna, *al-'Iraq: Amsuh wa Ghaduh* (Bayrut, 1966), chap. 20; *'Iraq al-Ghad* (Bayrut, 1968).

[56] For the various meanings of the term "Arab nationalism," see Anis Sayigh, *Tatawwur al-Mafhum al-Qawmi 'Ind al-'Arab* (Bayrut, 1961).

Chapter 9

FREE THOUGHT AND SECULARISM

Liberate your mind from all inherited traditions so that you will not find it difficult to discard a view or a doctrine to which your heart had been comforted or your mind accepted, if they appeared to you contrary to realities.
Isma'il Mazhar

Before discussing the subject of free thought, the question of whether this topic is relevant in a book dealing with Arab political trends must be answered. Religion and politics have always been closely interrelated in Islam, and thus a study of liberal religious thought is deemed necessary. However, no aspect of Arabic thought has been so inadequately treated by Muslims as secular free thought, save to condemn its advocates. This was partly because of the triumph of orthodoxy, but mainly because of the censorship imposed on thinkers who tended to depart from the official creed, notwithstanding some attempts to conceal unorthodox views in seemingly orthodox treatises.[1]

Today, the fate of free thinkers in the Arab world is not much better than in the past; most of those who hold unorthodox views have been reluctant to speak openly because of state

[1] For a discussion of free thought in classical Islam, see 'Abd al-Rahman Badawi, *Min Ta'rikh al-Ilhad fi al-Islam* [A History of Atheism in Islam] (Cairo, 1946); and *Shakhsiyat Qaliqa fi al-Islam* [Uncommitted Personalities to Islam] (Cairo, 1946). For the practice of concealing unorthodox views in orthodox writings, see Leo Strauss, *Persecution and the Art of Writing* (Glencoe, 1949), chap. 2.

censorship and traditional intolerance toward innovations. Association with Western free thought brought them under attack by orthodox thinkers first for their views and then as denounced traitors to their culture, which made their position even more difficult. State censorship, often invoked under popular pressures, does not always result in imprisonment or execution, though popular commotion may reach a high pitch reminiscent of past centuries. Nonetheless, the impact of free thought on current religious and political thought has proved to be far-reaching.

Secularization of Islam: 'Ali 'Abd al-Raziq

Ever since the Kamalist regime took action to separate the state from religion—an action often referred to as the "secularization of Islam" (which indeed was inspired by a Western movement for separation of church from state)—the term "secularization" has acquired in the Arab world the connotation of undermining religion. Thus, any secular proposal intended to reform an Islamic institution has been rejected on the ground that it aimed at the "secularization of Islam." But does "secularization" necessarily mean always the separation of religion from the state (or the religious from civil authorities), and could this not be achieved in fields which have nothing to do with religion? Although in its classical form religion formed the very basis of Islam, modern-age Muslim rulers have been able to adopt certain secular reform measures without serious opposition. For instance, when the Ottoman sultans introduced military, financial, and administrative reforms, they were able to secure the approval of religious leaders. But when the Kamalists moved to abolish the caliphate and separate religion from the state, Muslim reaction was prompt and violent.

Secularization may, therefore, take several forms: first, the adoption of measures which have little or nothing to do with Islam; second, the adoption of measures which are in principle consistent with Islam but are not dealt with in such detail as would fit existing conditions; third, the adoption of measures which may substitute certain aspects of Islam that have become obsolete; fourth, the separation of religion from the state.[2] The last step, obviously the most revolutionary, is the one Turkey undertook in 1924 which became the subject of much controversy in the Arab world. Before World War I, Farah Antun, whom we have met before as a liberal writer and an advocate of utopian socialism,[3] advocated complete separation between religious and civil authorities; his views caused little reaction.[4] Turkey's unilateral action of disestablishing the caliphate had an adverse reaction in the Islamic world and in 1926 a Muslim conference was held in Cairo to discuss the issue. Egypt took the matter more seriously than other Arab countries because of her pre-war attachment to the Ottoman caliphate and because some of her leaders (including the King) hoped that the seat of the caliphate might be transferred from Istanbul to Cairo.[5] An avalanche of books and articles protested the Turkish action; but only four—two for and two against the action—discussed the issue seriously. Rashid Rida, though suggesting certain modifications, put forth the most impressive argument in favor of the caliphate;[6] and Mustafa Sabri, an Ottoman functionary who settled in Egypt after the Kamalist Revolution, wrote an angry attack on Kamalist leaders accusing them of atheism.[7] The two works supporting the abolition of the caliphate were 'Abd al-Ghani

[2] Cf. my "From Religious to National Law," *Modernization of the Arab World*, ed. J. H. Thompson and R. D. Reischauer (Princeton, 1966), p. 49.

[3] See p. 91, above.

[4] Farah Antun, *Ibn Rushd wa Falsafatuh* [Ibn Rushd and His Philosophy] (Cairo, 1903), pp. 151–60, 160–72. In his work, *al-Saq 'Ala al-Saq* (Paris, 1852), pp. 134–40. Ahmad Faris al-Shidiaq also spoke about the separation of religion from the state.

[5] King Fu'ad of Egypt expressed an interest to be a candidate; he gave up the matter in face of opposition, although he supported the 'ulama of al-Azhar in holding a conference in Cairo. See Fakhr al-Din al-Ahmadi al-Zawahiri, *al-Siyasa wa al-Azhar* [Politics and the Azhar] (Cairo, 1945), pp. 207–17.

[6] See p. 69, above.

[7] Mustafa Sabri, *al-Nakir 'Ala Munkiri al-Ni'ma Min al-Din wa al-Khilafa wa al-Umma* [Woe to Those Who Deny the Favor of Religion and the Caliphate and the Nation] (Cairo, 1924).

Sani's Arabic translation of a book prepared by a committee of experts under the supervision of the Turkish Government to justify the action of the Turkish Grand National Assembly in separating religious from civil authorities,[8] and a far more important work by 'Ali 'Abd al-Raziq.[9]

Raziq (1888–1966) belonged to an influential family whose members had taken an active part in the Liberal Constitutional Party. He studied at al-Azhar University and went to England to study at Oxford shortly before the outbreak of World War I. He served as judge in a religious court and gave lectures at al-Azhar University on Arabic literature.[10] In 1925 when he published his book on the caliphate, he was dismissed from his office as judge; later he entered politics and became Minister of Waqf. Raziq's book on the caliphate might not have stirred a violent reaction had it appeared at a time when the Egyptian monarch was not showing an interest in the caliphate. Moreover, it was written by a member of a family known for its opposition to the King, although there was in the book no direct attack on the Egyptian monarchy.[11] Due to court instigation, Raziq was dismissed from office and the Minister of Justice, who belonged to the same political party, was forced to resign.[12] Raziq declared in the press that he was delighted to be dropped from the body of al-Azhar 'ulama and that he would wear European dress. After retirement, he resumed practice of law and took part in politics.[13]

The political repercussion resulting from Raziq's book at-

[8] 'Abd al-Ghani Sani, *al-Khilafa wa Sultat al-Umma* [The Caliphate and Sovereignty of the Nation] (Cairo, 1924).

[9] 'Ali 'Abd al-Raziq, *al-Islam wa Usul al-Hukm* [Islam and the Sources of Authority] (Cairo, 1925).

[10] 'Ali 'Abd al-Raziq, *Amali 'Ali 'Abd al-Raziq* (Cairo, 1912).

[11] There may be a few insinuating sentences against oppression and despotism of modern monarchies in Islamic lands construed to have been an attack on the King, but there are no direct references to the Egyptian monarchy (see *al-Islam*, pp. 26–27).

[12] 'Abd al-Aziz Fahmi, Minister of Justice, objected to the action of the Council of 'Ulama of al-Azhar as contrary to the constitution and also held that the Council had no power to act on penal questions. See 'Abd al-Aziz Fahmi, *Hadhihi Hayati* [This is My Life] (Cairo, 1963), pp. 153–58.

[13] For a brief account of Raziq's life, see Fathi Ridwan, "'Ali 'Abd al-Raziq wa al-Islam wa Usul al-Hukm," *al-Majalla* (January, 1966), pp. 3–11.

tracted the attention of the scholarly world and led to a lively discussion of secularism and the relationship between religious and civil authorities. No work for a long time had been so carefully scrutinized and its impact on secular thought so profound. Since the substance of the book has been adequately studied by a number of writers and summarized by others,[14] it might be more significant to discuss Raziq's ideas on secularism and free thought. Since Raziq did not publish further and did not reply to his critics, the present writer sought direct contact with him to discuss some relevant points.

Raziq's book is based on two premises: first, the caliphate is not inherent in Islam and therefore not necessary; and second, the separation between state and religion is based on the assumption that Islam, like Christianity, is a religion with a universal message. In support of the first premise, Raziq argued that the two authoritative sources of Islam—the Qur'an and Traditions—were silent on the matter; vague references to the subject, if rightly interpreted, give no ground for caliphal authority. Nor does the consensus of the community (*ijma'*) provide any guidance and the caliphate itself becomes the cause of dissent and rebellion among Muslims. Likewise, the argument that the material welfare and religious practices of Muslims are dependent on the caliphate is not a satisfactory argument, since authority needs not be in the form of the caliphate as defined by Muslim scholars. Any form of authority serving Islamic welfare at any particular time is satisfactory. "We have no need," said Raziq, "for the caliphate, neither in our religious nor temporal affairs; the caliphate has always been and continues to be a misfortune to Islam and Muslims, and the source of evil and corruptions." [15]

[14] French translation, "L'Islam et les bases du pouvoir," by L. Bercher, in *Revue des études Islamiques*, VII (1933), 353–91; VIII (1934), 163–222. An English translation is being prepared by Christopher Ross as a doctoral dissertation at the School of Advanced International Studies, The Johns Hopkins University. See Charles C. Adams, *Islam and Modernism in Egypt* (London, 1933), pp. 261–68; Albert Hourani, *Arabic Thought in the Liberal Age, 1798–1939* (London, 1962), pp. 184–88; Muhammad Husayn, *al-Itijahat al-Wataniya fi al-Adab al-Mu'asir* [Nationalist Trends in Contemporary Literature] (Cairo, 1956), II, 74–85.

[15] Raziq, *al-Islam*, p. 36.

From this premise Raziq proceeds logically to the next—the separation of religious from civil authority. The Prophet, he maintains, exercised political power necessitated by the special circumstances of his time; but his action should not be taken to imply that he attempted to found a state or that it was part of his religious mission, a mission which was "prophetic" and not "temporal." Muhammad's mission was completed with his death. After him, the community was bound to organize some form of government because it could not revert to the former state. The election of Abu Bakr set a precedent for the caliphate, but his position was political and not religious. It was in succeeding generations that a religious significance was attached to this office—a significance which the caliphs found in their interest to encourage. From this Raziq concludes that the caliphate had outlived its usefulness and might be allowed to vanish as political circumstances have radically changed.

Concerning the separation of religion from state, Raziq opined that Quranic legislation relating to civil matters did not call for the association of religious with civil authorities. After the abolition of the caliphate, all civil affairs must come under the jurisdiction of secular authority and all laws, except specifically religious laws, should be modified to conform to existing conditions. However, he told me that the laws of inheritance as specified in the Qur'an were inherently sound and should be administered without change by the state. Other laws, inadequate for modern society, should be allowed to lapse. For instance, penal laws, based on a tribal society, were no longer compatible with the modern age. The Prophet never insisted that he was the best informed on civil matters; he made it clear to his Companions that he was not immune from error. Only the rules regulating the spiritual life of Muslims are valid for all time and unchangeable; all other matters should be regarded as secular and subject to change by the state in accordance with society's needs.

All questions, including civil and political matters, on which the Prophet expressed an opinion, have been incorporated in the Prophet's Traditions, but Raziq maintained that the Prophet never said all his opinions were divinely inspired. On the contrary, he said that in all non-religious matters he was liable to err; only his religious instructions were inspired and required observance. Therefore, a distinction must be made between Muhammad's role as Prophet and his conduct as political leader, just as such a distinction was made concerning David, Solomon, Christ, and other prophets. For this reason, Raziq said, the Caliph 'Umar found it necessary to issue civil and political decrees after the Prophet's death; it was taken for granted that he had the right to do so after consultation with the Prophet's Companions.

Concerning purely religious questions, Raziq believed that Islam, like Christianity, is a spiritual and universal rather than a national religion. In a strictly theological sense, Islam, like Judaism, stresses the oneness of God more clearly than Christianity; but he said that the Prophet paid greater tribute to Christianity than to other religions. Raziq viewed the Prophet like other men: he had a family, was married to several wives, was respected although his actions as a political leader were often challenged, and, like other men, he was mortal and aware of his failing health toward the end of his life even though he died suddenly.

Raziq's views on the caliphate, while advocating complete secularization, provided legal validity for the newly established national political systems in the Arab world. Yet the new Egyptian regime penalized him for providing such secular justification. There were, of course, political reasons for the action against him, but in the eyes of religious leaders the matter went deeper. Raziq's argument in favor of the separation of religion from the state meant not merely the exclusion of the 'ulama from the exercise of their official functions, judicial and otherwise, but also of relieving the state from any responsibility on moral and spiritual issues. These views were construed to undermine the moral basis of society and to deprive the 'ulama from the right to ask the state to fulfill its moral responsibility. For this reason Raziq was condemned as a disbeliever (*mulhid*) even though he persisted in his Islamic belief.

Moderns vs. Ancients: Taha Husayn and Mustafa Sadiq al-Rafi'i

Raziq's work on the caliphate advanced no new method of thought. The cause of secularism in a broader sense was served more profoundly by a new group of thinkers who espoused a Western mode of thought designed to free the mind from traditional method of criticism and outmoded literary style. This group, calling itself "modern," stood in opposition to another one, styled as "ancient."

The "moderns" (*al-mujaddidun*) came into prominence shortly after World War I, but in fact this modernist trend had begun before the war. In 1907 a new political party, known as the Nation's Party (*Hizb al-Umma*), was formed to pay attention to cultural and social questions of the day, questions not discussed by other political parties. The organ of the party, *al-Jarida* (The Journal), edited by Ahmad Lutfi al-Sayyid, opened its columns to writers who were thoroughly imbued with Western thought. Some were disciples of Muhammad 'Abduh, but others had received their education in Europe. Two of these, Taha Husayn and Muhammad Husayn Haykal, both of whom later played a prominent role in the modernist movement, were inspired by Lutfi al-Sayyid's modernist views. A year later, in 1908, the Egyptian University was founded to provide a modern Western method of instruction for young men who could not receive their education in European universities, and European scholars were invited to lecture. The first graduate of this university to receive a doctoral degree of letters was Taha Husayn.

Following World War I the modernist movement continued to grow in strength and its younger members took the lead in advocating, irrespective of Islamic traditional standards, a completely Western mode of thought. Two important events strengthened this trend: First, the formation of the Liberal Constitutional Party which stressed liberalism in order to cultivate relations with the educated class and to counterbalance the influence of its rival nationalist party—the Wafd. The editor of its organ *al-Siyasa* (Politics) was Muhammad Husayn Haykal, a protégé of Lutfi al-Sayyid and a graduate of law from the University of Paris. Haykal started a weekly supplement of *al-Siyasa* devoted completely to literature and culture; it became the leading organ of modernist thought and a forum for Taha Husayn and other liberal thinkers. Haykal distinguished himself as the author of a two volume study on the life and works of Rousseau [16] and later as a literary critic. His dual task was to secure his party's support for modernism and to encourage modernist writers to contribute to his papers.[17]

The second major event which enhanced the position of the modernists was the reorganization of the Egyptian University which received grants from government funds when in 1924 the leaders of the Liberal Constitutional Party, then in power, attached it formally to the Ministry of Education. Lutfi al-Sayyid, the spiritual father of the modernists, became the rector of the university and Taha Husayn was appointed a member of its faculty. Haykal and Husayn, with Lutfi al-Sayyid's moral support, tried vigorously to speed up the modernist movement by drawing more heavily on European thought. To Lutfi al-Sayyid, the age was one of preparation rather than achievement, "an age of translation and not of composition," in his own words; but to Haykal and Husayn, who received more thorough French training, it was an age of progress and creativity surpassing mere translation.[18] Husayn, the real leader of the modernist movement, an advocate of liberal—even free—thought and later to be called the Dean of Literature, had to bear the brunt of conservative attacks.

[16] Muhammad Husayn Haykal, *Jean Jacques Rousseau* (Cairo, 1921–23), reprinted in a one-volume edition (Cairo, 1965). A third unpublished volume is included in this new edition.

[17] For the life and thought of Haykal, see his *Mudhakkirat* [Memoirs] (Cairo, 1951–1953), 2 vols.; Ahmad Lutfi al-Sayyid (ed.), *Muhammad Husayn Haykal* (Cairo, 1959).

[18] Both Lutfi al-Sayyid and Husayn Haykal took an active part in politics from their early careers and might well be regarded as "intellectual politicians," especially Haykal; Husayn, not a politician at heart, entered into a political career late in life, but he made his imprint more profoundly in literary circles. The role of the two intellectuals, Lutfi al-Sayyid and Haykal, will be examined in a forthcoming volume on *Arab Contemporaries*.

He was born in 1889, in a small village not far from Cairo, and at an early age lost his sight. He was sent to al-Azhar where he spent a few years before he went to the newly founded Egyptian University and acquired a thorough knowledge of religion and Arabic literature in the traditional manner. At the university he was initiated into and attracted by modern European scholarship. The fruit of his study was his book on the life and works of the blind sceptic poet, Abu al-'Ala' al-Ma'arri, in the introduction of which he began to attack the traditional modes of thought.[19] He was sent for further training to France on the University's educational mission; there he specialized in literature and classical studies, and wrote his doctoral dissertation on Ibn Khaldun.[20] While studying he married a French woman who gave him invaluable assistance; he confessed that he saw through her eyes.[21] Upon his return to Egypt he was appointed to the newly established chair of classical studies and later, when the University was reconstituted, became professor of classical Arabic literature. It was in this period that he became very active in literary circles, as a popular lecturer at the university and a contributor to *al-Siyasa*. He was also drawn into the political conflict that had raged between Sa'd Zaghlul, hero of the Egyptian Revolt of 1919 and leader of the Wafd Party, and 'Adli Yakan, Prime Minister and leader of the Liberal Constitutional Party. Husayn took the side of the latter. Lucid and biting in writing, he was encouraged by the Liberal Constitutional Party to criticize Zaghlul, but he had later to pay a price for his attack on the national hero.

It was not only Husayn's literary and political views that aroused the critics of the traditional school. At the very outset, his appointment to the faculty of the university gave the

[19] Taha Husayn, *Dhikra Abi al-'Ala' al-Ma'arri* [In Memory of Abi al-'Ala' al-Ma'arri] (Cairo, 1915).

[20] Taha Husain, *Etude analytique et critique de la philosophie sociale d'Ibn Khaldoun* (Paris, 1917); translated into Arabic by Muhammad 'Abd-Allah 'Anan.

[21] Taha Husayn, *Mudhakkirat* [Memoirs] (Bayrut, 1967), p. 179. These memoirs throw more light on the profound influence of this French woman on his preparatory work while studying in France than other works.

signal for the opening of a campaign by all conservative elements first against his teaching of classical literature to which he saw Islam indebted as no Muslim scholar was prepared to recognize, and then against his critical study of ancient Arabic literature which aroused the fury of religious elements. Ever since he was a student at al-Azhar, Husayn had displayed, in educational-literary circles, an audacity in attack on conservative elements that prompted their opposition to his method of study of Arabic literature. A number of writers representing various shades of opinion took issue with him, but only one carried the literary duel to official grounds, in both the Parliament and the Cabinet and forced the University to withdraw one of his books from the bookshops. This was Mustafa Sadiq al-Rafi'i.[22]

At the outset, the issue between Rafi'i and Husayn took the form of a polite display of literary talent. Early in 1923 Rafi'i contributed to *al-Siyasa* a short literary piece in a highly ornate style and invited literary critics to comment on it. Husayn pointed out that it represented the style of the fifth or sixth century of the Islamic era (eleventh or twelfth century A.D.)—a style which he regarded as not compatible with modern standards. Rafi'i replied to this that Husayn gave his own personal opinion and could not speak for others about modern standards.[23]

These literary exchanges prompted others to express their opinions about Rafi'i's literary views, some approving and others criticizing, provoking Husayn to rejoin.[24] Husayn then wrote a leading article in *al-Siyasa*, distinguishing between two schools of thought, calling one the "ancient" school, to which, he pointed out, Rafi'i belonged; and the other, the "modern" school, to which a number of writers, including himself, who had received European education belonged. The existence of these two schools in any society, he said, was a natural phe-

[22] For the life and works of Rafi'i, see Muhammad Sa'id al-'Uryan, *Hayat al-Rafi'i* [Life of al-Rafi'i] (Cairo, 2nd ed., 1947).

[23] Rafi'i's article, Husayn's comment, and Rafi'i's reply are reprinted in Taha Husayn, *Hadith al-Arbi'a* [Wednesday's Talks] (Cairo, new ed., 1962), III, 5–9.

[24] See *al-Siyasa*, Cairo, July 4, 1923 (cited in *ibid.*, p. 10).

nomenon, and the lively discussion between the two schools is always a healthy sign for progress. But, he added, if society were to achieve progress, the "moderns" will have to attain victory over the "ancients," and these moderns will in turn become ancients to be superseded by another set of moderns. This, he said, is the rule of social life, as demonstrated in the history of many other nations.[25] In several other articles on classical Arabic literature, Husayn applied his method of literary criticism, and there was no doubt that he became the leading literary critic of the modernist school. At home in both classical Arabic and modern literature, he often displayed disdain for writers who, in his opinion, belonged to the ancient school.[26] Because of Husayn's growing influence among the new generation the "ancients" began to challenge his leadership of the "moderns." In vain were occasional criticisms leveled at him in the press and in religious circles; for, as his replies demonstrated, he stood up to the challenge and tried to silence his critics with impressive arguments and an elegant style. However, his enemies continued to attack him.

Their opportune moment came when Husayn published his work on pre-Islamic poetry in 1926, in which he gave full expression of his modern method of literary criticism.[27] The

[25] *Ibid.*, pp. 10–13, 22–36.

[26] In his articles on the early 'Abbasid poets, Husayn described two phases in their life: an outward in conformity with religion, and an inward in which they led a licentious life, in violation of the laws of morality and religion. Moreover, he said that the life of these poets mirrored the spirit of an age in transition from the austere Arabian to the then modern civilized life. This way of life was reflected in the court as well as in literary and religious circles. These views were challenged by critics on the ground that Husayn did not give an accurate picture of the time, relying on some sources and rejecting others. Husayn replied that he did not want to bestow on Islamic history a halo of sacredness and that a realistic view of history indicates that the early 'Abbasid period was the natural product of complex social forces of the time. He then pointed out that he arrived at these views by applying a modern critical method (Husayn, *Hadith al-Arbi'a* [Wednesday's Talks] [Cairo, new ed., 1964], I, 11–12, 35–36, 58–62, 63–70).

[27] Taha Husayn, *Fi al-Shi'r al-Jahili* [On Pre-Islamic Poetry] (Cairo, 1926). Withdrawn from sale on account of public criticism, it was revised and published as a study on pre-Islamic literature. See Husayn, *Fi al-Adab al-Jahili* [On Pre-Islamic Literature] (Cairo, 3rd ed., 1933), p. 63.

substance of the book had been given in the form of lectures to his students at the university. The main theme was that the bulk of the so-called pre-Islamic poetry was not pre-Islamic but the product of early Islam. He was almost certain of this conclusion, he said, after a thorough study of the subject, although he had had some doubts about the genuineness of pre-Islamic poetry before he began his investigation. "The greater part of what we call pre-Islamic literature," he said, "does not belong to the pre-Islamic period at all, but was forged after the rise of Islam. It is, therefore, representing the life, trends and predilections of the Muslims rather than the life of the pre-Islamic period." [28] What remains, he added, of genuine pre-Islamic literature is very scanty and cannot be depended upon for a correct picture of that period. There were several motives, he asserted, which led to the attribution of later Islamic poetry to pre-Islamic poets—to support political or religious claims, to gratify national rivalries, to serve the purpose of narrators and story-tellers, and to embellish the evidence of tradition transmitters, theologians, and Quranic commentators.[29]

These views may not have aroused opposition, had Husayn not insisted on a scientific method which led him to doubt matters connected with religion. "I propose to apply to literature," he said, "the philosophical method laid down by Descartes." According to this method, he added, we should not accept anything that ancient writers said about our literature and history except after investigation. In order to study Arabic literature in accordance with this method, we should be unbiased and take no sides, whether as orthodox or as heterodox protagonists. "When we study Arabic literature and history," he pointed out, "we must forget our national feelings, our religious sentiments, and all that is connected with them." [30] This method led him to reject the story concerning the Black Stone (to be found at the Sacred Mosque of Makka), the historical existence of Abraham and Ishmael, notwith-

[28] Husayn, *Fi al-Shi'r al-Jahili*, p. 7; *Fi al-Adab al-Jahili*, p. 63.
[29] Husayn, *Fi al-Shi'r al-Jahili*, pp. 42ff.; *Fi al-Adab al-Jahili*, pp. 113ff.
[30] Husayn, *Fi al-Shi'r al-Jahili*, pp. 11–12; *Fi al-Adab al-Jahili*, p. 66.

standing that these have been mentioned in the Qur'an and the Old Testament.

Husayn not only accepted the Cartesian method of philosophical doubt which was decried in conservative circles as contrary to established beliefs but, perhaps more shockingly, he rejected the evidence of sacred scriptures as true historical facts. These views were denounced as direct attacks on religion, and several writers of the ancient school wrote to refute them.[31] The storm might have passed without further harm had not Rafi'i, one of his principal opponents, entered the battle to avenge previous grudges.

Rafi'i, equally at home in classical Arabic literature, was perhaps more audacious and biting in style than Husayn and could be abusive and profane in attack. His critical essays were read not so much because they expressed orthodox views but because of their elegance and literary style.[32] The debate between Rafi'i and Husayn was, at the outset, literary—despite personal recriminations; neither of them really had won completely the first round. There was considerable interest both in Husayn's as well as in Rafi'i's views and an appreciation for their style.

Two factors seem to have tipped the balance in favor of Rafi'i. First, the Liberal Constitutional Party, in power when Husayn was under attack, was involved in a struggle with the Wafd Party, and it was reproached for its support of Husayn and his liberal group because Husayn himself had taken a stand against the leader of the Wafd Party. Second, Husayn expressed certain views which were outwardly literary but were construed as, in reality, an attack on religion, and he was denounced as an "atheist," agent of Christian missionaries, and traitor to Islam and his mother country.

Rafi'i was at heart a conservative writer and honestly re-

[31] Muhammad Farid Wajdi, *Naqd Kitab al-Shi'r al-Jahili* [Critique of the Book on Pre-Islamic Poetry] (Cairo, 1925); Muhammad al-Khidr Husayn, *Naqd Kitab fi al-Shi'r al-Jahili* [Critique of the Book on Pre-Islamic Poetry] (Cairo, 1926); Muhammad Ahmad al-Ghamrawi, *al-Naqd al-Tahlili li-Kitab fi al-Adab al-Jahili* [Analytical Criticism of the Book on Pre-Islamic Literature] (Cairo, 1927).

[32] See Muhammad Sa'id al-'Uryan, *Hayat al-Rafi'i*, pp. 158–59.

garded Husayn's attack on Arabic literature as an attack on religion. Husayn's remarks on the Qur'an, a scripture regarded by Rafi'i as a miracle of literary perfection, were entirely unacceptable and were regarded as a great insult to Arabic literature. He published his fiery articles against Husayn in *Kawkab al-Sharq*, the organ of the Wafd Party. These articles were read as masterpieces of literary criticism, although parts of them were profane and often degenerated into scathing and personal attacks. Rafi'i played on religious sentiment and pictured Husayn as the most dangerous atheist in Islam. He asked the Government to take action against the man who lectured blasphemy and disbelief to his students and corrupted them with European and Christian views.[33]

Husayn was advised to keep quiet until the storm passed; he even wrote a letter to the Rector of the University professing Islam and stating that his views in literature had nothing to do with religion. This did not avail, for the Azhar 'ulama were behind the movement demanding action against Husayn. The subject was raised in Parliament and led to a verbal duel between 'Adli Yakan, the Premier, and Zaghlul, leader of the Wafd Party. The opposition sought to censor the Government, but the issue was finally resolved by a suggestion to refer the matter to judicial investigation in order to placate public commotion.

This attack on Husayn, though it shocked him, did not change his views on secular thought; it did, however, compel him to use more subtle methods of secularization. For almost a decade, he wrote mostly literary works, choosing Islamic themes, written in a lucid and artistic style. In 1938, he published *The Future of Culture in Egypt*,[34] in which he identified Egypt's cultural heritage with the Mediterranean world and called for further modernization. The book dealt essen-

[33] Mustafa Sadiq al-Rafi'i, *Taht Rayat al-Qur'an: al-Ma'raka Bayn al-Qadim wa al-Jadid* [Under the Banner of the Qur'an: The Battle Between the Old and the New] (Cairo, 1926).

[34] Taha Husayn, *Mustaqbal al-Thaqafa fi Misr* (Cairo, 1938), 2 vols.; abridged translation by Sidney Glazer, *The Future of Culture in Egypt* (Washington, D.C., 1954).

tially with educational problems and governmental control of educational institutions designed to raise academic standards and improve methods of instructions. The work unmistakably stressed secular education and the substitution of secular for religious institutions. For this reason, the work was attacked by conservative and religious writers, especially the Azhar 'ulama, who accused him again of trying to undermine religion; but these elements could no longer arouse public commotion, since Husayn had become more influential in the country and the tone of his writing less inciting.[35] It is deemed outside the scope of this work to discuss the purely literary and educational views of Husayn, since these have been studied elsewhere. Husayn made a deep imprint on the secular movement from the time he began his university career and challenged traditional modes of thought.[36]

Agnosticism: The 'Usur Group

The moderns, essentially men of letters concerned with new methods of literary criticism, did not intend to attack religion, but they could not avoid being involved in religious controversy. The frontal attack on religion was reserved to men who displayed greater versatility and broader range of interest: The 'Usur group.

The appearance of this group was made possible by the growing interest in Western scientific knowledge which *al-Muqtataf*, a periodical edited by Ya'qub Sarruf, began to spread in the Levant and Egypt in the later part of the nineteenth century. Following his study of physical sciences in the Syrian Protestant College (later the American University of Bayrut), Sarruf founded *al-Muqtataf* in Bayrut in 1876 and

[35] For an attack on this book, see Muhammad Husayn, *al-Itijahat al-Wataniya*, II, 213–26; Muhammad al-Bahi, *al-Fikr al-Islami al-Hadith* [Modern Islamic Thought] (Cairo, 2nd ed., 1960), pp. 173–84.

[36] For his life and thought, see Pierre Cachia, *Taha Husayn* (London, 1956); Albert Hourani, *Arabic Thought*, chap. 12. See also Sami al-Kayyali, *Ma' Taha Husayn* [With Taha Husayn] (Cairo, 1951–1968), 2 vols.; *Taha Husayn*, ed. al-Abyari *et al.* (Cairo, n.d.).

then moved it to Cairo in 1885.[37] Although not an original writer, Sarruf influenced young men to study Western science and philosophy, and his periodical became the medium for the spread of scientific knowledge in the Arab world. Before he published his works on the theory of evolution and religion, Shibli Shumayyil had made his reputation as a free thinker through his writings in *al-Muqtataf*, and had attracted others, like the 'Iraqi poet Jamil Sidqi al-Zahawi, and Salama Musa, the utopian socialist, to take an interest in liberal thought.[38] It was under the influence of Sarruf that a young Muslim thinker, Isma'il Mazhar, became interested in Western liberal thought and founded a periodical specifically devoted to free thought.

Mazhar, born in 1891 to a well-to-do family, received his education in Cairo and England. His brother-in-law, Ahmad Lutfi al-Sayyid, who encouraged liberal thought among the modernists, had a great influence on him, but his interest in Western science attracted him to Sarruf's circle and he began to write in *al-Muqtataf* rather than in *al-Siyasa*. He translated Darwin's *Origin of Species* and wrote articles on science and positive philosophy before he founded *al-'Usur*.

In 1926 Mazhar published an article in *al-Muqtataf* on "the scientific mode of thought," [39] in which he stated that the mode of thought which dominated the Arab mind in the past and persisted to the present was metaphysical, not positive or objective, because of the preoccupation of Muslim thinkers with idealist and abstract subjects rather than with real objects. He tried to apply Auguste Comte's three modes of thought—the theological, metaphysical, and positive—and con-

[37] Sarruf founded *al-Muqtataf* in collaboration with Faris Nimr, but after these two men had settled in Egypt Nimr became editor of the daily *al-Muqattam*, and Sarruf of the monthly *al-Muqtataf*. For a brief account of Sarruf's life, see Philippe de Tarrazi, *Ta'rikh al-Sahafa al-'Arabiya* (Bayrut, 1913), I, 124–29.

[38] See pp. 91–94, above. For an account of Shumayyil's views on science and philosophy, see Hourani, *Arabic Thought*, pp. 245–53.

[39] Isma'il Mazhar, "Islub al-Fikr al-'Ilmi," *al-Maqtataf*, vol. 68 (1926), pp. 137–45, reprinted in Mazhar's *Ta'rikh al-Kikr al-'Arabi* [History of Arab Thought] (Cairo, 1928), pp. 91–102.

cluded that despite the recent revival of learning in the Arab world no thinker, including Jamal al-Din al-Afghani, had yet applied positive scientific method to modern problems. He maintained that no political event, including the 'Urabi Revolt of 1880 and the Revolution of 1919, had yet declared principles embodying a positive outlook on life comparable to that introduced by the French Revolution in European thought. He concluded that the so-called modernist views, advocated by the literary group (without actually naming Husayn or Haykal) had not yet been crystallized into a positive movement, although he admitted that modern Arab thinkers have been struggling to break away from metaphysical influences.[40]

In 1927, the first issue of *al-'Usur* (The Ages) was published by Mazhar who stated in his leading article that this review was to be devoted to literature, science, and philosophy. It was to examine the questions of the day with complete freedom from preconceived ideas which, he said, often restrained writers from speaking out freely. The immediate purpose of this critical review was to present an objective analysis unencumbered by ulterior motives, whether pecuniary or political, that caused so many literary and other writers to fail in their duty to the public. Lack of objectivity, he pointed out, had become more apparent in Egypt under the new parliamentary system, and it may well have been one of the evil effects of that system. Mazhar said that democratic freedoms without responsibility led to similar results in other countries —and this applied to Anglo-Saxon as well as to Latin countries but was perhaps more evident in the latter than in the former; in the Oriental Semitic (i.e. Arabic) countries this trend was particularly noticeable, since they closely resembled the Latin countries. It was not Mazhar's objective to undermine Egypt's parliamentary system, because he believed in

[40] This article elicited several critics who reproached Mazhar for his disparagement of Arab thought, and one of them, Mustafa al-Shihabi, stated that not only the Arabs but other nations had experienced such a metaphysical mode of thought (see Mazhar, *Ta'rikh al-Fikr al-Arabi*, pp. 103–20).

parliamentary democracy in principle. Rather, he desired to expose unscrupulous and self-seeking men who sought to exploit the parliamentary system by false and devious means. To put an end to these evil influences he felt compelled to call the attention to these practices by asking men to rid their minds of traditional modes of thought and to adopt new critical techniques. The ultimate objective of *al-'Usur* was to strike at the sources of evil by an attack on religious and traditional modes of thought, as the motto of *al-'Usur* expressly states.[41]

No sooner had *al-'Usur* appeared than it became the rallying point of writers advocating free thought and was read widely in the Arab world. Some, like Husayn Mahmud, wrote on Western free thought—about Bertrand Russell's agnostic ideas and others–and other writers, like 'Umar 'Inayat, wrote on the history of religion and traditional ideas treating them almost as mythologies.[42] Jamil Sidqi al-Zahawi and Anwar Sha'ul, two poets from Baghdad (the latter an Arab poet of Jewish faith), wrote verse pregnant with agnostic ideas; Ibrahim Haddad, who bore the mantle of free thought in Bayrut after *al-'Usur* was succeeded by *al-Duhur* (also means The Ages), contributed similar articles. Above all, it was Mazhar, with this group of free thinkers in Cairo (some of whom had not been known before), who contributed outspoken articles on religious beliefs which no writer before ever dared to publish. In an article on man's relationship with God, Mazhar pointed out that among man's misconceptions was the belief that God created man after His image, but in reality God was conceived by man in a manner reflecting his own image. With regard to prophets, he stated that all God's chosen prophets were from a limited area confined between the Taurus Mountains and the Indian Ocean and between the Mediterranean and the Persian Gulf. Why did God choose

[41] Isma'il Mazhar, *al-'Usur,* I (1927), 1–16; Mazhar, *Risalat al-Fikr al-Hurr,* I, 7; and Mazhar, *Risalat al-Fikr al-Hurr,* II, 13–26.

[42] See, e.g., Husayn Mahmud, "al-Tajarib al-Diniya," and "al-Mu'minun," *al-'Usur,* IV (1929), 260–65, 433–36; and 'Umar 'Inayat on the Yazidis (*ibid.*, pp. 246–49).

all His prophets from these lands, he asked? Was it because the people of this region were a "chosen people" or because they so indulged in disbelief that He had to send so many prophets to admonish them? Why did God allow the peoples of other lands to follow such "false prophets" as the Buddha and Confucius and let them be misguided by them? These and other misconceptions, he said, have led him to believe in the free thought which European thinkers began to adopt from the period of Enlightenment.[43]

Unlike the literary modernists, the *'Usur* group was composed of freelance writers who, holding no government posts, were not inhibited by bureaucratic restrictions and who, avoiding politics, were not the target of political attacks. They were, accordingly, immune from the pressures of religious leaders which one political party might exploit against another as had happened in the cases of 'Ali 'Abd al-Raziq and Taha Husayn. Small wonder that the liberal thought of Raziq and Husayn was eclipsed by the free thought and agnosticism of the *'Usur* group. Thus, one of the *'Usur* writers criticized Taha Husayn for his failure to state clearly his views about the Qur'an. If Husayn believed that the Qur'an was not revealed to the Prophet, said the critic, why did he not have the courage to say so? Similarly, the same critic asked Shaykh 'Ali 'Abd al-Raziq, who stated in his book *al-Islam wa Usul al-Hukm* that Islam was not founded on sound principles and that it could not provide the basis for a democratic system, why did he fail to say so directly instead of calling for the separation of religious from civil authorities? Thus Raziq followed the same pattern of early Christian theological controversies at Ephesus, Khalcedon, and Nicaea in discussing the nature of the Prophet's mission as to whether it was temporal or divine. "Why did he not say clearly and directly," the critic asked, "that the sources of authority in Islam are no longer valid and that democratic principles are superior to the Islamic?" The reason why these men did not speak openly their mind, he added, was partly because they lacked

[43] Mazhar, *al-'Usur*, II (1928), 913–24.

moral courage and partly because they were not fully convinced of the validity of their claims.[44]

Mazhar also contributed short articles and notes commenting on current issues or reviewing previously or newly published works.[45] Of the former, he criticized Taha Husayn's works indicating Husayn's lack of objectivity in his failure to provide sufficient evidence for the views presented in his book on pre-Islamic poetry. He pointed out factual errors in the book owing to Husayn's heavy dependence on Western Orientalists rather than on original Arabic sources.[46] He also criticized Rashid Rida, the leading disciple of 'Abduh, for an article in *al-Manar* (1931) in which he denounced atheism and the attack on religion which a group of writers were spreading without specifying the name of the group or the review. In a sarcastic reply, Mazhar said how empty was Rida's claim to defend religion, since he was making his living on the gold lavishly given to him by Ibn Sa'ud, King of Saudi Arabia, for support of his reactionary rule in Arabia. He also reminded him of the private life of some of the 'ulama, to whom Rida belonged, but which Rida failed to criticize despite their degrading conduct; instead, he said, Rida criticized the alleged atheists who corrupt young men by diverting them from religion. "Don't you believe," Mazhar said, "that the conduct of those shaykhs is more damaging to Islam than these modernist atheists?" [47]

Most amusing perhaps were the articles about a leading literary figure and poet, 'Abbas Mahmud al-'Aqqad, under the scathing title "on the skewer," (*'ala al-saffud*) presumably intended to be a critique of contemporary literature. The articles were anonymous, although it became known later that they were from the pen of none other than Mustafa Sadiq al-Rafi'i, the great critic of Taha Husayn.[48] For the

[44] See *al-'Usur*, II (1928), 1113–14.

[45] These short studies have been reprinted in a separate volume (see Isma'il Mazhar, *Fi al-Naqd al-Adabi* [On Literary Critique] (Bayrut, 1965).

[46] *Ibid.*, pp. 69–73.

[47] *Ibid.*, pp. 105–11. See also Mazhar's article in defense of free thought on the occasion of a debate between Rashid Rida and Mahmud 'Azmi in 1930 (*al-'Usur*, VI [1930], 360–65).

[48] *Ibid.*, p. 51; see Sa'id al-'Uryan, *Hayat al-Rafi'i*, pp. 183–88, 189–96.

editor of *al-'Usur* to invite one of the leaders of the "ancients" to write a critique on a leading modernist must have, indeed, seemed strange. But Rafi'i knew that *al-'Usur* was the organ of an agnostic group and his acceptance to contribute to it meant that he tacitly approved of *al-'Usur's* newly adopted method of criticism. Mazhar, on the other hand, was more interested in Rafi'i's style and critical competence as a means to temper the literary arrogance of writers like al-'Aqqad.[49] At bottom personal jealousy may have been the underlying reason which prompted both Rafi'i and Mazhar to resort to the use of character assassination and not merely to debunk 'Aqqad as a writer.[50] In the meantime, Mazhar reviewed al-'Aqqad's book on "God" and pointed out that the study of God in accordance with one religious system must be distinguished from a study in an objective manner uninhibited by religious belief. Man, he said, is just as motivated by doubt as by belief, and he refuted the grounds on which al-'Aqqad explained belief in God. The review stated that there was no positive evidence for the existence of God, just as al-Zahawi pointed out in a verse, which may be paraphrased as follows:

> Man's ignorance of the nature of things, prompting him to seek an explanation of the [universe's] puzzles, established God in an effort to answer these puzzles, yet He Himself became the greatest of [man's] puzzles.[51]

Mazhar's criticism was not confined to Arab writers; he also commented on Western writers, like Sir Oliver Lodge for his attempt at reconciling science with religion, Will Durant, for his inadequate treatment of some philosophers, including Hume and Hegel, while he dwelt on others like Voltaire and Spencer; he did, however, compliment Durant for a thorough

[49] See Mazhar's introduction, in *'Ala al-Saffud* [reprinted] (Cairo, 1930); al-'Uryan, *Hayat al-Rafi'i*, pp. 183–207. This critique was first published in *al-'Usur*, V (1929), 18–26, 177–87, 353–62, 506–20, 567–609.

[50] Rafi'i's biographer admitted the personal motive in the writing of " 'Ala al-Saffud," although Rafi'i himself said that al-'Aqqad's criticism of his *I'jaz al-Qur'an* [Miracle of the Qur'an] prompted him to criticize al-'Aqqad because it implied an attack on religion. It seems rather unusual that in the defence of religion, an attack on al-'Aqqad should be published in an agnostic periodical (see Sa'id al-'Uryan, *Hayat al-Rafi'i*, pp. 190–91).

[51] Mazhar, *Fi al-Naqd al-Adabi*, pp. 7–31.

understanding of Spinoza.[52] His review of Frank Crane's *Why I am a Christian* was indeed devastating. He stated that this book, unlike Bertrand Russell's *Why I am not a Christian* (which one of the 'Usur group had translated), tried unconvincingly to prove the existence of God. Since both Russell and Crane, he said, were honest men regardless of their religious beliefs, he wondered why should men waste so much time on such vain and controversial religious questions.[53]

The 'Usur group set very high standards which necessarily brought it into sharp conflict with many other groups. It was attacked by religious groups for its *ilhad* (atheism), by modernists for its hypercriticism, and by moderate thinkers for its acceptance of Western thought without discrimination.[54] Four years after the appearance of *al-'Usur,* scarcely any well-known writer escaped criticism, unless he professed agnostic views. Mazhar, though a learned and a highly motivated man, failed to win many supporters in his drive for free thought. He was essentially an idealist who refused to compromise with reality. He came out into prominence in the literary world suddenly and withdrew into oblivion after the abrupt suspension of his journal, having exhausted his personal and material resources.

In 1930, the world economic crisis hit Egypt as severely as it had hit other countries. Mazhar had invested almost all his fortune in his literary enterprise which brought him fame but not material remuneration; he could no longer bear the burden. In 1929–30 he twice proposed to organize an Egyptian Agrarian Party and appealed to Nahhas Pasha, leader of the Wafd Party, to lead the nation in a drive to improve the social and economic conditions of the country, but Nahhas showed

[52] For criticism of Sir Oliver Lodge, *Reason and Belief* (London, 1910), see Mazhar's review of the book in *Fi al-Naqd al-Ababi*, pp. 143–47; and for Mazhar's review of Will Durant, *Story of Philosophy* (New York, 1926), see *ibid.*, pp. 149–52.

[53] *Ibid.*, pp. 93–95.

[54] See protest of a Christian priest (*al-'Usur,* IV [1929], 544–45) and Mazhar's reply (*ibid.*, pp. 657–64); and criticism of Habib al-Zahlawi, a Lebanese writer (*al-'Usur,* V [1929], 610–14); and Mazhar's reply (*ibid.*, pp. 614–17); and *Fi al-Naqd al-Adabi,* pp. 51–58.

no interest in proposals which appeared as too impractical and idealistic. Mazhar's plan for a new political party combined elements of free enterprise and socialism which no political leader was then prepared to accept.[55] Despairing of any hope to enter politics, a field in which he had shown no special talent, and severely hit by the economic crisis, he was forced to suspend *al-'Usur*. He withdrew to the country where he lived in solitude for almost two decades, concentrating on the preparation of a scientific dictionary; he returned to resume life in Cairo for a short while after World War II. He made an attempt to return to the literary world when he was invited to edit *al-Muqtataf* in 1945 but he was forced to give that up when *al-Muqtataf* itself was suspended in 1949. Afterwards he contributed but little to the press, until his death in 1962.

Upon the suspension of *al-'Usur* in 1931, Ibrahim Haddad, a Lebanese writer, sought to espouse the cause of free thought in Bayrut with the publication of *al-Duhur*.[56] It lasted but two years and, like *al-'Usur*, was suspended for financial reasons. This periodical, milder in tone, could not match in quality its predecessor; but the 'Iraqi poet Jamil Sidqi al-Zahawi published in it his most remarkable philosophic poem—the "Revolt in Hell," emulating al-Ma'arri's *Risalat al-Ghufran* (Treatise on Repentence) and Dante's *Divine Comedy*. In this epic, al-Zahawi expressed his sceptic views about Islamic beliefs, treating them like ancient mythology.

Al-Zahawi was born in Baghdad in 1863 and witnessed the vicissitudes of his country's progress from Ottoman days to independence. He served in the Ottoman administration in Baghdad, Istanbul, and the Yaman, and became a member of Parliament shortly before World War I. He also served in 'Iraq after the establishment of the national government and became a member of the Senate. He died in 1936.[57]

[55] For text of Mazhar's proposals and program, see *al-'Usur*, V (1929), 482–91, 491–94, 495–504.

[56] *al-Duhur* (plural of *dahr*) is a synonym of *al-'Usur* (plural of *asr*).

[57] For Zahawi's life, see Rafael Butti, *al-Adab al-'Asri fi al-'Iraq al 'Arabi* [Modern Literature in Arab 'Iraq] (Cairo, 1923): Nasir al-Hani, *Muhadarat 'An Jamil al-Zahawi* [Lectures on Jamil al-Zahawi] (Cairo, 1954); Mahir Hasan Fahmi, *al-Zahawi* (Cairo, n.d.).

Since his Istanbul days, al-Zahawi had been known as a liberal thinker advocating the adoption of Western science and philosophy and calling for the emancipation of women. He came under the influence of Turkish writers advocating positivist philosophy, and fell under the influence of *al-Muqtataf* to which he contributed in verse some of his liberal ideas. Known as an agnostic long before *al-'Usur* made its appearance, he wrote his epic on the "Revolt in Hell" for *al-'Usur* but it was published instead in *al-Duhur.*

The "Revolt in Hell" is perhaps the most impressive literary piece that al-Zahawi had written. The influence of al-Ma'arri and Dante is evident, but Zahawi's epic is not a mere imitation; he developed his own imaginary journey and gave his own account of Hell.

The journey begins in the grave when the corpse is visited by two Angels, Munkar and Nakir, whose task was to cross-examine man before the Day of Judgment. They asked searching questions about God and the belief in the Hereafter. Zahawi tried to escape the inquiry by giving the usual answers of a believing Muslim—he said he believed in God, in the Hereafter, in the Resurrection and the Day of Judgment, and finally in Paradise. What about Hell, he was asked? Zahawi said that he had once believed in it and then denied it, but, afraid of the two Angels, he hesitated to give his real views. Suspecting that he was a sceptic, the two Angels persisted in their cross-examination; Zahawi tried to change the subject and gave his views about the emancipation of women. Pressed about his real belief in God, he cited the orthodox articles of the faith, and as evidence of his belief, he invoked the doctrine of pre-destination. "But if man is not free," he asked, "why should one expect penalty for his doing wrong?" This question led to an argument on the nature of God, and he revealed some unorthodox views. Suddenly realizing that he had departed from the orthodox doctrine, he told the two Angels: why do you not ask me what I have accomplished in life instead of what personal views I held about God and the Hereafter? He gave an account of his career in the service of his country and his struggle in the defense of women and the poor, but to no avail. The two Angels were interested in religious beliefs and not in worldly affairs. He tried to reason with them, and finally said that he was a believer in Islam. But this confession came too late, because he had already admitted disbelief.

He was taken from the grave to Hell. On the way he had a glimpse of Paradise, where everything the believer desires exists in abundance–honey and milk and women. With brilliance, he described the *Sirat*, the sword-edge bridge between Earth and Paradise. He then proceeded to the fire of Hell. On the way he saw at a distance Layla, the poetic nymph of his youth. He also saw Arab literary celebrities–the agnostic poets Bashshar, Abu Nuwas, and al-Ma'arri. He saw in another spot Socrates, Plato, and Aristotle. And finally he saw al-Hallaj, the mystic martyr, who was beheaded for his passion in seeking union with God.

Having seen Hell crowded with scientists, philosophers, and poets, he felt that it was irrational to believe that all these sages should be damned to perdition and suffer eternal fire. Surely, they should be able to invent a tool capable of suppressing the fire and arresting the guardians of Hell. Revolt in hell, the vision of a sceptic poet, turned out to be true. The guardians appealed to God for help and an army of angels descended to suppress the revolt. The confrontation between rebels and angels, though leading to a fierce battle, was won by the rebels demonstrating that an ingenious instrument of theirs was more effective than divine power. Zahawi's epic leads to the inescapable conclusion that it is ironic that God should condemn to eternal fire men of science and learning who served mankind faithfully. His idea of the invention of a tool to overcome divine power implied his preference for reason over belief. This epic, the product of Zahawi's mature thought, showed that the old man remained agnostic to the very end of his life.[58]

[58] For a study of Zahawi's thought, see G. Widmer "Der Iraqische Dichter Jamil Sidqi Az-Zahawi," *Die Welt des Islams*, vol. 17, no. 12, 1935; and Jamil Sa'id *al-Zahawi wa Thawratuh fi al-Jahim* [al-Zahawi and His Revolt in Hell] (Cairo, 1968).

The 'Usur preaching of agnosticism proved to be short-lived, but it taught a lesson to liberal thinkers to follow more subtle methods in spreading liberal ideas. From the thirties to the end of World War II, religious and conservative elements became very active and the cause of free thought appeared almost lost, but after World War II there was a revival in free thought and some of the liberal thinkers of the early interwar years, including Mazhar, began to reappear and revive interest in free thought. The movement, now led by other men, has not yet gathered full momentum, but is gradually gaining ground.

It may be surprising that the most radical sceptic after World War II should come from Saudi Arabia, the cradle of puritanical doctrines. 'Abd-Allah al-Qusaymi, after a short visit to Cairo, settled in Bayrut. His first book, the title of which can be translated as "These are the Shackles," [59] reflects his reaction against Islam's stagnation, which he describes as "credal ignorance," calls for free thought, and condemns all traditional religious values. He published a few more books expounding with greater vigor the same theme.[60] Essentially a humanist, he sought the emancipation of the human mind and heart from all belief systems, Islamic or Western, and asserted a will to power which must be organized and strengthened. The essence of this will exists in Western activism and enables man's inner impulses to perfect himself. In his first book, al-Qusaymi specifically discussed the plight of the Arab individual, but in his other works he dealt with the servitude of mankind as a whole and sought its emancipation from every kind of civil or religious shackles which impeded man's inner force for freedom and progress.

Less radical an attack on traditional shackles but more subtle an approach is to be found in the writings of the 'Iraqi sociologist 'Ali al-Wardi, whose main goal is to emancipate the common man from religious practices and legends, originally designed to embody ethical values, but which have lost

[59] 'Abd-Allah al-Qusaymi, *Hadhihi al-Aghlal* (Cairo, 1946).

[60] These are: *al-Alam Laysa 'Aqlan* [The World is not Rational]; *Hadha al-Kawn, Ma Damiruh* [This World: What is its Conscience]; and others.

all their meaning. Not an agnostic at heart, he did not despair of Islam, but stressed its ethical and cultural values—the only elements capable of survival.[61]

Legal Secularism: Sanhuri

The radical secularism which Raziq, Husayn, and the 'Usur group advocated was construed as an attack on religion in varying degrees and produced a violent reaction leading to the revival of lay religious movements manifested in the founding of the Muslim Brotherhood and other religious associations. However, the secularization movement, though arrested in certain domains, continued in areas over which religious leaders had no direct control. As a result, changes in Arab society continued on two different levels—religious and secular—without a serious attempt to reconcile the two. On the contrary, there were often conflicts between the two, manifested in advocating two opposing ways of life and generating a crisis of conscience. The secularists maintained that conflicts could be brought under control by separating religion from the state, relegating the former to the individual level and thus resolving the crisis of conscience, and permitting social change to take its course under state control uninhibited by religion.

At the time of the controversy over Raziq's theory of the caliphate, 'Abd al-Razzaq al-Sanhuri, an Egyptian, was then studying law in France and addressing himself to the question of relationship between civil and religious authorities. His inquiry was published in a book on the caliphate in which he rejected Raziq's theory that political authority was not an integral part of Islam, but he saw no reason why the caliphate, which had undergone changes in the past, could not continue to change and develop into an Oriental League of Nations.[62]

[61] See 'Ali al-Wardi, *Wu'az al-Salatin* [Sultan's Preachers] (Baghdad, 1954); *Mahzalat al-'Aql al-Bashari* [Comedy of Mankind's Mind] (Baghdad, 1955); *Dirasa fi Tabi'at al-Mujtama' al-'Iraqi* [A Study of the Nature of the 'Iraqi Society] (Baghdad, 1965), and others.

[62] A. Sanhoury, *Le Califat: son evolution vers une Société des Nations Orientale* (Paris, 1926).

The caliph, he suggested, would become the titular head of the congregation of Islamic states, whose jurisdiction over religious matters would remain supreme, but in civil and temporal affairs the heads of state and government would be directly responsible. The religious portions of the *shari'a*, essentially devotional duties, would be separated from the civil parts and placed directly under the jurisdiction of civil authorities. Performance of religious duties would become the direct responsibility of the caliph and equally applicable to all countries. However, Sanhuri's views, though of theoretical significance, became of practical value only a decade later when he had an opportunity to apply them to civil law.

'Abd al-Razzaq al-Sanhuri was born in Alexandria in 1895. He completed his legal studies in Cairo while working as a junior government functionary. In 1920 he went to France for further study, where he wrote his dissertation under the guidance of Edward Lambert of the University of Lyon, and returned in 1926 to teach civil law in the Egyptian University Law School. Ten years later he became Dean of the Law School; in the meantime he became involved in politics, which led to his dismissal in 1936. He served in Baghdad for a year as Dean of the Law College and this new experience enriched his understanding of Arab legal institutions as well as it proved to be invaluable to his later contribution to Arab legal development. In that year he was invited by the 'Iraqi Government to prepare a draft civil law for 'Iraq which prompted him to return to his original theme of modernizing Islamic law to fit the legal development of an Arab state. It is in legal reform that Sanhuri's contribution will endure, although he made certain ventures in politics which elevated him to cabinet rank. Back in Egypt, he participated in various activities, until he became President of the Council of State in 1949. In that capacity, he co-operated with the Revolutionary leaders in the hope of contributing to the development of his country, but he came into conflict with them which precipitated his early retirement in 1954. During the last decade he has devoted almost all his time to research and writing on civil law and has given lectures on Islamic law at the Higher Institute of Arabic Studies of the Arab League in Cairo.

In 1936, while still in 'Iraq, a committee of which Sanhuri was a member, was appointed by the 'Iraqi Government to prepare a draft civil law for 'Iraq. Although the work was interrupted, the committee adopted Sanhuri's proposals regarding the sources for the proposed civil law code. It was agreed that both Islamic law and Western law, in addition to 'Iraq's experiences as reflected in its own laws, would be the sources for the new 'Iraqi civil law.[63] The work was resumed when Sanhuri, back in 'Iraq in 1943, completed the draft civil code for 'Iraq. Before this law was formally enacted in 'Iraq, it was adopted, with modifications, by the Syrian Government in June 1949. Meantime, a new civil code for Egypt was enacted in October 1949, derived mainly from Western law and from Egypt's own experiences, in the preparation of which Sanhuri took a leading part, when the Egyptian national courts assumed full jurisdiction following the abolition of the Mixed Courts. Profiting from the two new civil codes of Syria and Egypt, the 'Iraqi Government, making a final revision, formally adopted in June 1951 Sanhuri's draft as the 'Iraqi civil code.

Before analyzing Sanhuri's experimentation in blending Western and Islamic law, let us review the legal situation in the Arab world before the adoption of Sanhuri's codes. The Arab countries were divided into three categories: 1. The countries that followed traditional Islamic law without changes, such as Saudi Arabia in conformity with the Hanbali law, and the Yaman applying Zaydi law, a subdivision of Shi'i law. 2. The countries that followed Islamic law with certain modifications, essentially in accordance with the Hanafi school, as codified by the Ottoman Government, called the "*Majallat al-Ahkam al-'Adliya*" (Digest of Civil Law) and applied to the former Ottoman territories—'Iraq, Syria, Palestine, Transjordan, and Libya. Although these countries fell under British and French control after World War I, the *Majalla* remained in force except in Lebanon, where a new civil code based on the French *Code civil*, was enacted. 3. The

[63] See Sanhuri, "Memorandum to the Chairman of the Civil Law Commission," *Majallat al-Qada'*, II (1936), 221ff.

Arab countries that adopted the French civil code consisting of Egypt, Lebanon, Tunisia, Algeria, and Morocco. These countries (except Morocco, which was independent before French occupation), detached from the Ottoman empire before the *Majalla* was issued, adopted the French Civil Code either voluntarily, as in the case of Egypt, or under French influence after France had extended her control to them.

This situation remained essentially unchanged until World War II, but the experience of the Arab countries during the inter-war years, especially the Fertile Crescent and Egypt, demonstrated that neither a purely Western nor a purely Islamic law proved satisfactory without modifications. As in other domains of life, a conflict ensued between two schools of thought: the new denounced the old as incompatible with modern conditions, and the old, witnessing a sudden break with the past, demanded the full restoration of Islamic law.

A new approach combining the best of the two was therefore needed. Sanhuri championed the cause of a novel moderate approach combining Western and Islamic law, hoping that the blend might ultimately lead to a synthesis of the two. There was, indeed, already support for this new approach. There were critics who began to revaluate Western law; they could see that Western legal concepts, transplanted into a new social milieu, could not be expected to achieve results similar to those achieved in the West. Western law, though it did not interject itself uniformly throughout society, came into direct conflict with Islamic law in fields in which the latter had a strong hold. For this reason, some began to ask whether Islamic law could not be modernized to a point where it would not come into conflict with Western law. Perhaps the modification of Western law and the modernization of Islamic law might be achieved so that the two systems might be brought into harmony and a synthesis of the two might be accomplished. While thinking along these lines was entertained, Sanhuri toyed with the idea of applying this approach in the drafting of the new civil code for 'Iraq based on Islamic and Western concepts.

Sanhuri's experiment was not unprecedented. Ever since

the Ottoman empire began to implement the Tanzimat decrees, new legislations consisting of Western laws (such as commercial and penal codes of 1850 and 1858), had been adopted. Such attempts prompted a few modernists to codify Islamic civil law. The *Majalla,* an Islamic civil code (although by no means consisting of all aspects of a civil code) was prepared and promulgated in 1869. Derived in the main from the Hanafi school of law (although recourse had also been made to other schools), it marked a significant landmark in the development of an Islamic civil code. The Western influence is shown particularly in the form in which the *Majalla* was drafted.[64] A similar attempt, made in Egypt by Qadri Pasha in his *Kitab Murshid al-Hayran,* codifying the law of contract, according to the Hanafi school, was not unlike the *Majalla* in its content or a European code in form. Although this was an unofficial codification, since Egypt had adopted the French Civil Code, it was regarded as authoritative and used as a textbook in government schools.[65] But neither the *Majalla* nor Qadri Pasha's codes made significant changes in substance. Such changes were reserved for the following generation. It was Sanhuri who advanced the process a step forward.

The two countries—'Iraq and Egypt—that showed readiness to change their civil codes represented two extreme trends: Egypt adopted a completely Western (French) civil code and 'Iraq clung to the *Majalla.* Sanhuri made no attempt to draft entirely new codes for these two countries. Moderate in temper and pragmatic in approach, he did not call for revolutionary changes in either country. He recognized the difficulty of achieving radical change, and tried in each case to introduce some of the elements lacking in the others–to introduce elements of Western law to 'Iraq, where it was essentially Islamic; and to introduce Islamic law to Egypt, where it was essentially French. The two codes of 'Iraq and Egypt became models for

[64] See S. S. Onar, "The Majalla," in M. Khadduri and H. J. Liebesny (eds.), *Law in the Middle East* (Washington, D.C., 1955), chap. 12.

[65] For the life and works of Qadri Pasha, see Tawfiq Askarus, "Muhammad Qadri Pasha," *al-Muqtataf,* 48 (1916), 253–63; Muhammad Husayn Haykal, *Tarajim Misriya wa Gharbiya* (Cairo, 1929), pp. 109–18.

other countries—Syria adopted the Egyptian model, modified by the 'Iraqi approach; and Jordan and Libya adopted the 'Iraqi model, modified by the Egyptian.

It is evident that this experiment, varying in the degree of application from one Arab country to another, was perhaps most successful in introducing legal reform along secular lines, especially in 'Iraq, where Western and Islamic law were almost equally represented. Sanhuri's remarkable success may be attributed to the fact that he started to apply his method to that part of the law where it aroused little or no opposition from conservative elements. He wisely abstained from discussing controversial issues which might bring him into conflict with the 'ulama. Without going into a theoretical discussion on how Islamic law generally should be modernized, or even trying to give a rationale of his scheme, he proceeded in a practical way to show how a synthesis between Islamic and Western law could be achieved. For this reason, he succeeded where Raziq had failed.[66]

Toward an Islamic Reformation: Mustafa 'Abd al-Raziq and Khalid Muhammad Khalid

Having discussed the possible secularization of other aspects of life, we have reached the point where a question bearing directly on Islam as a religion might be raised: Is it possible to resolve Islam's religious crisis by some kind of reform? Some have pointed out that Islam had never experienced a Reformation which could have introduced basic changes compatible with the modern age, while others have stressed advantages of a more evolutionary approach. Revolutionary change, regardless of its inherent advantages or disadvantages, is now being experienced in many Arab countries. If the Islamic religion is to be reformed slowly—by many small revo-

[66] In his old age, Sanhuri proposed somewhat a more conservative approach in the drafting of an Arab civil code, consisting of an entirely Islamic legal raw material, derived from all schools, living or defunct, adapted to modern Arab life drawing on Western experience in drafting legal codes (see Sanhuri, "al-Qanun al-Madani al-'Arabi," *Majalat al-Qada'* [1962], pp. 7–33.

lutions rather than by a single major one—the ultimate outcome might well be salutary though the process is long and painstaking.

However, the problem is not merely procedural. Like Christianity, Islam is a universal religion which historically was closely tied with political authority. Christians were able to separate church from state and reform the church, but since Islam has no church, it is more difficult to relegate religious authority to a central religious institution which has never existed. The caliphate was abolished and could not develop into a central religious authority as the Kamalist regime first proposed. The Turks replaced Islam as a political identity by nationalism, but religious reform has yet to be introduced.

Similarly in the Arab world, Islamic identity is being gradually replaced by nationalism without revolutionary change. No matter how sincerely Arab nationalists continue to profess faith in Islamic religious and ethical values, they are committed to a second loyalty, even if Islam commands their primary loyalty. But once the principle of dual loyalties is established, religion is likely to be eventually superseded by nationalism as the primary loyalty. It is evident that religious leaders are not today opposed to nationalism, presumably because religion is recognized as an element of nationalism. Thus religious leaders have tacitly accepted in principle the subordination of religious to civil authority. Whether a formal separation of religious from civil authorities is necessary seems to be inconsequential and need not, as the experience of England has demonstrated, be done. In view of the absence of an organized "church" in Islam, some form of state supervision over religious institutions may be necessary to guide and coordinate religious activities; state supervision may encourage religious leaders to accept religious reform so that religious institutions do not lag behind the progress achieved in secular institutions.

The next stage in an Islamic reformation is to reform the "church"—its institutions, doctrines, and ethical values. Such reform is obviously more difficult in Islam than in Christianity, again because there is no central religious organization, and because each Islamic country might choose to follow a different course. Not even al-Azhar, the oldest religious educational institution, could claim supreme religious authority in Egypt and enforce a reform program on other religious institutions. Nor was the attempt to reform al-Azhar itself an easy problem, although some changes in structure, procedure, and academic standards have been introduced. These changes started with Muhammad 'Abduh, who laid down the first plan for modernization, and culminated more recently with Shaykh Muhmud Shaltut (d. 1964), who changed al-Azhar's academic program from purely religious and classical to a completely modern by the inclusion of medicine, physical sciences, and modern languages.[67] Some critics, devoted to religious and classical studies, regretted the adoption of a secular program of studies, since there were secular educational institutions already in existence. They maintained that the religious aims would have been better attained if reforms were limited to the religious and educational program. The author put these questions to Shaykh Shaltut, who replied: Before secular institutions were established, al-Azhar had taught all branches of knowledge, including the French language, and if this institution is to catch up with progress, it should at least resume the functions it had fulfilled in the past. Shaltut seemed to think that progress in religious instruction was inseparable from progress in other branches of knowledge, and insisted that there is no conflict between science and religion. For this reason reform in religion can be achieved only if the students of religion were exposed to modern scientific studies.[68]

However, because of the strong hold of traditionalism and because a radical change might undermine its spiritual leader-

[67] For a brief history and development of al-Azhar, see Bayard Dodge, *al-Azhar* (Washington, D.C. 1961); 'Abd al-Hamid Yunus and 'Uthman Tawfiq, *al-Azhar* (Cairo, 1946); Muhammad al-Khafaji, *al-Azhar fi Alf 'Am* (Cairo, 1954).

[68] Some of Shaykh Shaltut's own interpretations of Islam may be found in his *Tafsir al-Qur'an al-Karim* [Commentary on the Qur'an] (Cairo, 1960), *al-Islam: 'Aqida wa Shari'a* [Islam: Beliefs and Law] (Cairo, n.d.) and others.

ship throughout the Islamic world, al-Azhar has maintained an essentially fundamentalist outlook on religious matters. Few of its 'ulama other than 'Abduh and Shaltut expressed radical ideas. Al-Azhar, though often repudiating progressive ideas, has shown willingness to accept them later and even paid tribute to those who had expounded them. 'Abduh's views, it will be recalled, were at first rejected by Al-Azhar's 'ulama, but they are now accepted by them. The views of Shaykhs al-Maraghi, al-Zawahiri, and Shaltut are in turn being gradually adopted.[69] It is evident that neither al-Azhar nor any other great centers of religious learning are willing or capable of taking the lead in radical religious reform. Such leadership has come from outside the walls of these institutions, though much of this leadership was originally associated with them.

Radical religious ideas have been advocated by some Muslim thinkers, without an attempt to play the role of a Luther. But reformers like Ahmad Khan, or even Iqbal, have been unacceptable to the Arabs because it has been feared that they may stir schism; Arab reformers have, accordingly, tried to plead for reform without attacking basic doctrines. They have preferred to follow the examples of Erasmus and Melanchthon rather than Luther and Calvin. We have already discussed the role of 'Abduh as a religious reformer; but his disciples failed, as noted before, to provide reform measures for twentieth-century Islam. Since World War II several Arab thinkers, each stressing a different approach, have paid special attention to religious reform. Some, like 'Allal al-Fasi of Morocco and Khalid Muhammad Khalid of Egypt, were not very original, although they were influential in public life; but others, like Mustafa 'Abd al-Raziq of Egypt and Bin Nabi (Bennabi) of Algeria, more original in ideas, have not yet had any real impact. The significance of these men lies in trying to achieve an Islamic Reformation by an evolutionary rather than by a revolutionary process. The views of only two will be

[69] See Muhammad Kamil al-Fiqqi, *al-Azhar wa Atharuh fi al-Nahda al-'Adabiya al-Haditha* [al-Azhar and Its Impact on Modern Literary Revival] (Cairo, 1956), 3 vols.; 'Abd al-Mit'al al-Sa'idi, *Ta'rikh al-Islah fi al-Azhar* (Cairo, 1943).

scrutinized here: Mustafa 'Abd al-Raziq and Khalid Muhammad Khalid.[70]

Mustafa 'Abd al-Raziq, older brother of 'Ali 'Abd al-Raziq, was highly refined and of moderate temperament. Like his brother, he studied at al-Azhar, but later he studied in France and attended the lectures of Durkheim, rather than in England where his brother had studied. As a disciple of 'Abduh, he was interested in religion and devoted his life to the study of Islam. After a brief career in the Department of Justice, he was appointed in 1927 to the faculty of the Egyptian University. For a decade he taught and published studies in which he expounded Islam as a highly rational and progressive religious system. In 1938 he became Minister of Waqf and seven years later was appointed Rector of al-Azhar. His influence in the dissemination of liberal religious ideas went beyond his lecture audiences but fell short of attracting public attention. He died in 1947 at the age of 62.[71]

In two works, one devoted to Islamic philosophy and jurisprudence and the other to Islamic religion, Raziq, under the influence of French rationalism, carried 'Abduh's liberal interpretation of Islam one step further.[72] In the first, after a summary of divergent views of Western writers on Islam, especially of Renan, he demonstrates beyond doubt the role of reason in the development of Islamic religion from the beginnings of Islam. After an examination of the opinions of theologians and philosophers who were agreed on the essential teaching of religion, he shows the influence of philosophical writings on the development of religious thought despite the critical attitude of the theologians toward philosophy.[73] In law, Raziq traces the role of reason in the use of opinion (*ra'y*) as a source of law and the juristic method of reasoning

[70] For the views of 'Allal al-Fasi, see E. I. J. Rosenthal, *Islam in the Modern National State* (Cambridge, 1965), chap. 7; and for Bin Nabi, see Malek Bennabi, *Vocation de l'Islam* (Paris, 1954).

[71] For a brief account of his life by his brother 'Ali, see 'Ali 'Abd al-Raziq, *Min Athar Mustafa 'Abd al-Raziq* [Some Posthumous Writings of Mustafa 'Abd al-Raziq] (Cairo, 1957), pp. 5–77.

[72] Mustafa 'Abd al-Raziq, *Tamhid li Ta'rikh al-Falsafa al-Islamiya* [An Introduction to the History of Islamic Philosophy] (Cairo, 1944); *al-Din wa al-Wahi wa al-Islam* [Religion, Revelation and Islam] (Cairo, 1945).

[73] Raziq, *Tamhid*, pp. 101–23.

(ijtihad) in the development of Islamic law.[74] This method of analysis shows the influence of Raziq's European training, in particular in his use of the concept of historical development to reveal what Islam really means.[75]

In the other work, Raziq tries first to explain the relationship between religion and revelation and points out that Islam is regarded as one of the higher religions based on revelation. He cites the opinions of several Western writers, including Durkheim, on religion and concludes that no satisfactory definition of religion exists. It is perhaps too presumptuous, he says, to try to deny the existence of so ingrained a phenomenon as religion in human nature before one can fully understand the elements that form it or know how this phenomenon developed. Raziq then turns to define revelation on which religion, especially Islam, is based. He cites the development of the various meanings of direct and indirect revelation from the Prophet's time to the modern period, stressing, as did 'Abduh, the inner feeling of inspiration, based on genuine conviction that such an inspiration is equated with revelation. Such a modernist view, he maintains, is implied in the writings of Muslim philosophers and may well be regarded as the real basis of the Islamic religion.[76] From this point, Raziq proceeds to examine the meaning of Islam, citing the opinions of Muslim thinkers derived from the authoritative sources; he concludes that Islam is a religion based on belief in the validity of a set of basic principles as set forth in the Qur'an, embodying the Prophet's revelations. These principles were laid down, he says, to achieve the individual's welfare and inner satisfaction in accordance with reason and free will. He arrives at this meaning of religion by drawing on Islamic religious and philosophic writings and not on European thought. Islam, he says, is not an outward manifestation of actions, but the inward expression of intentions, the source of which is the spirit. This idea is based on the Prophet's saying: "Actions are the expression of intentions, and every one is [judged] in accordance with his intention." [77]

[74] *Ibid.*, pp. 136ff.
[75] See Albert Hourani, *Arabic Thought*, p. 163.
[76] Raziq, *al-Din wa al-Wahi wa al-Islam*, pp. 21 and 80.
[77] *Ibid.*, pp. 101–2.

Raziq's interpretation of religion seems to reflect a genuine belief in the value of religion and may well provide the basis for a "reformed" belief in religion relevant to contemporary Arab society. However, Raziq had no intention to initiate a reform movement, nor had he appealed to any group. He was satisfied that modernist interpretation of Islam should be proposed, leaving its propagation to others.[78]

If Raziq is taken to represent an Erasmus in Islamic Reformation, Khalid Muhammad Khalid possessed certain qualities of a Luther. A graduate of al-Azhar University, he was thoroughly at home in Islamic studies and wrote with a crusading zeal for reform. His style carried conviction and his terse sentences, though often repetitious, resembled public sermons. He became well-known to the public only after his first book, the title of which means "From Here We Start," was published in 1950.[79] At a time when censorship was strict and criticism of the monarchical regime and its functionaries, civil or religious, might lead to arrest and imprisonment, Khalid, with great moral courage, attacked both religious and social institutions. This book, obviously written by a man with religious convictions, attacked false beliefs and corrupt religious leaders. After several tedious months of waiting, the book was published in several editions and read not only in Egypt but throughout the Arab world including the most conservative parts of Arabia. Khalid, then teaching in one of Cairo's high schools, resigned to devote all his time to writing and preaching. Though he contributed to the Revolution of 1952 by spreading revolutionary ideas, he has preferred to remain outside official circles to avoid official restraints. After the Revolution, President Nasir, one of Khalid's admirers, admonished his followers to let Khalid speak out his mind freely. Nasir protected Khalid even when he made critical remarks about his military regime.[80]

[78] See 'Ali 'Abd al-Raziq, *Min Athar*, pp. 20–22, 68–70.

[79] Khalid Muhammad Khalid, *Min Huna Nabda'* (Cairo, 1950); trans. Isma'il R. al-Faruqi, *From Here We Start* (Washington, D.C., 1953).

[80] See Khalid's remarks in the meetings of the Preparatory Committee which prepared the National Charter (see p. 167, above).

In his writings, Khalid deals with three main subjects: religious authority, jurisprudence (*fiqh*), and religious ethics. In his first book, noted above, he touched on several issues, although he concentrated his attack on religious leaders calling and denouncing their priesthood (*kihana*) as no longer compatible with the modern demands of life. "What sort of religion," he asked, "is it which these men are calling for?" and he replied, that it is the religion of priesthood, or false religion—not true religion. "It seeks to exploit the peoples' devotion to [true] religion and, accordingly, it puts on the appearance of the latter, thus violating its sacredness."

Khalid believes that true religion is indispensable to mankind; it must be the true religion that meets man's social demands. What is that religion? Two prerequisites must be satisfied, if religion is to maintain its "glory" and "power" in the hearts of men. These are as follow:

> First: it must act and react in accordance with the change of human needs, and of life in general, if man is to be able to draw therefrom a permanent support against his newest problems and exigencies and receive its blessing in his continuous advance and progress.
>
> Second: Religion must safeguard and preserve its general and essential characteristics, the ultimate purpose for which God has granted and sanctified it—namely, to bring about the real happiness of man in the atmosphere of noble equality—a purpose which religion proclaimed at its beginning and has sought so long to actualize.[81]

"The bulk of the Islamic religion," Khalid told the present writer, "is essentially jurisprudence and law; it is therefore this side of religion which needs to be reformed and modernized in accordance with existing conditions, and to be embodied in codes laid down by the state." He laid great emphasis on ethical values which, in his eyes, are the essence of religion; thus, he devoted most of his works to values rather than to principles. These values, he said, were not only the essence of Islam but also of Christianity; and he demonstrated that early Prophets, including Christ and Muhammad, had

[81] See Khalid, *From Here We Start*, pp. 30–32.

as their chief goals the setting of an example by their own model conduct.

As a religious reformer, Khalid had often been reminded that his propositions on reform should be addressed to the Rector of the Azhar, one of the custodians of Islam, and not to the public. Khalid invariably replied pointing out the futility of approaching al-Azhar or other religious organizations because of the influence of the priesthood on them even if their heads were in favor of reform. He therefore wrote for the public, to prepare an opinion favorable to reform which, in turn, would impress upon the 'ulama of al-Azhar and other institutions the need for reformation. Khalid's message was, accordingly, not to reformulate religious doctrines, but to explain old ones and urge the public to bring pressure on religious authorities to reform Islam.

Islam, according to Khalid, is essentially a social system; it is inherently rational and democratic. It does not long tolerate conditions in which some Muslims live in abundance and the rest in poverty. Religious leaders, for their own selfish interests, have in the past supported a corrupt ruling class; thus only enlightened religious leaders are motivated by the precepts of true religion. Religious and civil authorities should be separated, but the 'ulama must be represented in national assemblies to advise the civil authority on religious matters.

It is evident that Khalid's main concern was with religious ethics and social justice; he had obviously discarded basic doctrines and reduced the function of religion to "guidance, liberation from oppression and corruption, and fraternity." Thus he was interested in social and religious values and not in religion *per se*; he did not pretend to be a theologian. In the present trend toward an Islamic Reformation, his role is significant in that the Arab world is in need of a religious reformer who would prepare the public to discard traditional religious beliefs before it can accept the ideas of a Mustafa 'Abd al-Raziq.[82]

[82] For a background of contemporary Islamic religious thought, see H. A. R. Gibb, *Modern Trends in Islam* (Chicago, 1947); and Kenneth Cragg, *Counsels in Contemporary Islam* (Edinburgh, 1965).

Chapter 10

A NEW SOCIAL DEMOCRACY?

God commands justice and kindness and giving to kinsmen; He forbids indecency and disreputable conduct and greed.

Qur'an XVI, 92

We have seen that the debate concerning the prospects of reform and progress has passed through essentially three stages of development. First, to recapitulate briefly, the debate in the initial stage was concerned about whether reform should draw exclusively on Western or Islamic sources. Second, the debate centered on what particular set of ideas or ideals, especially from the West, were to be introduced without being adapted to existing conditions; this debate culminated in evaluating the assimilation of imported ideas and on the possibility of blending them with Islamic concepts in an effort to create a synthesis of two or more ingredients.[1] The third stage, beginning after World War II, is the most constructive and the one with which Arab thinkers have been most pre-occupied today.

Arab endeavors to achieve reform, like the endeavors of other countries, are considered by some to have changed only the outward form but not the very basis of society, and by others to have provided a new elite capable of achieving reforms compatible with Arab needs and aspirations. Needless

[1] See chap. 1.

to say, the latter viewpoint stresses elements of change brought about by Arab revolutionary leaders while the former, stressing the elements of continuity, is followed in countries preferring peaceful rather than revolutionary change. The Arab countries are therefore divided, from the viewpoint of revolutionary leaders, into two groups with respect to social change: the first, advocating revolutionary change, consists of Egypt, Syria, 'Iraq, Algeria, the Sudan, the Yaman, and Libya; the second, stressing peaceful change, consists of the rest of the Arab world. However, Arab experimentation with revolutionary processes and indeed the experimentation of other countries advocating revolutionary change has demonstrated that, despite the desire to achieve progress quickly, such a change is necessarily slow and compels revolutionary leaders to undergo prolonged "transitional" periods. Traditional Arab countries, no less anxious to achieve progress quickly, have preferred to follow peaceful evolutionary processes despite popular pressures brought on their leaders to identify with Arab revolutionary methods. It is too early to foretell which of the two approaches will eventually result in constructive reform with a minimum degree of wasted time and energy, not to mention other sacrifices, notwithstanding the fact that the revolutionary process did not come out of free debate about its merits, but was the product of complex internal forces that had long been in the making. Arab choice of a revolutionary procedure will have been perhaps justified if the social polity that will ultimately emerge is based on tested principles. The hardships and insecurity which the Arabs have endured during the period of violent change might be worth the experimentation if the achievement meets cherished aspirations, even though the motivation of revolutionary leaders were not devoid of political ambition. Some counter-revolutionary steps—indeed, a chain of revolutionary and counter-revolutionary acts—especially in Syria and 'Iraq, might be regarded as natural and perhaps necessary if they were to lead ultimately to stability and progress. If, however, the revolutionary and counter-revolutionary processes fail to achieve the desired development, the new leaders might be compelled to embark on new experimentations, revolutionary or otherwise, and the cycle of change might continue indefinitely without real progress.

To achieve reform, Arab leaders will have to decide first what particular set of ideas and reform measures to adopt or reformulate and then, perhaps more important, to secure the consent and active participation of the people who are the object of the reform. In his *Politics,* Aristotle often affirms that citizens must be educated in the spirit of the constitution under which they live. Aristotle's remark may well remind us of the close relationship that must exist between polity and public and, in a broader sense, between operative ideas and society. It is proposed that unless the Arab citizenry is adequately "educated" to be ready for participation in the political processes, peaceful or revolutionary, the newly adopted systems, social or political, cannot possibly work and will not endure. Arab revolutionary leaders often sought to formulate the political systems they adopted in accordance with a foreign ideal or model (or a blend of the two) considered to be compatible with their country's needs, but they failed to enlist genuine popular participation even when they tried to do so.[2] In the Arab countries that have followed peaceful or evolutionary processes, the ruling elites have been able to secure partial popular participation and modify or adapt the political processes to their country's needs without violent change. In either case, if the emerging systems are to endure and achieve society's needs and aspirations, popular participation is deemed absolutely essential to establish legitimacy through public consent.

In reviewing the various ideas and ideals which Arab reformers have so far proposed, one may discern certain trends which are unmistakably emerging and are likely to command public respect, despite the ravages of social or political upheavals.

To begin with, nationalism is the fundamental concept on which all Arab thinkers are agreed and it may be regarded as

[2] See chap. 6, above.

the very basis of the emerging social polity. Even the communists, who desire an association with an international movement, are willing to acknowledge a national element in their program. In the past, Islam provided a superstructure within which all loyalties, ethnic or cultural, were superseded, and it remained the basis of unity in principle until nationalism began to supplant it. The reintroduction of Islam as an element in nationalism, as noted before, is a tacit recognition of the overriding principle of nationalism; thus Islam, by becoming a component, is no longer an opponent to nationalism.

However, the danger to nationalism is not because Islam is regarded as one of its elements but because it is identified with confessionalism. In countries like 'Iraq, Lebanon, and the Sudan, where large religious minorities exist, nationalism has not yet been accepted as a primary loyalty because of the existing parochial and confessional feelings. The idea of nationalism, though stressed by the ruling elites, has not yet penetrated to the masses to supersede religious and, consequently, confessional loyalties. In countries where strong ethnic minorities, like the Kurds in 'Iraq, exist, the problem is rendered more complicated, because the stress on Arab nationalism, though it might reduce confessionalism, tends to create tension between Arab and Kurdish nationalism.[3] 'Iraqi rulers have wavered between the broader notion of Arab nationalism and the narrow concept of 'Iraqi nationality, because the former has been strongly opposed by Kurds and the latter, though it might reconcile Kurds and Arabs, is not likely to supersede confessional feeling. As a result, some aspects of confessionalism may indefinitely continue in some Arab countries, especially in Lebanon and 'Iraq, as long as Arab nationalism continues to be identified with religion; but if nationalism develops along secular lines, it is likely that it might supersede confessionalism. In the Arab countries where no important ethnic or religious minorities exist, religion may become a valuable ingredient of nationalism; but in countries

[3] Cf. my *Republican 'Iraq* (London, 1969), pp. 3–5, 173ff.

where religious or confessional feeling is deeply rooted, a secular form of nationalism would be absolutely necessary to supersede indigeneous counter-currents, as Sati' al-Husri rightly observed.[4]

The principle of secularism, fully accepted by Turkey, has not yet been formally adopted by any Arab country. It has been relatively easy for the Turks to establish a secular state, because Islam has been renounced as part of their national heritage. But for the Arabs, who rightly regard Islam as an integral part of their historical heritage, it cannot so easily be disclaimed. And yet all Arab countries, including the traditional ones, have consciously adopted some form of secular measures to repair or modernize their traditional systems. The process of transformation of existing institutions from Islamic into secular is continuing without serious interruptions, notwithstanding that a formal step to separate religion and state has not been deemed necessary. Whether any Arab country would be prepared to follow in the footsteps of Turkey is difficult to foretell, but all countries seem to be unmistakably heading, in varying degrees, toward secular systems without so labelling them. Some Arab countries, where confessionalism is ingrained in the social order, may need a greater emphasis on secularism than others, to overcome their internal division; yet both Lebanon and 'Iraq, to mention but two instances, have found it exceedingly difficult to abandon confessionalism for political and not necessarily for religious reasons. Thus, the reduction of confessional feeling is dependent on the reform of existing political institutions no less than on the prospect of growth in religious tolerance that would blunt religious and confessional cross-currents.

Falling behind Turkey in the secularization movement, some of the Arab countries, especially the revolutionary ones, have made greater strides toward radical ideological goals than Turkey by adopting socialist reform measures. It may seem surprising that the Arab countries which showed reluctance

[4] See p. 204 above.

to accept full secularism should be inclined to adopt radical leftist doctrines not all compatible with Islam. However, Arab countries have been divided on the question of Islam's compatibility with collectivist doctrines. Some thinkers, as noted before, argued in favor of radical doctrines and maintained that Islam, opposed to the disparity between rich and poor, is at bottom a socialist system; others, especially those opposed to the materialist view of collectivism, argued against it and held that Islam is based essentially on free enterprise.[5] It is evident that Islam possesses elements common to both collectivism and free enterprise just as it is opposed to certain aspects of them. As a system which assesses all values of life in terms of divine revelations, it is opposed to materialism. To the pious Muslim who conforms to religion and the sacred law, collectivist doctrines appear to reduce life to a mechanical process, stressing mundane rather than spirtual values. In theory this opposition is undoubtedly true, but the same argument could be advanced with equal truth on behalf of Christianity, Judaism, and Confucianism, although doctrinal incompatibility has not prevented Christians, Jews, and Chinese from becoming socialists and communists. Idealist thinkers, stressing distributive justice, advocate socialism; but the realists, trying to increase production more rapidly and efficiently by free enterprise, are opposed to socialist doctrines. While Arab thinkers are still debating the issue, certain elements of either system that are not incompatible with Arab traditions are being consciously adopted to meet Arab needs and aspirations. A modicum of the two systems may well command greater public respect, although only 'Iraq has tried fitfully to maintain a balance between the two views in her experiment with a hybrid system.[6]

In the realm of theory, Isma'il Mazhar, whom we met before, came out strongly in favor of a hybrid economic system, long before 'Iraq began to experiment with it. He called this system "social equilibrium" (*al-Takaful al-Ijtima'i* or

[5] See p. 126, above.
[6] See my *Republican 'Iraq*, chap. 10.

al-Ishtiraki) and maintained that neither free enterprise nor socialism had so far succeeded in building a stable society. Free enterprise, permitting exploitation and disparity, subordinated society to the individual, while socialism, stressing restrictive measures and thereby limiting individual freedom, subordinated the individual to society. The system of "social equilibrium," which Mazhar proposes, is designed to limit the individual's oppression of the society as well as the society's oppression of the individual. This system provides equal opportunities to all under a system of safeguarded freedom. Social equilibrium, according to Mazhar, is compatible with the doctrine of human evolution, because it leaves no room for excessive wealth or poverty. Early civilizations, including the Islamic, he maintained, had declined mainly because of the absence of equilibrium (*takaful*); when extremism became difficult to check, the decline and disintegration of those civilizations occurred. Equilibrium, providing for moderation and individual security, is capable of insuring continuous progress and development and, therefore, likely to command public appeal.[7] Mazhar's views are shared by many Arab thinkers who seem to be prepared to tolerate certain restrictions on individual liberty in order to achieve equitable distribution of wealth rather than to tolerate disparity. Even opponents to collectivist doctrines are prepared to accept moderate socialist measures. For this reason, the adoption of moderate socialist principles may be regarded as a corrective approach to social reform and may well contribute to the emergence of a stable and enduring social order.

The question has often been raised whether social reform could be achieved through democratic procedures. A relatively short period of Arab experience with parliamentary democracy convinced the Arabs that this sytem was entirely unsatisfactory, despite the fact that its failure was due to complex factors and not merely because adequate social reforms had not been achieved. Arab thinkers were not slow in pointing out that, before the democratic system can work,

[7] Isma'il Mazhar, *al-Takaful al-Ishtiraki* (Cairo, 1961).

certain prerequisites—an educated public, organized political parties, an enlightened leadership, and so forth—must be fulfilled, and that the principal aim of the constitutional regimes that had been adopted after World War I was independence. This aim, as Edmond Rabbath pointed out to his satisfaction, had been fully achieved.[8] It was, however, realized that parliamentary democracy carried with it the germs of corruption; the cry for trying other political systems was soon echoing from many directions. Seeking temporary measures to provide the necessary prerequisites for a truly democratic system, Arab reformers advocated revolutionary processes: these processes are today the hope, as well as the despair, of many Arabs.

Before they resorted to revolutionary change, it was the declared aim of the leaders to establish a truly democratic system, based on popular representation and free elections. That system was to insure liberty, equality, and basic civil rights as well as to protect private property. However, the experiences of Egypt, Syria, and 'Iraq demonstrated that revolutionary processes can become ends in themselves and not merely means to another form or other forms of government. In spite of this, Arab thinkers still assert that the ultimate aim of revolutionary change is to achieve a form of democracy which is different from previously established democratic regimes: a form embodying ideals which have become fashionable such as a greater role of the state in social reform, collectivism, and the enlistment of mass support for public action.[9]

The adoption of various social principles combining Western liberal ideals as well as ideals of other societies may be regarded as a healthy approach to evolve a political system suitable for Arab society. The Arabs often speak of liberty and equality as two inseparable words meaning the same thing, but if they were to choose one of the two, it seems that

[8] Edmond Rabbath, "al-Dimuqratiya fi al-Bilad al-'Arabiya," *al-Dimuqratiya fi al-'Alam al-'Arabi* [Publications of the Lebanese Society of Political Science] (Bayrut, 1959), III, 48.

[9] For a discussion of the new ideas of democracy in the Arab world, see Malcolm Kerr, "Arab Radical Notions of Democracy" *St. Antony's Papers: Middle Eastern Affairs* (London: Chatto and Windus, 1963), pp. 9–40.

the choice of the great majority would be in favor of equality. Therefore, the adoption of certain socialist measures which would achieve an equitable distribution of wealth would be acceptable even if it led to restrictions on individual liberty. It follows that a political system which would insure the principle of equality with a minimum of liberty is likely to have greater public appeal than a system which insures individual liberty at the expense of equality. Does this mean that the modicum of liberty will remain indefinitely subordinated to equality? Once a large measure of distributive justice is achieved, it is likely that individual liberty would be in greater demand, and some form of a balance between liberty and equality might be achieved which would insure freedom and prosperity—a welfare state. If social democracy could achieve this welfare state, it may well be the ultimate outcome of the present Arab political trends, a blend of diverse principles and measures originated from different, if conflicting, sources.

Will the Arabs be able to achieve this blend and maintain an equilibrium between diverse principles? In the past, the Arabs have demonstrated an ability to adopt foreign elements of culture and create their own synthesis. The emerging Islamic civilization remained for centuries flexible enough to meet the essential demands of society. At the time of decline, the Arabs were no longer able to maintain that capacity. They became content with the social order they had inherited from their forefathers. Today the Arabs are in need to revive that capacity of assimilation if they are to create a new blend of culture capable of meeting modern demands. If they can meet this new challenge, a new political system may well emerge which would be a native form of social democracy, suitable for the Arab social milieu. One thing is certain: this system will have to evolve rather than to be imposed. Its ingredients necessarily will have to stem from the emerging political trends, embodying the ideas and ideals that have long been the subject of debate over social reform. In the recent past, the Arabs always have looked abroad for the panaceas of their ills; now they are beginning to look inward. Not until they are cured from within—socially and economically no less than politically—can they live a salutary way of life. The Prophet, in a Quranic injunction, reminded his people: "Verily God changeth not that which is in a people until they change that which is in themselves." The Prophet also admonished his people to take a "middle" position, presumably on matters concerning public affairs. "We made you a nation in the middle," one of the divine revelations has it. Commentators may have given different interpretations to this cryptic message, but all seem to agree that an element of moderation was implied in it.[10] The Prophet, perhaps noting Arab oscillation from one extreme to another, admonished moderation. Having oscillated between traditional and radical ideologies, the Arabs today, perhaps more than ever before, are in need for moderation, to put their house in order and build up a stable, progressive society.

Closely related to the emerging Arab social order is the question of relationship between each Arab country and another—the question of regional integration or Arab unity. No social order in any Arab country will endure unless the nature of the relationship between that country and the others is defined and collectively accepted. Will the Arab countries remain separate independent units or should they unite into some form of union, federal or unitary?

The Arab nationalists have always maintained that, since the Arabs were bound by a community of interests and aspirations—geographical, historical, and cultural—they should be able to form some kind of union. Half a century ago, when the Arab world was still under foreign control, no Arab nationalist ever questioned the feasibility of Arab unity. They held that European powers, by following a policy of *divide et impera*, prevented them from achieving unity. A quarter of a century after independence, the Arab countries have not yet achieved unity, even though plans for unity have been seriously considered. There must exist therefore certain inherent forces, more influential than foreign influence, working against unity.

[10] *Qur'an* XIII, 11; and II, 137. See Tabari, *Tafsir*, ed. M. Shakir (Cairo, 1955), III, 142.

Before Islam began to spread and provide a common ground for unity among diverse ethnic and cultural groups, the whole of Southwest Asia had been the scene of a constant struggle for power among rival empires, from the times of the ancient Pharaohs to Roman rule. Islam unified the whole area, including North Africa, by providing a new symbol of unity—a superstructure within which diverse ethnic and cultural groups were superseded by a higher existence within the Islamic ecumenical system. The *Pax Islamica* reigned supreme for several centuries so long as the central authority was able to enforce public order, but the rise first of provincial governors and then of *de facto* independent sultans reflected the inherent centripetal forces existing within the Islamic structure. The outward unity of Islam continued (though it remained symbolic after the fall of the 'Abbasid caliphate) until a permanent split into three—and later more—units occurred in the sixteenth century and the internal contest for power among rival local rulers took the form again of a struggle for domination among rival states. From the sixteenth to the nineteenth century there were hardly more than four Islamic sovereignties—the Ottoman empire, Morocco, Persia, and the Mughal empire—with the whole of the Arab world falling under Ottoman rule. The rise of nationalism, which began to undermine the ecumenical basis of Islamic polity, contributed further to the fragmentation of Islam and the Arabs sought secession from Islamic unity and formation of a separate national existence. With this ideal in mind, the Arabs demanded independence and unity after World War I. When the European powers divided the Arab world into spheres of influence, the movement to achieve unity was set in motion. The controversy over Arab unity that raged among Arab thinkers was essentially a debate on the ways and means of achieving that unity.

It is true that nationalism is a unifying force which tends to help peoples with common interests to unite into a single nation and perhaps into a single state. Turkey and Persia, confined within essentially well-defined borders, have been able to achieve a relatively high degree of national unity. But the Arab peoples, though possessing one language, inherited historical traditions reflecting more diverse ethnic and cultural divisions than Turks and Persians possessed; therefore, Arab nationalism did not provide as unifying a force as Turkish and Persian nationalism. Indeed, the various ethnic and religious groups in the Arab world created cross-currents which ran contrary to unity. Moreover, the spread of the Arab people over a vast territory, extending from North Africa to the Persian Gulf, necessarily gave rise to conflicting local interests accentuating ethnic and religious divisions.

Small wonder, therefore, that when Arab leaders met to discuss Arab unity, the various local and ethnic factors, often disguised in divergent methods, played a significant role in opposing any form of unity unacceptable to them. Nor were the leaders who were aware of the full strength of these under-currents, able to concentrate on achieving modest plans of unity, either a loose federal union of all or a unity between two (or more) of them.

Most damaging of all was the celerity with which Arab leaders had sought to achieve unity before detailed studies were available. Vague and emotional slogans of unity, supported by extremists, often prevailed over more practical approaches counseled by wiser men. During the inter-war years, the idea of the rise of a Piedmont or Prussia which would unify the Arab world by military action prevailed; at the time, long before Egypt entered the field to provide leadership, 'Iraq was looked upon as the most promising country to play that role. Later, though he did not want to unify the Arabs by military action, President Nasir made a direct appeal to the Arabs over the heads of their rulers: popular forces in each Arab country were to rise up and replace their rulers by others willing to join the United Arab State headed by Egypt. Neither approach proved practical, since the military or political ascendency of one country over others was unacceptable, as the short-lived Syro-Egyptian union demonstrated. Nor could the experience of a loose confederal union under the Arab League Pact provide a common ground for unity; the League became a ground for regional rivalry rather than an instrument for unity.

Egypt, displaying greater vigor in inter-Arab politics, proved to be an asset as well as a liability for unity. As a link between two continents, Egypt could provide leadership, but in offering it tried to reserve for her own use certain prerogatives which other Arab countries have been reluctant to concede. For this reason, whenever 'Iraq approached Syria to form a Fertile Crescent unity, Egypt opposed this move because such a union would reduce her preponderant position in the Arab world. Nor did 'Iraq look with favor at a Syro-Egyptian unity which would extend Egypt's influence to the Fertile Crescent. No objections to the internal unity of Arabia or to Northwest Africa were ever raised, although no scheme of unity has yet been seriously entertained by any state in either of these two regions.

No practical plan of Arab unity will endure, unless it provides an equilibrium among competing regions. The Arab world as a whole might be regrouped initially in four basic regions: the Fertile Crescent, the Arabian Peninsula, the Nile Valley (consisting of Egypt and Sudan), and Northwest Africa. Since the Nile Valley possesses relatively meagre resources, Libya might be persuaded to join in a union of this region. If a general plan of unity is ever to be achieved, it must begin on the regional level—each of the four regions to enter into a federal union as a first step, and each regional federation to join the others into a grand confederation composed of the four regions as a second step. As the confederation would draw closer together, it might form eventually a federal union. In the meantime, the four regional units might become unitary states linked together under the central control of the federal authority of the grand union. These are some of the problems for which a new generation of Arab thinkers will have to devote themselves.[11]

[11] For an exposition of Arab viewpoints on unity, see the proceedings of the Cairo Conference on Arab unity in 1963 entitled *Mahadir Jalsat Mubahathat al-Wahda* [Proceedings of Conversation on Unity] (Cairo, 1963). See also Amir Shakib Arslan, *al-Wahda al-'Arabiya* [Arab Unity] (Damascus, 1937); Sati' al-Husri, Akram Zu'aytar, and Kamil Muruwwa, *Risala fi al-Ittihad* [A Treatise on Unity] (Bayrut, 1954); Muhammad 'Izzat Darwaza, *al-Wahda al-Arabiya* [Arab Unity] (Bayrut, 1958). For critical studies, see Malcolm Kerr, *The Arab Cold War* (London, 2nd ed., 1968); and my "The Scheme of Fertile Crescent Unity," ed. R. N. Frye, *The Near East and the Great Powers* (Cambridge, Mass., 1951), pp. 137–77.

Chapter 11

THE ARAB WORLD ORDER

Had God not restrained one people by another, the earth would have been ruined.

Qur'an II, 252

The world view of any nation is shaped partly by the cumulation of traditions but mainly by a mixture of emotional and material elements often collectively called "national interests." These interests, though often taken to represent the common interests of the nation as a whole, are in reality a reflection of the narrow views and interests of one class or of a few influential elite groups. In Western countries, policy makers claim to weigh the national interests on a scale of rational and objective criteria and try by flexible but firm methods to pursue those interests in their intercourse with other nations, while the leaders of the new countries of Asia and Africa tend to consider the national interests in the light of intemperate and subjective standards. Arab leaders in particular have often appeared to foreign observers as intransigent and unrealistic in their assessments of foreign affairs because traditional and emotional influences outweigh other considerations. What are the factors which influence Arabs in forming their world views and making judgments on questions of foreign policy?

The Islamic Legacy

The original home of the Arabs was the cradle of a universal religion and a conquering state—the Islamic empire in whose establishment the Arabs played an important role. Within one century after the death of the Prophet, that empire extended from the Atlantic to the Indian Ocean. Although the object of Islam was the world, the Islamic state remained confined to a specified territory despite almost uninterrupted warfare on its frontiers. The territory under Islamic rule was known as the *dar al-Islam*, or *Pax Islamica*; the territory that remained outside the bounds of Islam was the *dar al-harb*, or the territory of war. Between these two divisions there existed a perpetual state of war, though not necessarily continuous fighting, called in accordance with Islamic doctrines the *jihad*, often popularly translated as "holy war." Whenever the *jihad* was dormant, diplomatic and commercial ties were permitted and believers and infidels crossed frontiers without difficulty. Peace treaties were necessarily of short duration, but they were often renewed by mutual agreement and observed with good faith. The law that governed Islam's intercourse with other nations, called the *siyar*, was a set of rules and practices derived from Islam's long experiences with other nations as well as from Islam's own legal and ethical system. According to this law, the *jihad* will come to an end only when Islam has engulfed the whole world and mankind lives in peace under the public order of *Pax Islamica*. This was the Islamic view of world order in the classical period.[1]

But it was not only Islam that viewed the world as the exclusive object of its public order. Western Christendom (the *Respublica Christiana*), a prototype of divine system, conducted its relationships with other nations in accordance

[1] For a discussion of the Islamic theory of international relations, see my "The Islamic Theory of International Relations and Its Contemporary Relevance," *Islam and International Relations*, ed. J. H. Proctor (New York, 1965), pp. 24–39.

with similar doctrines and entered into rivalry and competition with Islam which lasted during the entire medieval period. The fall of the 'Abbasid caliphate in the middle of the thirteenth century brought about a change in relationships; Western Christendom actively began a far-reaching progress in modifying its internal structure and eventually saw the rise of the modern state-system, while the Islamic world, menaced by Mongol invasions at its gates, took a defensive attitude and no longer presented a threat to Western Christendom. From the thirteenth to the sixteenth century Islam was at its lowest ebb of power and felt the need to come to terms with its rivals: it tacitly began to recognize the *de facto* existence of other political entities. Early in this period, Islam and Christendom both passed through a transitional span of coexistence which Don Juan, Crown Prince of the Kingdom of Spain, characterized as *guerra fria* (cold war).[2] Finally they agreed to permanent peace and conducted their relationships on the basis of reciprocity and mutual respect. The Arabs played no significant role in this development, and for four centuries their lands were controlled by Mamluk and Ottoman rulers.

In early modern times, the Ottoman Sultan, despite his military strength, showed a readiness to initiate peaceful relationships with European powers. In 1535 a treaty of alliance esablishing peace between the Sultan and the King of France was signed; other European princes were invited to adhere to this treaty, but they failed to respond. The circumstances were not yet conducive to a full understanding between Islam and Christendom, and the precedent established by the Ottoman Sultan for conducting his diplomatic intercourse with Christendom on the basis of peace and reciprocity led to no appreciable improvement in peaceful relationships.

[2] Don Juan Manuel, nephew of Ferdinand II and cousin of Alphonse X, distinguished between "hot war," which he said always ended by a peace treaty, and "cold war," which "does not bring peace." The latter concept, Don Juan held, characterized the situation of his time (thirteenth and fourteenth centuries) which was the era of continuous hostility between Christians and Muslims (see my *The Islamic Law of Nations* [Baltimore, 1966], p. 22).

Had European princes accepted the Ottoman empire as a member of the European community, the developing law of nations might have provided at an earlier time a common ground for the integration of Muslim countries with the Christian world and would perhaps have spared many unhappy encounters.

Western Domination

Ottoman control of Arab lands was not considered a form of foreign domination because the Ottoman sultans had adopted Islam and had governed Arabs as Muslim—not as Turkish–rulers, notwithstanding that their administration may have been oppressive and often corrupt. Before Arab lands fell under Ottoman rule, the Arabs marvelled at the expansion of Islamic territory in Europe at the expense of Christendom. The Ottoman sultans proved worthy successors to Arab caliphs and enjoyed Arab allegiance because they ruled in the name of Islam. The sultans did not interfere in the internal affairs of ruling dynasties (Mamluk rulers in Egypt, Syria, and 'Iraq; and Arab dynasts in Arabia) as long as the annual tribute was paid. Well entrenched in power and protected by the sultan, local rulers felt secure from foreign invasions. They were, however, unaware of the immense changes that had taken place in Christendom, and they seem to have had no idea about the corresponding decline in Ottoman power.

The first event to awaken the Arab world to the significance of European advances was Napoleon's invasion of Egypt in 1798. Before Napoleon descended upon Egypt, the Arab world was in a "splendid isolation" and removed from the mainstream of world events, although the Ottoman Porte was aware of European advances much earlier. When Nelson, pursuing Napoleon in the eastern Mediterranean, arrived at Alexandria and warned the Egyptians of an impending French invasion, he was bluntly told that Egypt belonged to the Sultan and that neither he nor the French could snatch it from him. The proud Mamluks, we are told by a contemporary chronicler, dismissed the threat by a remark that if the Franks ever landed their forces, "they would be trampled under their [Mamluk] horses." [3]

Following Napoleon's departure, Egypt as well as the entire eastern Mediterranean, South Arabia, and the Persian Gulf began to be drawn into the sphere of competition among the Great Powers and to feel direct European pressures. For over a century and a half, from the opening of the nineteenth century to World War II, one Arab country after another fell under the direct or indirect European control. While European penetration demonstrated the superiority of European over Islamic power, it also resulted in a feeling of injured pride; history had shown that, whenever an Arab country was exposed to a foreign invasion, its forces, despite valiant resistance, were routed. Only after World War II did European domination begin to recede, and the Arab countries to recover their independence.

Two major events had far-reaching effects on the morale of the Arabs and helped encourage their resistance to foreign pressures. The first was the Russo-Japanese War of 1904–5 resulting in the victory of an Oriental over a European and a Christian power. For over a century after Napoleon had invaded Egypt, the Arabs (as well as many other Muslim peoples) resigned themselves to the idea that, whenever they were confronted by a European force, humiliation and defeat were almost inevitable. The victory of Japan over Russia, demonstrating that an Oriental power can, by adopting European methods and technical know-how, defeat a European Power, restored to the Arabs confidence by giving them the hope that by following in Japan's footsteps they would be able to repulse European encroachments. Never before in Islamic lands had there been such unanimous acclaim for the victory of an Oriental over a European power, and the press reported with enthusiasm the progress of the war. Hafiz Ibrahim, a leading Egyptian poet, was not the only one who

[3] 'Abd al-Rahman al-Jabarti, *'Aja'ib al-Athar fi al-Tarajum wa al-Akhbar* (Cairo, 1322/1904), III, 2–3.

sang the praise of Japanese victory and pointed out the moral of the event. Japan provided an object lesson for many Arab writers to study her sudden rise to prominence and the secret of her victory over Russia.[4]

If Japan's victory raised high hopes, the Arabs had yet to be rehabilitated. After the Young Turks Revolution of 1908, the Arabs began to engage in nationalist activities which resulted in the separation of Arab lands from Ottoman sovereignty. In World War I, they sided with a European ally and raised a revolt which led to the liberation of their lands from Turkish rule. True, the general offensive against the Ottoman empire was carried out under British command, but the military operations in Arab lands started in the interior of Arabia and were conducted by a desert army and Arab officers who forced the Ottoman army to retreat from Makka to Damascus. The British authorities supplied material resources and expert advice and the Arabs provided the human resources. Had the Arabs been able, as a result of these events, to establish an independent Arab state, their rehabilitation would have been complete and their reconciliation with the West might have led to an enduring co-operation. In their new national life, the Arabs needed Western economic and technical assistance which the West might have given them to secure their goodwill. While agreeing to extend economic and technical assistance, the European powers insisted on political control and thus clashed with Arab nationalism. The Arabs may not have been able to put their house in order without foreign assistance, but it is doubtful that European intervention had brought about salutary effects to people who impatiently wanted unity and independence. One thing is certain: the European Powers lost Arab goodwill by denying them independence initially.[5]

Britian was not slow in realizing Arab national grievances: she tried to follow a more forward policy toward them by

[4] See *al-Muqtataf*, 30 (1905), 9–19; Armenius Vambery, "Japan and the Mohametan World," *The Nineteenth Century*, LVII (1905), 573–76.

[5] The Arab countries which remained independent were the relatively backward countries of the Arabian Peninsula.

agreeing, though slowly and piecemeal, to certain fundamental aspirations. The mandate over 'Iraq was terminated in 1932; the Jordan mandate and British residual privileges in Egypt were also brought to an end after World War II. Britain sought by these arrangements, as well as by subsequent withdrawals from other Arab dependencies, to satisfy basic Arab nationalist demands and hoped, once other pending issues (in particular that of Palestine) were settled, to open a new chapter in Anglo-Arab relations based on mutual interests and respect for sovereign rights. France was bound to follow in Britain's footsteps by giving up her Levant mandates and then eventually her North African dependencies.

For a full understanding with the Arabs, Britain finally decided to settle the Palestine problem. In 1937–38 attempts were made first by proposals for partition and then by local and municipal autonomy for Arabs and Jews, but these arrangements were unacceptable to the Arabs.[6] In May 1939 another plan was laid down designed virtually to put an end to Jewish aspirations for unlimited immigration by declaring that the Jewish National Home had been achieved.[7] But the new circumstances created by World War II prevented the implementation of this plan, although it came very near to meeting Arab demands.[8]

Following World War II, Britain made still another attempt to settle the Palestine imbroglio; in 1946 she laid down a plan by virtue of which Palestine would have become self-governing. To bring it into effect, Britain needed the co-operation of the United States, since American support had become absolutely essential to maintain peace and order in the Arab world. If the United States had supported Britain's plan to grant Arabs and Jews local autonomy, Palestine would

[6] These proposals were rejected by the Arabs and the British Government never formally accepted them. See *Palestine Royal Commission Report* (London, 1937), Cmd. 5479; and *The Palestine Partition Commission Report* (London, 1938), Cmd. 5854.

[7] See *Palestine: Statement of Policy* (London, 1939), Cmd. 6019.

[8] For a discussion of this plan and failure of its implementation see my "General Nuri's Flirtations with the Axis Powers," *Middle East Journal*, XVI (1962), 328–36.

have been spared bloodshed and violence. However, increasing Jewish pressures on American policy makers prompted the United States to support a policy of partition and subsequent creation of the state of Israel, despite increasing American interest in the Arab world. American support of Israel, though varying in degree from one administration to another, was considered diametrically opposed to Arab national interests and adversely affected the American image in Arab eyes. The immediate effect of American policy was, first, to frustrate Britain's attempts to come to an understanding with the Arabs without denying the basic claim for a Jewish National Home, and second, to open the way to another Great Power to fish in the troubled waters. Soviet penetration into the Arab world may not have been generated by the Arab-Israeli conflict, but Western support of Israel certainly provided the opportunity for Soviet desires to be fulfilled.[9]

Neutralism

Not less significant is Arab neutralist attitude in the present East-West conflict. This attitude evolved partly as a legacy of Islamic history and partly as the product of post-war circumstances.

The medieval bi-polar conflict between Western Christendom and Islam (first under the Arab caliphate and then under the Ottoman Porte) re-emerged after World War II in a new form as part of the East-West conflict between the Soviet Union and Western countries. Islam is no longer a partner in this conflict. The area of the medieval conflict, which centered essentially around the Mediterranean world, has now shifted northward to engulf the Eastern European and Western countries on both sides of the Atlantic. The Mediterranean area, the center of world power until early modern times, has been dwarfed by a vast northern area dominated by giant nations whose claim to ascendency is based on industrial power and dynamic new ideologies.

[9] See Bernard Lewis, *The Middle East and the West* (Bloomington, 1964), pp. 134ff.

With regard to their attitude toward the East–West conflict, the Islamic countries may be divided into two groups, Arab and non-Arab. The non-Arab countries, especially Turkey, Persia, and Pakistan (known to some Western strategists as the Northern Tier), have in various forms committed themselves to Western alliances, presumably designed as defensive against the Soviet threat. The Arab countries (the counterpart Southern Tier), have advocated both non-alignment, often designated as "neutralism," and resistance to all Western attempts to elicit commitments, because they never felt an immediate Soviet threat. Notwithstanding that some Arab countries tried to obtain Soviet economic and military assistance, all preferred to avoid entering into formal alliances with either side; some have opted for Western aid while others have preferred Soviet offers. Islam's historic encounters with Christendom ended with the fruitful lesson of coexistence and both systems became integrated into the modern community of nations. These experiences also demonstrated that the infusion of ideology into the relationships among states can be dangerous indeed. If relations among states are ever to be peaceful, they should be regulated on the basis of reciprocity and mutual interest and divorced from religious or ideological bias. It is paradoxical that in an industrial age when religious ideologies have finally been divorced from foreign policy, a new departure in the conduct of states has ensued under the impact of a new ideology which its followers appear to insist on reintroducing in the intercourse among nations.[10]

Unlike the Indians and some South Asian peoples who have displayed a pacifist attitude stemming partly from their own culture and partly from the present situation, the Arabs have never really believed in pacificism. Neither the Islamic heritage nor Arab traditions support a pacificist attitude, since Islam permitted the use of violence and Arab tribal tradition evolved from continuous inter-tribal warfare. Likewise, Arab neutralism today has been dictated neither by traditions nor by behavior patterns, since on neither doctrinal nor emo-

[10] See my *The Islamic Law of Nations*, pp. 69–70.

tional grounds do the Arabs refrain from the use of violence to achieve their political ends. Arab countries have varied markedly in their dealing with the West; these differences reflected partly their historical experiences in conflict between Islam and Western Christendom, and partly their opposition to communism. Therefore, the attitude of each Arab country must be explained more on local or circumstantial grounds than on ideological alone.

Having long been the object of foreign encroachments, the Arab countries (as well as other new countries) are keen to assert their newly won independence and to determine independently their foreign policy.[11] Attempts to align them with the West evoked negative responses, particularly when Arab leaders felt that those attempts were intended to divert their efforts from the immediate threat of Israel to another one which they considered more remote (Soviet Union). The Arabs, however, have been divided on the degree of aloofness from East and West. Arab communists and Pan-Arabs, not to mention other influential groups motivated by ideological drives, have displayed marked preference for one camp or the other, although for different reasons all have asserted a neutralist attitude.[12] Religious groups, while showing an aversion to communist teachings, have not favored a pro-Western policy. On the official level, however, the traditional countries, Saudi Arabia and Jordan in particular, have favored Western countries, although under the influence of ideological groups they failed to enter into a formal alliance with any one of them. Soon after 'Iraq and Jordan entered into a treaty relationship with the West, these ties were broken under the influence of extremists.[13] Revolutionary countries, stressing nationalism and full sovereign rights, have been more out-

[11] This attitude was clearly reflected in the desiderata of the Bandung Conference in 1955 (see G. M. Kahin, *The Asian-African Conference* [Ithaca, 1956], pp. 76–85).

[12] See F. A. Sayegh (ed.), *The Dynamics of Neutralism in the Arab World* (San Francisco, 1964).

[13] For a discussion of 'Iraq's entry into the Baghdad Pact and her withdrawal see Waldemar Gallman, *'Iraq Under General Nuri* (Baltimore, 1964); for Jordan's experiences with Britain, see General J. B. Glubb, *A Soldier With the Arabs* (London, 1957).

spoken in advocating a neutralist policy, notwithstanding that in reality they have oscillated from one camp to the other. For instance, President Nasir showed marked preference for the West after the United Arab Republic was established, and he received American economic assistance. But his dependence on Soviet economic and military assistance after the Arab-Israeli war of 1967 far exceeded any past commitment.

The communists and Ba'thists may be considered the two major groups which have displayed a definite ideological stand: the communists in favor of the Soviet Union and the Ba'thists in favor of the West in principle. However, neither has so far been willing or able to advocate a policy of commitment—the communists for fear of losing support of Pan-Arabs who favor a neutralist policy, and the Ba'thists because of lingering Western influence and Western support for Israel. Michel 'Aflaq, stating the Ba'th position in 1948, said:

> If the Arabs were free today from colonialism, foreign occupation, Zionist threat, and dismemberment and had to take a stand in the global struggle, a stand which would be closest to their ideals and national interest, they would take the side of the Western democracies rather than that of the Eastern dictatorships. They would choose this course because they so well know that freedom has been, is and will remain the very essence of their existence and the best guarantee for the development of their personality.
>
> The present status of the Arab world, however, and the inimical policies of the West regarding Palestine and other Arab issues dictate that the Arabs' interest can in no way be served by alliance with the Western bloc or any of its members.[14]

Arab leaders have often indicated their readiness to reconcile their differences with Western countries, if basic Arab demands were met. The attitude is demonstrated by Britain's recognition of fundamental national aspirations and particularly by a change in French policy after France had relin-

[14] See *al-Ba'th*, Damascus, January 21, 1948, cited in George Tomeh, "Syria and Neutralism," *The Dynamics of Neutralism in the Arab World*, ed. F. A. Sayegh, (San Francisco, 1964), p. 124.

quished control over her North African dependencies. Owing to close cultural and educational connections, the United States used to enjoy very high prestige in the Arab world. However, her position there began steadily to deteriorate because of her greater attention to and support of Israeli claims notwithstanding the increasing American interest in the oil of Arabia and North Africa.

Like the emerging countries of Asia and Africa, which have formed a "third force" designed to maintain a power balance between East and West, the Arab countries have shown a keen interest in playing the role of an equal partner in international relations rather than in becoming a pawn in the game of power politics among giant nations. In the realm of practical politics, some Arab leaders tried to play off the East against the West in an effort to gain certain concrete advantages from both sides; but most of them tried to avoid involvement in the East-West conflict. Opposition to Israel, however, had often prompted the Arabs to seek Soviet support, and thereby the East-West conflict is reflected by tensions within the region rather than by participation of the region itself in the global issues.[15]

Foreign Policy

Today the foreign policy of any country depends partly upon the strength of its position in the world, its economic resources, and the preparedness of its people to assume international responsibility. The success of its policy is dependent on the diplomatic ability of its leaders to win the greatest number of friends and supporters among the members of the community of nations. The Great Powers can win the support of other nations by offering military, economic, and technical assistance. But the position of small nations is very difficult

[15] For Arab views on neutralism, see Salah al-Din al-Baytar, *al-Siyasa al-'Arabiya* [Arab Policy] (Bayrut, 1960); Clovis Maqsud, *Ma'na al-Hiyad al-Ijabi* [Meaning of Positive Neutrality] (Bayrut, 1960). For a discussion on the neutralist attitude of new nations in international affairs, see R. A. Scalapino, "Neutralism in Asia," *American Political Science Review*, 48 (1954), 49–62.

indeed. They may choose to become clients of a giant state—or a bloc of states—and take sides in a world contest; thus they virtually become allies of one camp and enemies of the other. They may, on the other hand, follow a neutralist or a non-aligned policy and try to play off one side against the other with the consequential risk of losing the good will of both. Few countries can attain the position of an Austria, keeping a balanced position among rival powers, or a Switzerland, secure in permanent neutrality.

Similar to their varied attitudes toward the East-West conflict, the Arab countries can scarcely be said to have a unified foreign policy. However, there are two foreign policy objectives on which all Arabs are agreed—opposition to imperialism and to Israel's national claims.

Imperialism is viewed as essentially a form of economic exploitation—the need of capitalist states for raw material and protected markets, as defined by J. A. Hobson, Lenin, and others. True, imperialism began to recede after World War II, but European influence is still to be found in certain parts of the Arab world, and there is always the danger of some kind of encroachment on Arab rights by foreign powers. The Arabs are agreed in their opposition to foreign influence, although some have maintained close ties with one Western power or another on the basis of reciprocity and mutual interest. Other Arab countries have preferred to enter into commercial and economic connections with the Eastern bloc, preferring to purchase military and technical assistance from the Soviet Union rather than from Western Europe or the United States.

Perhaps more unanimous agreement is to be found in Arab opposition to Israel. The existence of Israel is considered a threat to all Arab countries, although some of them are more directly concerned than others. Since opposition to Israel is a deeper concern, which is not as likely to recede in the near future as opposition to Western imperialism, the subject merits a closer scrutiny in a separate section.

After World War II, the rise to statehood of several Muslim countries, such as Pakistan and Indonesia (to mention but two), has given impetus to the idea of reviving collaboration among Muslim states in international affairs. One would have expected that the Arabs would welcome collaboration among states that had been formerly part of an empire in the establishment of which they played an important role. Some Arab leaders have called for the holding of Islamic conferences and the formation of regional pacts and alliances among Muslim states. These leaders envisaged the possibility of co-operation in international councils to serve their common interests as well as to contribute to the development of a more stable and peaceful world order. This trend, called neo-Pan-Islamism, unlike the Pan-Islamic movement of the nineteenth century, has not aimed at the restoration of Islamic unity, nor the reinstatement of the Islamic system in international relations. It was perhaps not the wish of all Muslim states to co-operate as an Islamic bloc within the community of nations.[16]

Some Muslim countries, especially Pakistan and Indonesia, have supported Arab rights in Palestine during successive sessions of the United Nations; but the Muslim states as a whole have failed to form a bloc to protect their common interest or support Arab states in their military conflicts with Israel. Islam, though an important force that held peoples together in the past, has been recently supplanted by nationalism in the conduct of foreign policy, and Muslim states have often found themselves in opposite camps, especially when national interests ran contrary to Islamic solidarity. For instance, although Pakistan, Saudi Arabia, and Egypt were members of an Islamic organization designed to coordinate their activities in international affairs, Egypt supported India's claim to Kashmir against Pakistan's protest. In recent years Iran (Persia), another Muslim state and a former ally of Egypt and 'Iraq, has become the target of Arab attacks no less because of conflicting interests in the Persian Gulf than be-

[16] For a brief discussion of the Pan-Islamic movement in the nineteenth century and attempts at reviving it after World War II, see my "Pan-Islamism," *Encyclopaedia Britannica,* XVII (1961), 184–85; cf. T. Cuyler Young, "Pan-Islamism in the Modern World," in J. H. Proctor (ed.), *Islam and International Relations*, pp. 194–219.

cause of her recognition of Israel. As a result, Islam failed to provide a sufficient ground for solidarity among Arab and other Muslim states, although it is conceivable that Islamic states might seek co-operation if their basic national differences are resolved.

The Arab states are not in agreement among themselves concerning interregional questions. They have, it is true, established the Arab League, but failed to unite into a single state, as noted before, although Arab unity could provide a medium for a unified foreign policy. In the past, disagreement stemmed from dynastic rivalry and conflicting claims over leadership of the Arab world; today divergences in political systems and ideologies provide the major cause of disagreement. At bottom, failure to overcome local, confessional, and parochial feelings has kept each country separated from the rest, and the people, though they often applauded their leaders' call for unity and national solidarity, have failed to support them in practice. Disparity in economic resources, especially between the oil-producing countries and others, is another cause of disagreement, particularly because some of the oil-producing countries received royalties far in excess of their local needs while other countries which have launched ambitious programs of economic development desperately need capital for their implementation.[17]

Faced with occasional foreign threats, the Israeli threat in particular, Arab leaders have often met to iron out differences and substantial economic and diplomatic support has been given by one country to another. In 1956, and again in 1967, the Arab leaders have shown readiness to set aside local differences and to co-operate in the face of foreign dangers, but they have not yet shown sufficient unity of purpose nor full readiness to subordinate local to common national interests as demonstrated in recent Arab summit meetings. The Israeli challenge may bring about further collaboration and unity—indeed, Israel may well prove eventually to be the greatest unifying factor among the Arabs. Her superiority in skills is

[17] For a discussion on Arab problems of foreign policy, see Charles D. Cremeans, *The Arabs and the World* (New York, 1963).

bound to inspire them with the notion that unless they achieve reform and development swiftly they will never be able to stand up to the challenge.

Israel and the Arab World

Qui vicit non est victor
nisi victus fatetur.
Quintus Ennius

No work on the political trends in the Arab world would be complete without at least a brief discussion on Israel's relations with her Arab neighbors since it is impossible to study any major Arab question without discerning an inescapable bearing on Israel. We have already seen that the mainstream of contemporary Arab thought has been essentially the product of recurring crises generated by Western encroachments. No sooner did Western influence begin to recede and the Arab countries show preparedness to reorganize their internal affairs than they were confronted by another form of Western intervention—the establishment, in the heart of the Arab world, of a new body politic, foreign to its social environment and separating it territorially into two disconnected parts, and in whose creation and maintenance the Western powers had taken an active part.

People who have been the victim of cumulative injustices primarily because they refused to be assimilated are certainly entitled to being rehabilitated. Their choice of rehabilitation has been to call to life an ancient symbol of identity reshaped in the modern garb of a nation-state. Moved essentially by a guilt feeling, the Western powers pledged to fulfill the promises of the newly awakened Jewish nationalism by offering the Jews a territory to establish a "homeland." If these powers had offered the Jewish people an empty land, or, at any rate, a land with scanty population, to establish a state, the solution would have been both just and without harm to other peoples. But the powers could neither persuade the Jews to settle in a backward African territory nor were they willing to offer them part of their own metropolitan territories. Instead, the powers handed over a land for which they had neither a title nor the prior consent of its people; the sole reason for their choice of Palestine was Jewish historical connections traced back two thousand years. In this hasty arrangement, the Western powers inflicted no less an injustice by displacing and dispossessing another people than had been inflicted on those to whom they tried to repair past injustices. If guilt feelings had prompted them to do justice to their immediate victims, they have yet to correct the injustices inflicted on the victims of their victims.

In the process of erecting their homeland, the Jews who chose Zionism, despite their bitter experiences with injustice, cannot shrink from the responsibility for expelling the native people from their lands by force of arms—the very people to whom they owe the historic debt of religious tolerance and protection during the time when they were persecuted in varying degrees almost everywhere in the Christian world. No matter how valid is their justification to redeem an ancient homeland, these Jews cannot escape the moral responsibility for the harm they have done to another people, first for their resort to coercive actions in taking over a land without the consent of its people and, second, for inflicting an injustice in return for benevolence.

However, neither the Jews nor the Western powers meant to hurt the Arabs. It is maintained that a Jewish homeland, consisting of a wealthy and highly civilized people, could extend to the Arabs the capital and technical know-how which they need for the development of their barren lands. It is also held that there is sufficient land for both Arabs and Jews to live together in peace, and that the civil and religious rights of both can be respected. Even as a state, some Jewish leaders might argue, the Arabs would derive infinite advantages by regional co-operation and by diplomatic support in international councils as well as by technical and commercial connections.

The Arabs, while conceding possible material advantages, are concerned about other things. They began to display real apprehension when the gates of Palestine were thrown open to Jewish immigration after World War I. Jewish intentions were never made clear or definite. Arab fears were intensified when it became abundantly clear that the Jewish appetite for a national home was continually growing: first, by instituting a Jewish National Home in Palestine which promised no separate political entity, as defined in the Balfour Declaration of 1917; secondly, by the Partition Plan for Palestine which under the United Nations Resolution of 1947 separated Palestine into two political entities;[18] thirdly, by the emergence of an expansionist (in fact even if not in intent) Israeli state, as revealed in three Arab-Israeli wars of 1948, 1956, and 1967; fourthly, by resort to retaliations and periodic armed attacks whenever an Israeli claim is put forth *vis-à-vis* an Arab claim. These methods, humiliating far more than former foreign interventions were, seem to increase injured feeling among the Arabs. They are likely to produce more far-reaching social and political upheavals than have hitherto been witnessed.

A Jewish national home in Arab lands might have proven less objectionable, had the Jews genuinely tried to alleviate Arab fears and conciliate their adverse reactions. Not only did the Jews incite Arab fears by their threats to resort to force but also have gone far enough to alienate them permanently by their arrogance. The Oriental Jew, though occasionally the object of discrimination, was a familiar figure who succeeded in protecting his best interests by manipulating traditional practices in the same way as did his Arab counterpart; but the Westernized Jew, who looked condescendingly on the "uncivilized" Arab in much the same way as the earlier European did, utterly failed to win him to his side. No one has expressed more clearly this attitude of the Westernized Jew toward the Arab than 'Abd al-Rahman 'Azzam, then Secretary-General of the Arab League, in his explanation of Arab objection to Jewish imigration before the Anglo-American Commission of Inquiry, in 1946, when he said:

> Our Brother has gone to Europe and to the West and came back something else. He has come back a Russified

[18] The United Nations Resolution of 1947 laid down that Jerusalem should form a *corpus separatum* to be governed by a separate administration under United Nations supervision.

Jew, a Polish Jew, a German Jew, and an English Jew. He has come back with a totally different conception of things, Western and not Eastern. That does not mean that we are necessarily quarreling with anyone who comes from the West. But the Jew, our old cousin, coming back with imperialistic ideas, with materialistic ideas, with reactionary or revolutionary ideas and trying to implement them first by British pressure and then by American pressure, and then by terrorism on his own part—he is not the old cousin and we do not extend to him a very good welcome. The Zionist, the new Jew, wants to dominate and he pretends that he has got a particular civilizing mission with which he returns to a backward, degenerate race in order to put the element of progress into an area which has no progress. Well that has been the pretension of every power that wanted to colonize and aimed at domination. The excuse has always been that the people are backward and that he has got a human mission to put them forward . . . the Arabs simply stand and say "NO." We are not reactionary and we are not backward. Even if we are ignorant, the difference between ignorance and knowledge is ten years in school. We are a living, vitally strong nation, we are in our renaissance; we are producing as many children as any nation in the world. We still have our brains. We have a heritage of civilization and of spiritual life. We are not going to allow ourselves to be controlled either by great nations or small nations or dispersed nations.[19]

Something seems to have gone amiss in Jewish diplomacy, perhaps best expressed in a saying attributed to Moshe Sharett, Israel's second Premier, in which he warned his compatriots that they had succeeded in winning all peoples to their side save those with whom they chose to live. Dr. Judah L. Magnes, an American Jew and founder of the Hebrew University, made essentially the same point when he tried to persuade his people not to resort to military force during the first Arab-Israeli conflict (1948–49), if they were to retain permanently their foothold in Palestine. Even after three successful wars

[19] See Richard Crossman, *Palestine Mission: A Personal Record* (New York, 1947), pp. 109–10.

in pitched battles, Magnes' admonition is still true: Arab consent is necessary. The Arabs, continuously hurt by the Jews, will insist on saying "NO," to borrow 'Azzam's word.

Obviously the present crisis and its aftermath cannot be resolved by force alone. The Arabs, maintaining that time is not necessarily in favor of the other side, are prepared to wait, even though they have paid a high price for their refusal to concede to Israel complete military victory. They maintained that, in the words of Quintus Ennius quoted above, "the victor is not truly victor unless the vanquished admits it." They are a proud people and possess an impressive potential. Whenever challenged in the past, as we have already observed, they were capable of rising up to the task they were called upon to fulfill, if they were guided by an inspiring leadership, and their rising might "release a store of energy which could lead to a creation or to destruction." So long as Arab grievances and the vivid Arab sense of injustice remain unredressed, the Arabs will remain determined to fight the Israelis, as they previously fought and eventually defeated the Crusaders.

Like the Arabs, the Jews also possess fine qualities and some weaknesses; thereby they are capable of creation and of destruction. At the present moment, they are elated by military victory and they display more than ever before intransigence and presumptuousness, although the day of victory ought to be the occasion of magnanimity and foresight. In the last message which he gave to the Jewish people, Weizmann warned:

> The Jews are a small people, but also a great people. They are an ugly people, but also beautiful people. They are a people that builds and a people that destroys. They are a people of genius and at the same time a people of enormous stupidity. By their obstinacy they will drive through a wall, but the break in the wall always remains gaping at them.[20]

[20] See Richard Crossman, *A Nation Reborn* (London, 1960), p. 122. For the original in Yiddish, see *ibid.*, appendix C, p. 141.

Here is an impasse—a vicious circle which, unless it is broken, might involve the world in a nuclear war. Several approaches have been suggested, varying from an imposed solution by the Great Powers, which would guarantee the survival of Israel by permanent intervention, to the outright liquidation of Jewish national existence to Arab satisfaction. Neither is the latter possible in the present circumstances nor can the former endure forever unless Arab consent is obtained. Needless to say again, Arab consent is absolutely necessary for any settlement if it is to be lasting.

Several Western writers, known for their concern about the plight of both Arabs and Jews, have suggested proposals for a settlement of the Arab-Israeli conflict on the basis of the *de facto* partition of Palestine into separate territorial units. "After the third Arab-Israeli war," wrote Toynbee, "it is imperative that there should be not just renewal of the previous truce but a permanent peace settlement between Israel and the Arab states." This peace, he added, must not be imposed by force. "Only a peace settlement that is . . . accepted by both sides," he went on to argue, "can open the way for reconciliation and cooperation between them." [21] Other writers, such as General Sir John Glubb, endorsed the Partition Plan but insisted that Israel should give back to the Arabs the territory she has occupied in the June war, especially "that part of Palestine which formerly was united to Jordan," and that "money should be provided from outside so as to develop a reconstituted Jordan that all refugees could be settled there." [22] Still others called for either a loose federal or confederal union between Israel and her Arab neighbors or between Israel and the rest of Palestine reconstituted as an Arab state. The federal plan, aiming at co-operation between two peoples without fusing them into one political community, is envisioned to guarantee peace and security between

[21] Arnold J. Toynbee, "The Middle East, Past and Present," in *The Arab-Israeli Impasse*, ed. Majdia D. Khadduri (Washington, D.C., 1968), p. 45.

[22] General Glubb also insisted that Jerusalem should be "internationalized" (General Sir John Glubb Pasha, *The Middle East Crisis: A Personal Interpretation* [London, 1967], p. 47).

Jews and Arabs. It is taken for granted that each political unit will have to be fully self-governing in internal affairs but prepared to co-operate in economic and technical matters.[23]

These plans, though embodying the two essential requisites for peace—Israel's accommodation and Arab consent—are based on the principle of the partition of Palestine into separate political units. However, the implementation of these plans, in as much as they envision the existence of small states with possible outside intervention whenever the just claim of one party is not met by the other, gives little assurances to permanent peace and security. Some suggested the guarantee of the Great Powers so as to discourage internal frictions or outside encroachments. Guarantee by the Great Powers means permanent intervention; such a state of affairs, even under the auspices of an international organization, cannot remain permanent.

Peace, if it is ever to endure in this part of the world, can stem only from internal peaceful conditions. These conditions, as Magnes and Toynbee have rightly pointed out, must themselves be based on the principles of accommodation and consent. Neither the present nationalist mood in Israel nor in Arab Palestine can continue indefinitely; if Israel is ever to endure, its social order must of necessity change and its people would be bound to accommodate. A change in the mood of one people might invite a change in the other—the signal that a balance between accommodation and consent might be arrived at.

Several formulas for future settlement might be worked out, depending on many variables, permanent or circumstantial. In my view, the most permanent one would be that which is based on the renunciation by both parties of national ideologies and on an agreement to live as equal nationals in one Palestine State. No political community—exclusively Jewish or Arab—would be permanently acceptable to either Jews or Arabs. Neither the one nor the other would or should be prepared to live as a minority in such a political community.

[23] See Don Peretz, "A Binational Approach to the Palestine Conflict," *Law and Contemporary Problems*, 33 (1968), 39.

To be acceptable to both, the political community must be supranational within which Jews and Arabs (both Muslims and Christians) can with full freedom practice their own religious and civil rights.[24]

To achieve the ultimate goal of this political community Palestine must be reconstituted as an independent state. This state should be neither Jewish nor Arab, but a Palestinian state composed either of two "national homes" within one state or of one home for the two peoples, to which each individual might belong and in which he would be at once a Palestinian citizen and an Arab or a Jewish national. The full sovereign attributes of the state should be recognized and respected by all the Arab countries and the world.[25] It would have the right to enter into an economic union—a common market or otherwise—with one or more of the neighboring Arab countries as well as into a confederal union with them by free choice. If it wishes to be permanently neutralized along the lines of Switzerland, Palestine might become the trust of the community of nations.

Needless to say, this is not a proposal to settle immediate issues; it is a long view for future possibilities of "live and let live": for people who desire to live in peace and prosperity and foster art and culture, not ideologies.

[24] Judah Magnes and his followers advocated the principle of binationalism for Palestine over thirty years ago; some of his followers still insist that this principle provides a more permanent basis for peace, but others maintain that the binational approach is no longer practical (see Don Peretz, "A Binational Approach," *ibid.*, p. 32ff.).

[25] If the Arabs of Palestine desire some sort of an association with Jordan, then the two "national homes" in Palestine might form a sort of loose federal union rather than a unitary state.

INDEX